AN INTRODUCTION
TO
POLITICAL SCIENCE
METHODS

SECOND EDITION

AN INTRODUCTION TO POLITICAL SCIENCE METHODS

Robert A. Bernstein

James A. Dyer

Department of Political Science
Texas A & M University

PRENTICE-HALL, INC., ENGLEWOOD CLIFFS, N.J. 07632

Library of Congress Cataloging in Publication Data

Bernstein, Robert A. (Robert Alan), (date)
  An introduction to political science methods.

  Includes bibliographies and index.
  1. Political science—Methodology. 2. Political
science—Research. I. Dyer, James A. II. Title.
JA73.B42 1984   320'.01'81   83-26917
ISBN 0-13-493313-3

Cover design: Wanda Lubelska Design
Manufacturing buyer: Ron Chapman

Printed in the United States of America

10 9 8 7 6 5 4 3 2 1

ISBN 0-13-493313-3

PRENTICE-HALL INTERNATIONAL, INC., *London*
PRENTICE-HALL OF AUSTRALIA PTY. LIMITED, *Sydney*
EDITORA PRENTICE-HALL DO BRASIL, LTDA., *Rio de Janeiro*
PRENTICE-HALL CANADA INC., *Toronto*
PRENTICE-HALL OF INDIA PRIVATE LIMITED, *New Delhi*
PRENTICE-HALL OF JAPAN, INC., *Tokyo*
PRENTICE-HALL OF SOUTHEAST ASIA PTE. LTD., *Singapore*
WHITEHALL BOOKS LIMITED, *Wellington, New Zealand*

CONTENTS

Chapter Fifteen
PUTTING THINGS TOGETHER: THE RESEARCH DESIGN
AND REPORT   249

PREFACE

An Introduction to Political Science Methods introduces students without any background in methods or statistics to what social science research involves and to some of the basic methods used to do it. The approach is to teach by having them view the research process as if they were researchers trying to do empirical research. We believe that students learn better by doing things and confronting material in the context of real situations rather than dealing more abstractly with the subject.

We provide the student with numerous examples from a variety of types of research, both as examples discussed in the text and in three more complete examples of research articles. In the laboratories the students deal with data taken from existing research. We also provide material to help the student develop his or her own simple research project including a detailed outline of a research report and an example of a student paper.

The changes in the second edition reflect our own experience teaching several hundred students using the first edition, and comments of others who have used the book. We would particularly like to thank Mike Gant, who has provided us with a number of suggestions. We would also like to thank James Payne, Jon Bond and William Klecka, along with James Ward and Alan Monroe who provided useful reviews of the book. Finally, we owe a debt to the students who have played a very important role in developing our ideas and helping us to better communicate.

AN INTRODUCTION TO POLITICAL SCIENCE METHODS

INTRODUCTION

The goals of this text are twofold: to enable you to understand and evaluate reports on empirical research, and—at least in an elementary way—to prepare you to do empirical research of your own. *An Introduction to Political Science Methods* assumes that you have had no previous training in research methodology. For most of you, much of what is presented here will be quite different from anything you have studied before: You will learn a new vocabulary and perhaps even a new way of thinking about things.

The material in this book is relevant to you both as a social science student who must read, understand, and evaluate social science research, and as a member of a society in which empirical research plays an increasingly large role in our lives. Social science research is used to help make or justify decisions on issues like school busing, welfare programs, work-incentive systems, and local-government services. Almost every day your newspaper includes a story that focuses on empirical research—"STUDY SAYS BAN ON CONTRACEPTION HURTS CATHOLICISM" is a headline for such an article. Polls are presented informing us of what others in our society are thinking. Surveys determine which positions candidates will take, which products will be manufactured and sold, even which television shows will be continued. In almost any job, and as a private citizen, you will at some time need to be able to evaluate social science research.

Before we proceed, let us clear up a misconception that some students bring to a course like this. This introduction to political science methods has very little to do with mathematics. Though in this text we consider some statistics, it is not a statistics course. A small hand calculator will be useful for those with less well-developed arithmetic skills.

WHAT IS EMPIRICAL SOCIAL SCIENCE RESEARCH?

Empirical Research

What exactly do we mean by the phrase *empirical social science research?* You are familiar in a general way with research. Any inquiry or search for information is research. **Empirical research** means that we require observation of the world about us in order to verify the conclusions of the inquiry. This distinguishes empirical research from studies that rely on revelation, introspection, or appeals to authority. The typical college research paper primarily involves assimilating what various authorities have said about a subject. Though this is often a first step in doing empirical research, the conclusions in such a paper are not tested through actual observation, and therefore they are not examples of empirical research. When an Eastern mystic goes into a period of silence and introspection and emerges with a set of statements about how people can live more fully, these statements have not been tested by observation; they too cannot be considered empirical research.

It is clear that some kinds of questions cannot be explored through empirical research. What we might call moral questions are questions that probe how people *should* behave rather than how they *do* behave. The principal objective of such inquiries is the determination of what is good and what is evil. These inquiries are beyond the capabilities of the empirical-research process. Empirical research may provide useful information on how to go about achieving moral goals, once the goals have been derived, but it cannot by itself determine these goals.

Empirical Scientific Research

When the word *scientific* is added to the phrase *empirical research* two other considerations are added: explanation and generality. **Empirical scientific research** is an inquiry that seeks general, empirically verified explanations for some class of phenomena. The class of phenomena social science deals with is human behavior. In other words, empirical social science research is an inquiry that attempts to discover and verify general rules allowing us to understand why human beings behave the way they do.

When we say that social science seeks to explain behavior, what do we mean by *explain?* What we are trying to establish are the relationships among different things we observe. Suppose we observe that as nations become wealthier they spend more money on their military. We might suggest that the amount of money a nation has to spend at least partially explains how large an army that nation has. This is an important point we will consider in more detail in Chapter 1: Social scientists explain behavior in terms of how it is related to something else.

When we say we are looking for explanations that can be generalized, we mean that we are looking for the explanations that can be applied under the largest number of circumstances. Social science would rather find explanations that apply to all Supreme Court justices, not just a single one; to all judges, not just those on the Supreme Court; to all political officials, not just judges; and so on. Though it seems unlikely that a single explanation could be offered to explain all behavior of all government officials, we search for the most general explanation possible.

ORGANIZATION OF THE TEXT

We shall approach the study of empirical research by looking at the ways in which we empirically verify proposed explanations about human behavior.

In Figure I–1 we show an outline of the research process. This book is organized after the research process. The first step involves suggesting explanations and proposing statements that can be empirically tested. Chapter 1 discusses how to make empirically testable statements and Chapter 2 deals with the broader issues of finding explanations and supporting the proposed testable statements with existing literature. In Chapter 3 we explore how we determine what it is we observe in testing the statements. Chapters 4, 5, and 6 all deal with defining and measuring the things we need to observe when we test the statements. In Chapter 7 we discuss basic automated data processing. In Chapter 8 we show you how to describe the data that have been collected. How we actually go about testing the statements is taken up in Chapter 9. In Chapters 10 and 11 we discuss how to eliminate alternative explanations for finding support for the explanatory statements. At that point in the book, you will know enough to evaluate explanatory statements and know whether or not they are supported. In Chapters 12, 13, and 14 we introduce some important techniques for analyzing different types of data. Chapter 15 discusses the presentation of the research design and the culmination of the research process.

Each chapter assumes that you have mastered the previous chapters, and

FIGURE I-1 The Research Process

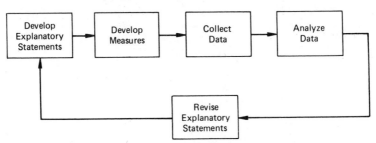

builds upon that knowledge. Review questions at the end of each chapter give you feedback on whether you have mastered the subject. If you have not, do not proceed. A shaky foundation cannot support a very strong building.

Laboratory exercises follow the text of each chapter. They allow you to use the knowledge you have acquired. Working through the exercises will aid your understanding and increase your retention of the material.

Research methodology can be learned only by practice, and it is valuable only if it can be used. We are not concerned with rote memorization. The ability to spout back specific definitions should not be a criterion for success; success comes with the ability to use the terms in actual practice. To help you learn the technical vocabulary we will be introducing, we have provided a glossary in the appendix.

Research Examples and Obstacles to Perfection

Examples of actual empirical research follow Chapters 1, 9 and 10. They show how others have handled some of the issues discussed in those chapters. Try to evaluate these articles as you read them. In your evaluation consider questions like these: Is the case convincingly presented? Could the research design have been improved? How would you have carried out the project?

When you evaluate, look for major problems in the case presented. Remember, however, that whoever did the research was limited in time, money, and other resources necessary for the project. All researchers face those obstacles when they do research. So if we fall somewhat short of perfection, we can expect no more. It's how far short we fall that determines whether or not the explanation will be accepted.

CHAPTER ONE

EXPLANATIONS AND HYPOTHESES

MAKING EXPLANATIONS

The research process begins with an observation of variation in behavior. You note, for example, that some people have voted for a school bond issue and others have voted against it. Or that some Supreme Court justices find abortion laws to be constitutional while others do not. Or that some countries have a higher inflation rate than others.

As social scientists, we assume that such variation is not just haphazard. The people who vote for the bond issue differ from those who vote against it. It is our task to explain which differences among people cause them to vote differently. Similarly, justices who find abortion laws to be constitutional differ from those who do not. Countries that differ with respect to inflation rates also differ in other respects. Our task is to explain which other differences among justices cause them to differ with respect to abortion, or to explain which differences among countries cause them to have different rates of inflation.

To Whom or What the Explanations Apply

The Theoretical Population. Explanations may apply to individual human beings or to groups of human beings—for example, organizations, communities, states, or nations. The group of objects to which an explanation applies is called the **theoretical population.** In the examples above, the theoretical population would have been individuals who vote on school bonds, Supreme Court justices, and nations.

When we gather data to see if an explanation is correct, each object on which the data are gathered should be part of the theoretical population. Those objects are referred to as **units of analysis.**

If we were gathering data on school-bond voting, as in the first example above, each voter would be a unit of analysis. Mary Smith might be one such unit. We would determine how Mary voted, plus other data about Mary that might explain her voting. A voter named Bill Jones might be a second unit of analysis.

If we were gathering data on inflation rates, as in the third example above, the unit of analysis would be the nation. The United States would be one such unit. The inflation rate in the United States would be determined, as well as other data about the United States. In this case the individual human being is not the unit of analysis. Individuals such as Mary and Bill make up the United States, but if we are seeking to explain why some nations have higher inflation rates than others, nations make up the theoretical population and it is nations that should be observed.

Given that one goal of science is generalization, the more widely applicable an explanation—that is, the more inclusive the theoretical population—the more valuable it is. An explanation applying to all people for all time would be more valuable than one applying to fewer people or for a more limited time. It is unfortunate that less inclusive explanations are usually easier to verify.

What We Are Explaining

Properties. Units in the theoretical population will differ with respect to many characteristics, attributes, or types of behavior. These we call the **properties** of the units. Age, number of years in the community, and position on the school-bond referendum are three properties of individuals who vote on such referenda. Religious affiliation, prestige of law school attended, and position on abortion are three properties of Supreme Court justices. The size of the government deficit, the degree of progressiveness of the tax structure, and the rate of inflation are three properties of nations.

Because the units of analysis vary with respect to the properties that are of interest to social scientists, the term *variable* is often used instead of the term *property.* Although the terms can be distinguished, their meanings are close enough to generally permit them to be used interchangeably.

Kinds of Properties. We distinguish two broad types of properties: **qualitative properties,** where units are classified by type, and **relative properties,** where units are classified by degree or amount. Religious affiliation is an example of a qualitative property. Each person is classified as a Protestant, a Catholic, a Jew, and so on, without any implication that one of those types is "higher" or has "more" religious affiliation than any other type. Protestants, Catholics, and Jews simply differ from each other with respect to this property, so we classify them as having different religious affiliations.

Age is an example of a relative property. Whether people are classified by actual age; as "older" and "younger"; as "over 50," "30 to 50," or "under 30"; or as "old" and "young"; the classifications are based on the number of years or relative number of years the person has lived. Some have more of this property and others have less.

In the examples we have been considering, "vote on the school bond issue" (for or against), and "decision on the constitutionality of abortion" (constitutional or unconstitutional) are qualitative properties. The relative properties are "number of years in the community," "prestige of law school attended," "size of government deficit," "progressiveness of tax structure," and "inflation rate."

When a property is divided into categories, students will occasionally confuse the property and the categories. For example, Democrats and Republicans might be identified as two properties rather than as two categories of a single property, political-party affiliation. A simple way of determining if the word is a property or a category is to ask a question in this form: What is the unit's _____? If it is a property, the sentence will make sense. If it is a category, the sentence will not make sense. To use the political-party example, "What is the unit's party?" makes sense. "What is the unit's Republican?" does not.

How We Explain Variation in Properties

Relationship Between Properties. As stated before, we assume that if units behave differently, it is because they differ with respect to one or more other properties. It is variation in other properties that causes or influences variation in the property we are seeking to explain. For example, variation in age may influence how people vote on school bond issues. Similarly, variation in religious affiliation may cause justices to vary in their opinions regarding the constitutionality of abortion laws. Variation in the size of the government deficit may cause variation in the inflation rate.

An explanation must state precisely what variation in one property will cause a particular variation in another. How does growing older affect voting on school bond issues? Which religious affiliations incline justices to view abortion laws as constitutional, and which do not? Do larger deficits increase or decrease the inflation rate?

A statement asserting that specific variation in one property results in or causes specific variation in the property we are seeking to explain is called a **hypothesis.** One hypothesis would be, "Older voters are less likely to vote for school bond issues than are younger voters." That hypothesis specifically relates variation in the properties "age" and "vote on school bond issues." If we verified it by actually comparing the ages and votes of citizens, it would be a partial explanation of why people differ in their voting.

Similarly, "Protestant justices are more likely to decide that abortion laws are constitutional than are Catholic justices" is a hypothesis explaining why justices differ on the abortion issue. "The larger the government deficit, the higher the nation's inflation rate tends to be," is a hypothesis explaining why some nations have higher inflation rates than do others. Each of these hypotheses would be subject to verification by examination of the properties of the units being analyzed.

In a hypothesis the property we are seeking to explain is called the **depen-**

dent property or **dependent variable;** the property that is asserted to cause variation in the dependent property is called the **independent property** or **independent
variable.** The dependent properties in the examples above were "vote on the
school bond issue," "constitutionality of abortion laws," and "inflation rate."
The independent properties were "age," "religion," and "size of government deficit."

An Important Assumption. At the end of every hypothesis we could, and perhaps should, write "all other properties being held constant." When we state
that older voters are less likely to vote for school bond issues than are younger
voters, we mean that if voters differed *only* with respect to age, then the older
voters would be the least likely to vote for bond issues.

Why State Hypotheses?

It is generally important in empirical work to assert what you think you
will find before you go out exploring. There are several practical reasons for this.
You waste fewer resources if you know exactly what you need to observe before-
hand; you don't overlook observing things that turn out to be necessary; you are
forced to find what previous scientific or other observation has already discovered, reducing the duplication of effort. More important, science proceeds by a
process of continual verification of offered explanation. It is only through this
process that we can claim generality for findings.

Let us consider the example of explaining party voting in elections. Suppose you gathered a lot of data on as many different properties as you could for
a particular election. You then analyzed the data and found all the possible associations. Then you proceeded to build an explanation based on the properties
you found to be associated. There would be two problems with your explanation.
First, your conclusions could have been based on factors that were highly unique
to the election; if so, they would not be open to generalization. Second, your conclusions could have been the product of measurement error.

The verification route would have required you to have first looked back at
what earlier researchers had learned about voting behavior, and what observers
had suggested about factors that caused voting behavior. You would have then
created a series of assertions about relationships that you expected to find. You
would have tested the assertions. Assertions verified in that manner would not
likely be based on factors unique to that election. Any assertions you found not
to be true could be brought into question and new explanations suggested. These
new explanations could then be tested by additional research, in which you
would use the new explanations as a basis for the assertions. It is through the
route of development of explanations, hypotheses, verification of the hypotheses,
revisions of the hypotheses, and retesting that a body of scientific knowledge is
generated.

CONSTRUCTING HYPOTHESES

Hypotheses should be clear, concise, and unambiguous. They should communicate the theoretical population, the properties, and the way in which the properties are associated. In addition, they should be as general as possible and must not involve value statements. Let us consider these requirements more closely.

Information Communicated in the Hypothesis

The Theoretical Population. Most often the theoretical population is implied by the context of the hypothesis and is not explicitly stated. For example, if we state that "Protestant justices are more likely to decide that abortion laws are constitutional than are Catholic justices," the theoretical population is implicitly Supreme Court justices. If, however, we want to restrict the theoretical population to liberal justices, then the hypothesis must include a statement to that effect—for example, "Among liberal justices, Protestants are more likely to decide that abortion laws are constitutional than are Catholics."

The Properties. A hypothesis must relate two properties of the units of analysis. Consider the hypothesis "The larger a nation's government deficit, the higher its inflation rate tends to be." This relates two properties: "size of deficit" and "inflation rate."

There are a number of important statements that do not relate two properties. Some of these may be important to a full explanation of behavior, and some we may test empirically to see if they are true. Statements like "People are avaricious" or "More people are Democrats than are Republicans" are not hypotheses because they each refer to just one property.

A statement relating three or more properties may be referred to as a **compound hypothesis.** Compound hypotheses tend to be unclear in intent, and are usually clarified by reduction to two or more hypotheses, each relating just two properties. An example of a compound hypothesis would be "The larger a nation's government deficit and the more progressive its tax structure, the higher its inflation rate is likely to be." There really are two hypotheses in that statement, one relating size of deficit to inflation rate and the other relating progressiveness of tax structure to inflation rate. We should test each separately to see if it is supported by the evidence.

The Relationship. The hypothesis should state specifically what difference in the second property is expected if there is a difference in the first property. It is not sufficient for an explanation to state that age affects voting, or that religion influences justices' decisions, or that deficits have an impact on the inflation rate. Hypotheses need to assert that specific variation in the independent property results in specific variation in the dependent property. Note how the hypotheses we have been considering specify the consequences of being older, of having different religious beliefs, and of larger deficits.

Occasionally a researcher may have good reason to believe that two variables are causally related, but cannot predict the direction of the relationship. Only when this occurs, should the direction not be indicated in the hypothesis.

Statements that refer to only one category of a property cannot specify a relationship completely. "Protestant justices tend to rule that abortion laws are constitutional" would be such a statement. That statement describes the behavior of Protestant justices, but fails to tell how it differs from the behavior of justices having other religious affiliations. The author of the statement probably means that Catholics are less likely than Protestants to rule in this way—but if that is what he means, that is what he should say. Without an explicit comparison we cannot tell if the author is even comparing Protestants and Catholics; he could be thinking of Protestant/Jewish differences or Protestant/atheist differences. Be sure to state completely how variation in the independent property causes variation in the dependent property.

Making Hypotheses General. Since the goal of social science is general explanation, we try to avoid hypotheses that refer only to specific situations. Generality is a matter of degree, and so it is not possible to state that only general hypotheses are worth verifying, or to determine where the line between general and nongeneral statements is to be drawn. Hypotheses should be as general as possible without going beyond the limits of what can be verified. A statement like this would not be considered very general: "England has a more stable government than China." A more general hypothesis would be "The greater the economic development of a nation, the more stable its government tends to be."

Avoiding Value Judgments. We have indicated that certain kinds of questions cannot be answered by empirical research. We cannot resolve questions of good and evil through empirical research. Therefore, we must avoid value judgments in stating hypotheses. For example, the statement "Countries should adopt democratic rather than dictatorial forms of government" involves a value judgement and cannot be empirically tested. Whether the statement is true or not depends on each individual's values. In contrast, the hypothesis "People have a higher per-capita income under democracies than they do under dictatorships" can be tested by observation. Some people might view higher per-capita income as a good thing, others might not. But whether some people have a higher per-capita income than others can be determined without recourse to value judgements.

Forms of Hypotheses

You can state hypotheses in a number of different ways, as long as all of the required information is contained. Some of the simplest forms are discussed below and examples are given. The examples are designed to serve as models for writing hypotheses. When writing your own hypotheses, substitute references to the properties you are relating for the nonitalicized phrases in the examples.

When Both Properties Are Relative. When both properties are relative, state what happens to the dependent property when the independent property increases. For example:

1. *If* military spending in countries *increases, then* the rate of economic development *tends to decrease.*
2. *As* the per-capita income in cities *increases, the* bond rating *tends to increase.*
3. *The more* education individuals have, *the less* frequently they will vote a straight party ticket.
4. An *increase* in social class causes people to vote for more conservative candidates.

When Only the Independent Property Is Relative. When only the independent property is relative, state the category of the dependent property that is most likely to result when the independent property increases. For example:

1. *As* the population of a city *increases,* it is *more likely* to adopt zoning ordinances.
2. *The more* money candidates raise, *the more* likely they are to be elected.
3. In nations, a decrease in economic satisfaction leads to revolution.

When Only the Dependent Property Is Relative. When only the dependent variable is relative, state which category of the independent property will result in more of the dependent variable. For example:

1. Female legislators *tend to get more* press coverage *than* do male legislators.
2. The rate of increase in GNP per capita *tends to be higher* in free-market economies *than* in centrally planned economies.
3. *If* cities *adopt* nonpartisan elections, *then* turnout for elections *tends to decline.*

When Both Properties Are Qualitative. When both properties are qualitative, state for each category of the independent property which category of the dependent variable is most probable. For example:

1. States that finance local school districts with local property taxes *are less likely than* other states to adopt a state income tax.
2. Lawyers in the legislature are *more likely to* vote against no-fault insurance *than are* nonlawyers.

Restricting the Theoretical Population. To restrict the theoretical population of any of these forms, simply precede it with a limiting parenthetical phrase, such as "Among developed nations," or "In competitive districts."

Errors In Hypothesis Writing

Here are examples of some common errors people make in writing hypotheses.

1. The statement has only one property:
   a. Hypotheses must relate two properties.
      Not a hypothesis: People are alienated from the political system. There is only one property in this statement, alienation from the political system. It must be related to some other factor for there to be a hypothesis.

      Better: People who are alienated from the political system are less likely to vote than those who are not alienated.
   b. The two properties identified must not be two words for the same thing. In other words, hypotheses should not be true by definition.
      Not a hypothesis: More tolerant individuals tend to be less prejudiced than less tolerant individuals.

      If we interpret the words *tolerance* and *prejudice* as they are normally used, the statement says that more tolerant people tend to be more tolerant than less tolerant people.
      Better: The more highly educated the person, the more tolerant he or she is likely to be.
2. The relationship is unclear:
   a. The relationship between the two properties should not be stated vaguely.
      Not a hypothesis: Economic development is related to level of literacy.

      We cannot tell from this statement whether literacy increases or decreases as a nation develops economically.
      Better: As a nation develops economically, its level of literacy tends to increase.
   b. Hypotheses must not simply describe units in one category of a property.
      Not a hypothesis: Families living in the central city have low median incomes.

      Comparison of units that differ with respect to both properties is critical to any hypothesis.
      Better: Families living in the central city tend to have lower median incomes than do families in the suburbs.
3. The statement lacks generality:
   a. Hypotheses should not use personal names or names of countries.
      Not a sufficiently general hypothesis: John Foster Dulles (secretary of state in the 1950s) was less credible than Robert McNamara (secretary of defense in the 1960s).

Case studies of great men often suggest hypotheses, but here as in any hypothesis the statement should be general.

Better: Foreign policies based on massive retaliation tend to be less credible than those based on flexible response.

b. Hypotheses should not be limited to a very specific period of time.

Not a hypothesis: The Supreme Court struck down fewer laws in 1940 than in 1935.

Again, the hypothesis should be more general. Historical studies often suggest hypotheses that could be tested.

Better: When the majority of the justices on the Supreme Court have been appointed by the incumbent president, the Court is less likely to strike down legislation than it is when less than a majority have been appointed by the incumbent president.

4. The statement makes a value judgment:

a. Hypotheses should not use words such as *should, ought, better,* or *worse.* These words indicate a value judgment is being made.

Not a hypothesis: Conservatives are better than liberals.

Such value judgments may conceal a hypothesis that could be made explicit.

Better: Conservatives are more likely to vote than liberals.

VERIFYING HYPOTHESES

We can never be absolutely certain that a hypothesis is true. We can rarely examine the entire theoretical population to see if the asserted relationship holds for all units. We can never hold constant all other properties that might cause variation in the dependent property. The best we can generally do is examine part of the theoretical population in some detail, in order to show that the asserted relationship exists for those units after several other potentially influential properties have been held constant.

Association

At the heart of verification is the demonstration that there is an *association* between the independent and dependent properties: that units differing with respect to the first property generally differ with respect to the second property in a consistent fashion. If older voters are more likely to vote against bond issues than are younger voters, we would say that there is an association between age and voting.

Association between two properties is essential in showing support for an explanation. If either property varies while the other remains constant, then one cannot be the cause of the other. For example, the "sinfulness of people" cannot be what causes war; sometimes people go to war and sometimes they do not, but the "sinfulness of people" is always present. Similarly, if there is no consistent way in which variation in one property is related to variation in the other property, then one is not the cause of the other. For example, height is not a cause of political ideology; even though both properties vary, there is no consistent relationship between the variation in height and the variation in ideology.

Not Every Association Explains

Causal Association. Demonstrating that there is an association between the independent and dependent properties for the units you are analyzing is not sufficient to verify a hypothesis. What we are searching for is a **causal association,** an association in which variation in one property causes (leads to, results in, influences, affects) variation in a second property. We want to be able to say that the differences in behavior came about *because of* the difference in some other property.

Many observed associations between pairs of properties are not the result of variation in one property causing variation in the other. For example, among nations there is an association between levels of pollution and levels of literacy. Yet it is unlikely that reading leads to pollution, or that pollution causes the populace to read. Variation in one or more other properties (possible industrialization) causes variation in both pollution and literacy. If those other properties were held constant (if only highly industrialized nations were observed, for example) there would be no association between pollution and literacy.

Holding Constant Other Properties. To verify a hypothesis, you must show that there is an association between the independent and dependent properties *after* you have held constant the variation in other possibly causal properties. For example, to verify the hypothesis "Higher-income voters are less likely to vote for school bond issues than are lower-income voters," it would be necessary to hold constant the ages of voters. We might do this by comparing voters of the same age but different incomes.

MULTIPLE CAUSATION

We live in a complex world. Human behavior and the behavior of human institutions is almost never explained by the variation in a single property. No single hypothesis is ever likely to be a complete explanation, Age, income, number of children in schools, and several other properties may all independently influence how citizens will vote on school bond issues. Religious affiliation, prestige of law school, number of years as a federal judge, and several other properties may all independently influence how Supreme Court justices will rule on abortion. Size of deficits, progressiveness of tax structure, percentage of labor force in unions, and several other properties may independently affect inflation rates.

Complete explanations, if possible, would require virtually unlimited sets of interrelated hypotheses. All research projects are limited by time and other resources, and will at best produce incomplete explanations. It is the accumulation of those incomplete explanations that advances our knowledge of human behavior.

RESEARCH EXAMPLE

We conclude with a brief example from published research that illustrates what we have been considering in this chapter. The extract, part of an article by Jon Bond that appeared in *Law and Policy Quarterly*, 2 (April 1980), 181–82 (used here with permission) illustrates how the author developed hypotheses in order to partially explain why proposals to add judges to the federal judiciary are more likely to pass Congress in some years than in others.

As you read the article, try to determine the theoretical population and the independent and dependent properties for each hypothesis. Note that the theoretical population is more restricted than we would like for a major research effort, but appropriate for a short example of this type. Note also that the dependent variable is the same in both hypotheses, because both seek to explain the same observed variation. In verifying each hypothesis (which he does later in the article), Bond holds constant each independent property and shows that the other independent property is associated with the dependent property.

THE POLITICS OF COURT STRUCTURE: THE ADDITION OF NEW FEDERAL JUDGES, 1949–1978

Jon R. Bond

An increasing case load in the federal courts creates a need for more judges. Congressional decisions to respond to these needs are inevitably influenced by politics.

Previous research on Supreme Court appointments reveals that political variables such as party control of the Presidency and Senate, and the timing of nominations influence presidential success in securing Senate confirmation (Scigliano, 1971: 97–98). Richardson and Vines (1971) suggest that similar factors may influence congressional decisions to add new federal judges. They note that omnibus bills adding new judges in 1949, 1954, 1961, and 166 closely followed presidential victories and were "intended to provide patronage for the administration, the Senate, and the state parties." These examples lead them to the broader conclusion that "the omnibus bills represent accumulations of judicial needs and judicial appointments saved for the periods following the national campaigns, when the need for party allocations of important positions is greatest" (Richardson and Vines, 1971: 49).

However, this conclusion is based on only four bills which passed during the first two years of the President's term *and* during the time the same party controlled the Presidency and Congress. Richardson and Vines do not examine any proposals which failed, and they say nothing about the success of proposals made late in the President's term or when the opposition party controls Congress. Using a more comprehensive and updated data set, this brief note tests two hypotheses suggested by their analysis:

*H*1.   Proposals to add new federal judges are more likely to pass if the party controls the Presidency and Congress than if different parties are in power.

*H*2.   Proposals to add new federal judges are more likely to pass during the first two years of the President's term than during the second two years.

The basis of these hypotheses is straightforward. Presidents almost always appoint members of their party to fill judicial vacancies, and Congress is naturally reluctant to give an opposition party President additional opportunities to reward his partisans with lifetime appointments. But timing is important also— regardless of party control, Congress is not likely to pass proposals to expand the judiciary late in a President's term. A Congress controlled by the opposition party has an incentive to delay action until after the election, in hopes of capturing the Presidency, and short delays are easier to justify than long delays. A Congress controlled by the President's party does not wish to be accused of playing politics with the judiciary, and adding new federal judges late in a President's term smacks of politics. Thus, we expect party control and timing to exert independent effects, but we also need to consider the combined impact of these variables.

References for Bond Article

RICHARDSON, R., and K. N. VINES (1971) *The Politics of Federal Courts.* Boston: Little, Brown.

SCIGLIANO, R. (1971) *The Supreme Court and the Presidency.* New York: Free Press.

LABORATORY EXERCISES

This laboratory is designed to give you practice in recognizing, analyzing, and developing hypotheses.

Task 1.   Indicate for each of the hypotheses below (a) the theoretical population; (b) the independent property; (c) the dependent property; and (d) two examples of data you could gather to test the hypothesis (for example, if the hypothesis is "Women are less likely to vote than men," you might interview American citizens after a presidential election to see who voted and to determine their gender, or you might get a sample of voting-age residents in a city and inspect voting lists from the last municipal election to see who voted and to determine gender from their name).

*H*1. Candidates who spend more money than each of their opponents during an election campaign are more likely to be elected than are those who spend less than their opponents.

*H*2. In comparing individuals over time, as their marginal income-tax rates increase, they tend to work fewer hours per week.

*H*3. The greater the population growth rate of cities, the more competitive city elections will tend to be.

*H*4. The longer members of congress serve, the more conservatively they tend to vote.

*H*5. The greater the freedom of press within nations, the more stable their governments tend to be.

Task 2. Evaluate the following statements. Indicate which are incorrect hypotheses and what is wrong with them.

*H*1. In socialist countries the government is more likely to own businesses than it is in nonsocialist countries.

*H*2. The government should lower taxes.

*H*3. There is a greater degree of political instability in Great Britian than in the United States.

*H*4. Poor, less well educated people are more likely to be liberal than are wealthy, better educated people.

*H*5. Workers from some industries are more likely to strike than are workers from other industries.

*H*6. Northern cities have high crime rates.

Task 3. Develop hypotheses as indicated:

a. a hypothesis relating two relative properties
b. a hypothesis relating two qualitative properties
c. a hypothesis relating a relative independent property and a qualitative dependent property
d. a hypothesis relating a qualitative independent property and a relative dependent property

Task 4. Especially in the nonscientific literature, explanations frequently contain statements that are hypotheses, imply hypotheses, or that can be restated as hypotheses. Those statements are often not called hypotheses by their authors, but can be recognized as such by social scientists. Find hypotheses in the following passage from the Supreme Court's decision in Brown *v.* Board of Education. Restate them in proper form.

> Segregation of white and colored children in public schools has a detrimental effect upon colored children. The impact is greater when it has the sanction of the law; for the policy of separating the races is usually interpreted as denoting the inferiority of the negro group. A sense of inferiority affects the motivation of a child to learn. Segregation with the sanction of the law, therefore, has a tendency to retard the educational and mental development of negro children and to deprive them of some of the benefits they would receive in a racially integrated school system.

REVIEW QUESTIONS

1. What is the major weakness (if any) in the statement of this hypothesis "Catholics tend to be liberal"?

2. What is the major weakness (if any) in the statement of this hypothesis "Deficit spending by the federal government tends to alter the inflation rate"?

3. What is the major weakness (if any) in the statement of this hypothesis "Because it is so difficult to manage, cities should find an alternative to the property tax"?

4. Write a hypothesis in correct form that might partially explain why Democrats running for Congress are successful in some districts and not in others.

5. Write a hypothesis in correct form relating socioeconomic status, as the independent property, to party identification, as the dependent property.

6. Hypothesis: People who hold bachelor's degrees in the liberal arts are more likely to vote for Democratic presidential candidates than are holders of non-liberal-arts bachelor's degrees.
   a. What is the theoretical population?
   b. What is the independent property? Is that property qualitative or relative?
   c. What is the dependent property? Is that property qualitative or relative?
   d. Give two examples of the type of units you would collect data on, and indicate the type of data you would collect in order to test this hypothesis.

7. Hypothesis: The higher the taxes are for cities, the higher the turnover rate will tend to be for city councilors of those cities.

a. What is the theoretical population?
b. What is the independent property? Is that property qualitative or relative?
c. What is the dependent property? Is that property qualitative or relative?
d. Give two examples of the type of units you would collect data on, and indicate the type of data you would collect in order to test this hypothesis.

CHAPTER TWO

DEVELOPING AND REPORTING EXPLANATIONS

In doing empirical research, we start by offering the best possible explanation of some phenomenon given existing knowledge. We can judge the adequacy of the explanation and the existing knowledge by testing the hypotheses that are part of the explanation.

Finding support for hypotheses from existing knowledge assumes that the causes of behavioral differences are not peculiar to the particular case being studied. Explanations offered in other research lead us to explanations in our own, and the findings from our research contribute to the body of knowledge that may help others explain yet other cases. It is this process that enables science to produce a body of literature that provides general explanations.

DEVELOPING EXPLANATIONS

Reasoning Behind Hypotheses

There are two general lines of reasoning you can take to develop hypotheses. The first is to derive specific hypotheses from more general explanations. General explanations are often called theories. **Theories** are general explanations that are constructed from interrelated sets of hypotheses. An example of a general explanation is cognitive-dissonance theory. It predicts that when people are confronted by information that is contrary to what they already believe, they will tend to ignore the information. It has been tested in many different situations and has generally been supported. A researcher might use this theory to develop the hypothesis that voters are more likely to ignore negative than positive information about the candidate they support.

The second line of reasoning is to derive hypotheses based on similar hypotheses supported by previous research. For example, in the research example at the end of Chapter 1, Jon Bond suggested the hypothesis that proposals to create new federal judgeships are more likely to pass if the same party controls the presidency and Congress than if they are controlled by different parties. To support this he cites previous research on success in Senate confirmations of Supreme Court nominees. Since the circumstances are similar, he argues that factors influencing success in confirmations of Supreme Court justices also influence the likelihood of new judgeships being created.

Since the goal of science is to produce general explanations, it is most useful to test hypotheses arising from general explanations. Testing those hypotheses will help confirm or cast doubt upon the general explanation. Often, however, our existing knowledge is such that we lack a general explanation that is useful in explaining variation in a property. In these circumstances it is necessary to use hypotheses based only on previous research that has not produced a general explanation. The knowledge gained in testing the hypothesis may help us to develop more general explanations.

Developing Hypotheses Having Different Independent Properties

As we indicated in the first chapter, a single hypothesis is almost always insufficient to explain variation in a property. Variation in a property is almost always caused by variation in several other properties. The researcher should develop several hypotheses, each relating a different independent variable to the dependent variable.

In the research example at the end of Chapter 1, two hypotheses explaining the likelihood of passage of proposals to add new federal judges were suggested. The dependent variable for both hypotheses was likelihood of passage. The independent variable in the first hypothesis was whether or not the same party controlled the presidency and Congress; the independent variable in the second hypothesis was whether the proposal was made early or late in the president's term of office. The two hypotheses together explain more of the variation in likelihood of passage than does either hypothesis by itself. To *completely* explain the likelihood of passage would require additional hypotheses.

Research often involves adding a new hypothesis to several that have previously been found to be explanations for a dependent variable. In such a case we must test all of the hypotheses in order to determine how important the new variable is relative to the existing ones in explaining the dependent variable.

An example may make this clearer. A researcher wanted to test the effect of the size of an interest group in a constituency on the roll-call votes of members of Congress. Specifically, he hypothesized that members of Congress from states with a smaller number of hunting licenses per capita would be more likely to support gun control than representatives from states with a greater number of hunting licenses per capita. He found a great deal of support in the literature for the notion that constituency interest did influence congressional voting on some issues. But he also found that there were other factors that explain much of congressional voting. The principal factors were the party and the ideology of the representative. Although there was little reason for him to be interested in yet another test of the effect of party and ideology on voting in Congress, he could not test the possible influence of numbers of hunters without considering those factors. The apparent effect of numbers of hunters could have been a function of different types of states tending to elect members of different parties or ideologies. Also, in evaluating the effect of number of hunting licenses he wanted to be able to compare its importance with the already established importance of party and ideology.

Sources of Explanation

A careful search of the literature is usually the most valuable source of general explanations and previous research that can be used to develop and justify hypotheses. A search of the literature will also identify hypotheses that have not been supported in previous research and also hypotheses that have been suggested but not tested. A very good place to begin a search of the literature is with basic textbooks on the subject. These will usually identify important work in the area and give a good overview of the subject.

The literature is not the only source of explanation. Exploratory research is often a valuable supplement to the literature in developing hypotheses. Casual personal observation is a common initial source of hypotheses.

The Professional Literature. An important part of developing a science is having a careful record of research that is accessible to researchers. Without such a record there is no way to build on previous research. Each field of science has several journals that regularly publish reports of research. In addition, there are books and other publications that report research findings of the people working in that field. These published sources, which we call the **professional literature,** are the primary source of explanations for most empirical research.

Journals.   In the field of political science there are general-purpose journals and journals that focus on specific subfields. Some cross-disciplinary journals and journals in related disciplines may also be of assistance. The major general-purpose journals are the official journal of the American Political Science Association, the *American Political Science Review,* and the journals of the regional associations:

Journal of Politics
American Journal of Political Science
Polity
Western Political Science Quarterly
Social Science Quarterly

Among the most useful journals concentrating on subfields are:

World Politics
International Studies Quarterly
International Organization
Comparative Politics
Public Administration Review
Urban Affairs Quarterly
Law and Society
Legislative Politics Quarterly
American Politics Quarterly

The most useful cross-disciplinary journals include:

Journal of Conflict Resolution
Public Opinion Quarterly
American Behavioral Scientist

The top journals in related disciplines include:

American Sociological Review
American Journal of Sociology
American Psychologist
American Economic Review

Some professional journals are more policy-oriented. They generally do not publish complete reports on empirical research, but they may suggest explanations to you. The most useful include:

Annals of the American Academy of Political and Social Science
Public Interest
Public Policy

Problems with the Professional Literature.   There are problems with the professional literature. A major problem, particularly for students and others who are not professional social scientists, is that the professional literature is often hard to read and understand without considerable prior knowledge. Specialized language is often used; references may be made to literature that the reader needs to have read to understand the work; complex methods of analysis may be used that require considerable methodological sophistication. It is probably true that some of the obscurity could be avoided, but for whatever reason, much of the professional literature is very hard to read.

Another problem with the professional literature is an extreme delay between the completion of research and its appearance in a professional journal or book. The **backlog time** (time between acceptance and publication of an article) for most journals now runs between one and three years. To find the full time between research and publication, one must add to the backlog time the time needed to write the article after the research is finished, the time to review the article before a journal will accept it (usually several months), the time to revise the article in line with reviewers' comments, and the time to review the final draft. It is a minor miracle if research is seen in the professional literature within two years of its completion. Delays of four or five years between completion and publication are not uncommon. To compound the problem, most professional articles in political science have a useful life span of less than six years. After that time they are unlikely to be cited in other research.[1]

A final major problem is the limited amount of space available for reporting research. This has two consequences. First, a number of reasonably sound research reports are unavailable to researchers. For example, the *American Political Science Review* usually accepts 10 percent or less of the articles submitted to it. This space limitation is especially a problem for reports viewed as too narrow for the professional audience as a whole. The second consequence is that the profession has set up an elaborate, if not always wise, method of evaluating articles: Most must be reviewed by at least three evaluators, an often lengthy process.

Informed Commentary. In the social sciences, whose subject matter may be of general interest to others, whether scientists or not, nonscientific sources often contain articles that are useful in developing explanations. We refer to these sources as **informed commentary.**

Political commentary by nonprofessionals is not likely to be as helpful in suggesting valid general explanations as is the professional literature. For one thing, nonprofessional commentary tends to focus on single cases of immediate interest, and the suggested explanations tend to be specific to those cases rather than generally applicable. For another, commentators rarely subject possible explanations to empirical testing. Often the explanations are suggested before an event and are not checked afterwards.

Despite that, newspapers and newsmagazines can be valuable sources of explanations. They frequently comment on topics not covered in the professional literature. They are also much more likely to be up to date than the journals and professional books.

News stories, editorials, and political analyses in the newsmagazines and newspapers are likely to suggest explanations. The political bent of the author or the publication may give you a clue as to which groups support a particular issue. You can follow up a commentary through the indexes by looking for other articles by the same author, or by tracking down work by others to which the commentary may have referred.

Exploratory Research. Another source of explanation is **exploratory research**—empirical research that proceeds without hypotheses and/or involves looking at a smaller amount or a different kind of data than would be appropriate for research designed to test hypotheses. Exploratory research should supplement the review of the literature, not substitute for it. A great number of explanations are possible for any observed behavior. The prior review of the literature should serve to focus your explorations in such a way as to determine which of the explanations is the most likely to be corroborated in later research.

Exploratory research takes many forms. Frequently the research involves a detailed analysis of a very small number of units, often the study of a single group. With a very small sample the researcher can gather information on a large number of properties without going to great expense. For example, a researcher may study her friends and acquaintances in order to gain insights useful in suggesting explanations. The availability of computerized data banks and computer analysis has made it somewhat easier in recent years to do exploratory research with larger samples. Data collected for other purposes are made available to researchers, who can use them to conduct exploratory research.

Exploratory research often makes use of laboratory analogies to the units of analysis. Sometimes this involves studying the behavior of laboratory animals in the hope that their behavior will be similar to that of humans. More often it involves studying the behavior of students under conditions simulating those of interest—again, in the hope that the laboratory behavior will be similar enough to outside-world behavior for the explanations suggested in the lab to apply outside.

Casual Observation. The most important *initial* source of an explanation is simply the casual observation of the researcher. Curiosity and an attentiveness to patterns of human behavior often combine to produce reasonable explanation. Consider the following introduction to a study on making judgments about guilt and punishment:

> The casual observations which led to the research reported below were made by one of the authors while he was in graduate school, mainly during a period of several months when he was also working as a "hacker" or taxicab driver in the Washington, D.C., area. This job provided numerous opportunities for informally questioning widely divergent types of people about current political news. No systematic procedure was followed, but a few notes were made and lengthy discussions about the observations with classmates and professors helped to crystallize a number of initial impressions. These discussions like the observations themselves were informal, but they were an important device for exploring the extent to which others had seen the same phenomena.[2]

This kind of observation is a form of exploratory research. We treat it separately in order to emphasize the important role it plays in scientific inquiry. Many, if not most, of our most profound explanations originate in the casual observations of an inquiring mind.

Casual observation offers a possible starting point for explanations, but it does not offer an excuse for avoiding a search of the literature or formal exploratory research. Perhaps others have made the same observations as you, and their work may help you develop (or discard) your explanation.

Increased understanding of human behavior does not come about solely from perusal of the work of other scholars. Yet it is unlikely to come about solely through casual observations by even our best minds. What is most likely to increase understanding is observation informed by and added to the body of knowledge that constitutes our discipline.

Finding Sources in the Literature

There are a variety of sources of information to help you find research reports and other information relevant to your research. Several of these sources may not be familiar to you. In this section we discuss methods for finding your way around the professional literature and informed commentary.

The Professional Literature. Since thousands of books and articles by social scientists are published every year, it is best to begin any search with one of the guides to published literature. These guides include bibliographies, indexes, and abstracts. More and more libraries are having these guides computerized, and for a fee they will retrieve a list of appropriate literature.

Among the most useful bibliographies and indexes to published professional literature in political science are:

The library card catalogue, subject guide—Remember to look under various related headings.

Social Science Index (formerly the *Social Sciences and Humanities Index*)—A quarterly index (since 1916), by author and subject, of articles in over 200 scholarly periodicals from the United States, Canada, and the United Kingdom.

Public Affairs Information Service Bulletin—A weekly index (since 1915), by topic and author, of periodical literature, pamphlets, some books, and government publications.

Social Science Citation Index: Subject Index—A semiannual index (since 1972) based on key words in the titles of articles.

Advanced Bibliography of Content: Political Science—Reproduces (since 1969) the complete list of articles from the table of contents of about 260 scholarly journals.

United States Political Science Documents—Annual index (since 1975) by author, subject, geographic area, journal, and proper names.

Combined Respective Index to Journals in Political Science 1886–1974—subject index, by field, key words, and author.

Most of these bibliographies and indexes directly list the complete citation necessary to find the literature you are after. However, some use a two-entry system. If the listing you find is incomplete, it leads you to a second list that has the
complete citation.

In addition to the bibliographies and indexes, there are guides to the literature that include short summaries of the contents of the work cited. These
guides are called abstracts. They are more useful than the simple lists of sources,
but have more limited coverage. The most useful are:

> *International Political Science Abstracts*—A quarterly journal (since 1951)
> abstracting about 1500 articles per year from more than 200 journals from
> around the world.
>
> *United States Political Science Documents*—Abstracts of articles indexed
> in the index volume cited above.

Abstracts for related fields may also provide you with useful information:

> *Sociological Abstracts*—A journal that appears eight times each year (since
> 1952.) It contains about 5000 abstracts per year. Abstracts of special inter-
> est to political scientists are classified under "Political Interactions."
>
> *Psychological Abstracts*—A monthly journal (since 1964), it abstracts
> about 9000 articles per year.
>
> *Key to Economic Science and Managerial Sciences*—Semimonthly ab-
> stracts.

The bibliographies, indexes, and abstracts will lead you to books, mono-
graphs, and journal articles. Of these, the articles are the most numerous, and
usually deal with specific, narrow topics. You may find that books (including
textbooks) will give you a better general start on an explanation; the journal articles are most useful in telling you what related hypotheses have been tested by
others.

Following the Thread. Once you have established an initial list of possible useful
sources, the next step is to find the sources. We assume that you know how to
find sources for which you have been given a citation. You go to the appropriate
journal or other source, and read and evaluate it. If the source is relevant to your
study, you make notes on its content. You should also note the works cited in
the article or book itself. This is often the major way of finding additional relevant sources. If the article or book is relevant to your study, it will usually include a number of other useful citations. Thus, you can add to your bibliography
simply by checking the citations made in articles you have already located. You
can see how the branching process can continue. You find a relevant citation, go
to the source, find another one there, go the next source, and so on.

This method of tracking down relevant material is particularly useful for finding citations to earlier work. But moving forward in time is another problem. What you would like to know is what later works cite an article you have discovered to be useful. To find this out, use both the *Citation Index* and *Source Index* volumes of the *Social Science Citation Index.*

First, look up in the *Citation Index* volume the author of the article in which you are interested. Under the author's name will be an entry for the article (if it was cited during the year indexed) and a list of abbreviated citations, which represent other sources that have cited the article; to get the complete citation for any of these sources, look up the author of the abbreviated citation in the *Source Index* volume. There you will find the complete citation, and also other works and other citations by the author who had cited the original article.

This method provides a way of finding additional articles that may be relevant. This is, of course, only the first step. Many of the articles will be irrelevant to you. Those that are not can be gleaned for additional citations.

Informed Commentary. As with the professional literature, the best place to start your search is with the indexes. Two of the indexes noted above may be helpful here as well: the card catalogue and the *Public Affairs Information Service Bulletin.* In addition, the *Reader's Guide to Periodical Literature* is of assistance in locating newsmagazine articles.

There are also a number of newspaper indexes. The *New York Times* and the *Times* (London) are the two English-language papers that have been indexed over a long period of time. They are also papers that emphasize national and international news, and they are not oriented exclusively to their own locale. The *Wall Street Journal* and the *Christian Science Monitor* have had their own indexes for several years. Starting in 1972, Bell and Howell Corporation began indexing selected regional newspapers. For the first time, information from a variety of regional papers have become accessible to researchers. Finally, there is an indexed microfilmed clipping file on public affairs called *News Bank.* The clippings are from the major newspapers in each state. This is an excellent resource, since it allows information that would not be reported nationally to be gathered from each state.

REPORTING EXPLANATIONS: THE LITERATURE REVIEW

A report of research always needs a detailed discussion of how this research fits into the existing body of research on the subject. This discussion is called the **literature review.** It includes a discussion of existing literature, both scientific and nonscientific, and any other evidence that may be relevant to the proposed hypotheses.

The literature review has two purposes. First, it presents reasons for believing the hypotheses being offered. Second, it shows how testing the hypotheses will contribute to the body of knowledge on the subject.

Reasoning Behind the Hypotheses

Before presenting empirical support for the hypotheses, the researcher should give convincing reasons why the hypotheses should be true. Merely showing empirical support for a hypothesis is not enough; the hypothesis must have reasoned support as well. If we searched, we could probably find a city somewhere on the globe where the rise and fall in rainfall matched the rise and fall in London gold prices. Merely showing an association between those two variables would not mean that variation in that city's rainfall causes the price of gold in London to change. No matter how good the empirical evidence for that association, no one should accept the hypothesis relating rainfall and gold prices because no reason can be advanced for why that hypothesis should be true.

The researcher should give the logic that leads to the formulation of each hypothesis. He or she should report, with complete citations, theoretical and empirical work by others that supports the hypotheses or the logic behind them. If there is research that tends to refute a hypothesis being offered as an explanation, the researcher should indicate why that research is less persuasive than the research supporting it.

Contribution to Knowledge

The literature review also allows the researcher to argue why it is important to do the research. He or she can show how the research will contribute to the existing knowledge, where it will fit in.

Advances in explanation usually come from filling in gaps in present knowledge. Part of an explanation may not have been tested, or there may be logical extensions of the explanation to be explored. Often there are unresolved controversies about what factors are causal or how important different factors are in the explanation.

Not all research advances knowledge by advancing new hypotheses. **Replication,** the retesting of hypotheses, is frequently justified. We may find that previous research findings are incorrect, that there are exceptions to what were thought to be generally applicable hypotheses, or that changes over time have altered the relationships found by others.

Endnotes

[1]W. Baum, G. Griffiths, R. Mathews, and D. Scherruble, "American Political Science Before the Mirror: What Our Journals Reveal About the Profession," *Journal of Politics,* 38 (1976), 895–917.

[2]Gene Bigler (Instituto De Estudios Superiores De Administracion, Venezuela) and Eric Veblen (Texas A & M University), "The Use of Informal Observation for Hypothesis Formulation and Measurement: A Methodological Case Study Based on the Use of Rules of Thumb in Making Judgments about Guilt and Punishment" (manuscript, 1977), p. 9.

LABORATORY EXERCISES

The purpose of this laboratory is to give you experience in using a literature review to support hypotheses.

Task 1. What follows is a fabricated literature review. Identify and evaluate the support offered for the hypotheses. Compare this literature review with the one presented by Bond in the research example at the end of Chapter 1.

FICTITIOUS REPORT

The nation is greatly concerned with how much children learn in the public schools. Recently Governor Mark White of Texas asserted that teacher salaries are a prime factor in determining learning, "If we pay our teachers second-class salaries, they won't produce first-class minds."[1] This research will test the hypothesis implicit in his statement: The more public school teachers are paid, the more their students learn.

Past empirical work supports that hypothesis. George Gregg's survey of Ivy League administrators showed that New York high schools have the reputation of producing the best students in the nation, and New York pays some of the highest salaries in the nation.[2] Furthermore, in most states the suburban schools pay their teachers more than do schools in the central cities, and children in the suburban schools learn more than do those in the central city schools—otherwise why would families with school-age children try to move to the suburbs?

Of course, teacher salaries are not the only factor influencing learning. The more public schools emphasize athletics, the less their students learn. As Paul Blake found, athletes tend to be much poorer students than average.[3] Student athletes cannot devote the time that is necessary to fully comprehend the advanced subjects now taught in high school.

This study will investigate the hypotheses relating both teacher salaries and emphasis on athletics to student learning. It will enable us to determine which is the more important factor.

Notes

[1] Television address, KBTX TV, Bryan, Texas, Jan. 28, 1983.

[2] George Gregg, "New York Schools Still Tops," *New York Times,* February 24, 1982, p. 16.

[3] Paul Blake, "Comparing Academic Performance of Athletes and Other Students," *Social Science Quarterly,* 50 (Jan. 1979), 423–429.

Questions for Evaluating the Literature Review

a. What are the hypotheses?
b. Are convincing reasons given for suggesting those hypotheses?
c. What kind of support (professional literature, informed commentary, or other) is offered for the hypotheses?
d. What evidence is there in the cited literature to support the hypotheses?
e. Is any evidence cited contrary to the hypotheses?
f. How is it shown that in spite of existing research, this additional research is needed?
g. What problems are there (if any) with the literature review?

Task 2. In this task you are asked to find topics in standard bibliographic references. You will be assigned one or more of the following topics by your instructor:

House of Representatives
traditional education
tolerance
diffusion model
measurement

a. Find each topic in the subject index in the *United States Political Science Documents (USPSD)* for 1980. Give a complete citation for the first article found under the topic heading. Using the abstract in *USPSD,* report a brief description of the contents of the article.
b. Using the *Social Science Citation Index* for 1981, find the first article listed that cites the article found above. Give a complete citation for that article.

REVIEW QUESTIONS

1. Assume that you have been assigned to explain why some members of congress are more likely to support the president than are others.
   a. Where would you look first to find previous research on that subject in the professional literature? (List two sources.)
   b. Once you had a list of articles on that subject, where would you look to find a summary of each article?
   c. If research on this topic had appeared in several general-purpose journals and you wished to look first at the most prestigious of those journals, which journals would you look at first? (List three.)

    d. Name a policy-oriented journal that might have had an article on this subject.

    e. If you wanted to find informed commentary on this subject, where would you begin your search? (List two sources.)

2. If an article for a professional journal and one for a newsmagazine were written at the same time, which would likely be published first?

3. Both the *Social Science Citation Index* and *United States Political Science Documents* require that you use two volumes to find the complete information that you are searching for. Briefly explain what those volumes are and why you use each one.

4. Note major weaknesses in the explanation below.

    The distribution of income is far more equal in some countries than in others. For example, in Sweden the highest-paid fifth of the workers gets just 25% of all personal income earned in the country. In Paraguay, the highest-paid fifth gets 60% of all of the income.[1] This report seeks to explain why income is more equally distributed in some nations than in others.

    Clearly, one determining factor is geography. Our first hypothesis is that the distribution of income is more equal in European nations than in African or Latin American nations. European nations are more industrialized than are African or Latin American nations. Industrialization encourages the development of a middle class.[2] And the larger the middle class, the more equally income is distributed.

    The type of government is also crucial in determining how equally income is distributed. Communist theory calls for a classless society.[3] Therefore, our second hypothesis is that the distribution of income is more equal in communist nations than in noncommunist nations.

    Finally, religion influences distribution. A good Christian is always willing to lend a hand to those in need. In Christian nations, charities are formed to take from the rich and give to the poor. That suggests our third hypothesis: the distribution of income is more equal in Christian nations than in non-Christian nations.

[1] *World Almanac* (New York: Harper, 1982).
[2] Paul Duncan, *Sociology of Development* (Chicago: Leeds, 1981).
[3] Karl Marx, *Collected Works* (Dallas: Hill, 1982).

CHAPTER THREE

UNITS OF ANALYSIS: SELECTING THE SAMPLE

Once we have established the hypotheses we plan to test, we need to determine what must be observed in order to test them. We must observe the behavior of appropriate units during analysis to test the hypotheses. There are three decisions to make in selecting the units to be observed: *what kind* of units to observe; *how many* units to observe; and *which* specific units to observe.

Our objective should be to select units that will allow us to generalize about the hypothesis. With that objective in mind, in this chapter we consider factors affecting the three decisions.

WHAT KIND OF UNITS?

The kind of units to observe usually derives directly from the hypothesis. If the hypothesis involves the behavior of people, we will want to observe people. If we are considering differences among nations, we will want to look at countries. In most cases, then, the selection of the kind of objects will be very easy to determine.

Occasionally it is impossible or prohibitively expensive to observe the kind of units to which the hypothesis refers. For example, the hypothesis may require observation of individuals voting on whether to legalize gambling, but there may be no current referenda on that subject. Or it may be that there is such a referendum, but you don't have the necessary funds to hire interviewers to get data on each of the voters. Suppose the hypothesis deals with the behavior of presidential advisors or Supreme Court justices and these individual will not grant you an opportunity to observe them. What can you do in these cases?

The best you can do is to draw a sample of units that are as close as possible to those specified by the hypothesis. If the units are similar enough, most of the scientific community will be willing to infer that the relationships found in the sample would also be found among the units to which the hypothesis refers.

Substituting Groups for Individuals

Let us consider the example of the gambling referendum. Suppose your hypothesis is that whites are more likely than nonwhites to vote for legalized gambling.

You find that there was a referendum on gambling in New Jersey in 1976. It is doubtful that most individuals will accurately recall how they voted (or even *if* they voted) in that referendum. In addition, it would be expensive to try to interview a large sample of individuals. However, you can find published information in newspapers indicating what percentage of voters in each *county* voted for and against the referendum. Also available are published data (from the census) on the percentage of nonwhites in each *county*. In a case such as this, the counties are often substituted for individuals as the units of analysis.

Such substitution would present no problem if each county were either 100% white or 100% nonwhite. If there were 1000 voters in a county that was 100% white, and 70% of the voters favored legalizing gambling, then you would know that 700 whites favored gambling, while 300 opposed it. Similarly, if only 40% favored it out of 1000 voters in a totally nonwhite county, you would know that 400 nonwhites favored gambling while 600 opposed it. You could correctly infer individual behavior from data based on groups of individuals, and therefore could test your hypothesis even though you couldn't observe individual behavior.

But it rarely happens that human groups are homogeneous with respect to any property you would be interested in measuring. In the example above, New Jersey counties are not 100% white or 100% nonwhite. If a county were 60% white, you might call it a "white" county. But if 70% of 1000 voters in that county favored legalized gambling, you would not know if the 700 progambling votes all came from whites, nonwhites, or a combination of the two. There would be no guarantee that 60% of the 700 came from whites. Similarly, if a 60% nonwhite county voted 40% in favor of gambling, you also could not tell the racial composition of that 40%. If the groups are not homogeneous, you cannot infer individual behavior with certainty from group behavior. Therefore, you cannot say with certainty that you have found support for your hypothesis.

This does not mean that one can never substitute groups for individuals. It does mean that the more homogeneous the group, the more certain we can be of inference to the individual level. Thus, if you must substitute group for individual behavior, you should include only those groups that are relatively homogeneous.

In the New Jersey example, you might have looked only at the results in counties that were more than 90% white or more than 90% nonwhite. If you consistently found that the 90% white counties gave gambling 70% support, while 90% nonwhite counties gave it only 40% support, you could justifiably conclude that your hypothesis was substantiated.

You should note that in eliminating heterogeneous counties, you have ignored people living in racially mixed neighborhoods. If nonwhites living in mixed neighborhoods are different from nonwhites living in homogeneous neighborhoods, or if whites living in mixed neighborhoods are different from whites living in homogeneous neighborhoods, the conclusion based only on homogeneous neighborhoods may be misleading.

It frequently happens that a researcher must observe groups when he would prefer to observe individuals. Such a substitution inevitably reduces confidence in the applicability of his results to the theoretical population.

Simulation

Suppose a medical researcher hypothesizes that a certain drug is safe for humans, but doesn't want to risk human lives in testing it. She might begin by testing to see what the drug does to mice, monkeys, and other animals that resemble humans in some important respects. If she closely *simulates* (or duplicates) the conditions under which humans would take the drug, and if animal reactions are close enough substitutes for human reactions, then she will have some confidence that the results she finds with animals will be similar to those that she would find if the drug were given to humans.

Suppose you have a hypothesis that presidential advisers act less rationally in crisis than in noncrisis situations. Further, suppose that the advisers will not let you observe them during crises. Your problem is similar to that of the medical researcher; the units you need to observe are unavailable. You might try to solve your problem as the medical researcher solved hers: by simulating the situation you wish to observe and substituting other units that you believe will react to those conditions as would presidential advisers.

For example, you might compare the relative rationality of students in crisis and noncrisis situations. If students act less rationally during crises, you would hope to convince your audience that advisers, too, would act less rationally during crises.

How convincing the results of simulation are depends on:

1. how closely the conditions can be simulated (in the above example, how realistic the crisis and noncrisis situations are).
2. how similar the reactions of the substitute units are to those in the theoretical population (in the above example, how similar the reactions of students and advisers are).

Observation based on a simulation will not be as convincing as observation of actual behavior. Still, although we bar from the market drugs based on animal simulations of human reactions, simulations are accepted for some purposes in medical science. Similarly, simulations may be accepted for some purposes in political science.

Summary

In selecting the kind of units to observe, the first choice should always be those specified by the hypothesis. That is, the observed units should be a part of the theoretical population. Only when this is not possible should other kinds of units be substituted. If groups are substituted for individuals, the groups should be relatively homogeneous. If simulations are used, conditions and actors should be as similar to the actual conditions and actors as possible.

HOW MANY UNITS?

Once the kind of unit to observe is determined, the researcher must decide how many of those units ought to be observed. We almost never look at all of the units in the theoretical population. Even if the entire theoretical population were available, the cost of obtaining information on it would usually be too great for us to observe the whole population. Instead, we use a **sample,** or subset, of the theoretical population.

It is usually not necessary to observe all of the objects before we can draw quite accurate conclusions about how all of them behave. Assuming the objects are selected in an appropriate manner (more will be said about this in the next section), only a very small part of the theoretical population needs to be studied to reflect the behavior of the total population. For example, a pollster can interview about 1000 people in the United States and reflect what the responses of the entire population would have been within $\pm$ 3% accuracy 95 times out of 100. This kind of accuracy is adequate for testing most hypotheses.

There are two reasons that we need only a small part of the population in order to generalize about the entire theoretical population. First, we can often assume that all of a population behaves essentially the same. Therefore, examining the behavior of a relatively small group allows us to generalize to the behavior of the population. Second, we can pick a sample in which the observed characteristics are distributed as they are in the population as a whole, or in which we know specifically how the characteristics in the sample differ from those in the population.

Though it is clear that we can avoid observing the entire theoretical population, determining how many to study is not an easy matter. How many objects need to be observed depends on three things: the degree of accuracy needed for the analysis, the number and distribution of categories for each property, and the total number of units in the theoretical population.

Accuracy Needed

The greater the number of observations, the more confidence we have in conclusions based upon them. When the number is small enough, we simply do not believe the results.

Suppose a researcher told you that he did a sample of one person and concluded that John Doe was going to win the next presidential election. You would have reason to be skeptical, and to demand that he enlarge the sample. Each additional case increases the accuracy obtained. However, after many cases the additional accuracy derived from adding one more to the sample is small enough to make the cost of collecting data not worthwhile. If a researcher has already sampled 2000 people, there would be virtually no increase in accuracy from adding another person to the sample.

There are precise ways of estimating the size of samples that are needed for given levels of accuracy, if we know the kind of analysis to be undertaken and the properties we expect to find. These methods get fairly complex, so we will not consider them here. What is important is that people reading the study find the sample large enough to accept the findings. In later chapters you will learn ways to test how likely it is that a relationship observed in a sample reflects a relationship in the population. Using these tests, you can determine, given what the properties were and the kind of analysis you did, whether the sample was large enough to be accepted according to the general criteria imposed by social science.

The Number and Distribution of Categories for Each Property

What you must compare in order to test your hypothesis greatly influences sample size. Particularly important is the number of categories of a property. The greater the number of categories, the larger the sample you need to achieve the same degree of confidence in the results. For example, if the hypothesis requires a comparison of sexes (only 2 categories), you can use a smaller sample than you could if the hypothesis required a comparison of occupations (20 categories).

The distribution of the categories within the sample also influences sample size. The more evenly distributed the categories, the smaller the sample you need to get the same level of confidence. There must be enough observations in *each* category for us to be confident of results comparing one category with others. A sample of 1000 would not allow us to confidently compare men and women if it included 999 men and only 1 woman. A sample that included 500 of each would maximize confidence in the results.

Size of the Theoretical Population

The third and least important determinant of the size of the sample is the size of the theoretical population. The size of the sample needed is not influenced by the total number in the population once the number in the population is very large—say, over 5000. For any large population, the size of the sample is simply a function of the level of accuracy needed and the number and distribution of the categories. As the theoretical population gets smaller, the number needed for the same level of accuracy also gets smaller. At the same time, the *proportion* of the population needed to be sampled for the same accuracy increases. Suppose we needed to look at 50 objects out of 100 to get a certain level of accuracy. We might need to look at 8 objects out of 10 to obtain the same level of accuracy. When the theoretical population was 100, we needed 50% of the objects in the sample; when it was only 10, we needed 80%.

How Many Units: Some Suggestions

Though we have given you the considerations affecting the decision on the size of the sample, we have not given you detailed instructions for making that decision. This is in part because the calculations are too complex for this book, and in part because people doing social science research usually determine the size of the sample by the data and resources available. Since there are tests that, when given after the analysis is completed, easily determine whether the sample was large enough for the researcher's purpose, we do not have to worry too much about erroneous results based on too small a sample. For the researcher whose sample is too small runs the risk of doing a lot of work only to find it is not acceptable.

A useful guide to the size of samples is the size that other researchers have typically used. A report on several hundred studies by Seymour Sudman indicates that nationwide samples of individuals usually include 1000 to 2500+ people. Samples of individuals in smaller areas are usually based on 200 to 1000+. Samples of groups of people (cities, institutions, and so on) usually include 200 to 1000+ groups at the national level and 50 to 500+ at the lower levels.[1]

There is obviously a great deal of variation in the sample sizes used. We suggest that if you are doing surveys of individuals in which great precision is not necessary and there are few categories for each property, 200 to 300 respondents are probably sufficient. Where greater accuracy is needed, or where the properties are more complex, a sample of 1000 should generally be enough. Samples of more than 2000 respondents are rarely needed.

Samples of nations and states are typically limited by the number of units in existence at different times and by the number of units for which there are data on the properties you are measuring. You should generally include as many as possible in your sample. Counties, cities, and other institutions may be more plentiful. Where you will be taking a sample of institutions, we suggest that you try to include at least 100 units for relatively simple analysis and at least 200 for more complex problems.

WHICH UNITS TO OBSERVE

For a sample to be useful for generalization about the theoretical population, there must be a known relationship between the distributions of the properties in the units picked to be observed and the distributions of the properties of the population. We often use a **representative sample,** which is a miniature of the population. It is smaller than the population, but the distributions of the properties are similar. In the case of the representative sample, the distributions of the properties in the sample and the population can be assumed to be approximately the same.

Some samples that are not representative of the entire population are useful. A **weighted stratified sample** is a sample in which some units of analysis are deliberately oversampled and some are deliberately undersampled. That is, we select more of one type of unit and less of another than should be in the sample if the population was to be represented. A **stratum** is just part of the population that has the same characteristics on one or more variables. As an example of a weighted stratified sample, from a population that has 15% minorities and 85% nonminorities we might draw a sample containing 50% of each. This sample is stratified by minority and nonminority status of the people; minorities are oversampled and nonminorities undersampled.

Although a weighted stratified sample is not representative of the population, it must be representative of the units within each of the strata. That is, the sample of minorities must look like the population of minorities and the sample of nonminorities must look like the population of nonminorities.

Weighted stratified samples are useful whenever relatively rare parts of the population are to be studied. In the preceding example, if 500 people could be studied and we needed to be able to compare minorities and nonminorities, a representative sample would have only about 75 minorities to compare with 425 nonminorities. The weighted stratified sample, containing 50% of each, would result in a comparison between 250 of each. Because the accuracy of a sample increases at a decreasing rate as more units are added, the accuracy gained by increasing the minority sample from 75 to 250 is greater than the loss in accuracy from decreasing the nonminority sample from 425 to 250.

In order for a sample to be useful in testing hypotheses, there must be enough units in each category of the independent variables for accurate comparisons to be made. When the numbers in the categories are too small, then either the size of the sample must be increased or a weighted stratified sample must be used. Often the cost of increasing the size of the sample is prohibitive, so a weighted stratified sample may be the only practical solution.

When the analysis involves comparing the strata, there is nothing further we need to do to generalize to the population. For example, if we had hypothesized a difference between minorities and nonminorities, it would not make a difference that the size of those groups was not proportionate to their size in the population.

When we are using a weighted statified sample but are not comparing the strata, we must weight the units in order to compensate for the over- and under-sampling that was done. We determined the weight for each strata by dividing the number that should have been in the sample had it been representative of the population by the number that actually are in the sample. For the minorities that would be 75/250, which gives a weight of .3; for the nonminorities it would be 425/250, which gives a weight of 1.7. The weights indicate how many times a unit in the sample is counted when the sample is to be used as a representative sample. Each minority person in the sample would count .3 and each nonminority would count 1.7. That is, it takes a little over 3 minority units to add one case to the analysis, and each nonminority would add 1.7 cases to the analysis.

SELECTION OF THE UNITS

There are a variety of methods used to actually select the units used in the sample. The methods we discuss here are some of the most common.

Samples of Convenience

It is common to pick a sample of units that happen to be readily available to the researcher. We call a sample determined by its availability a **sample of convenience.** The professor who studies the students in an introductory class because she has access to them is using a sample of convenience. Researchers studying the community in which they live, or an organization to which they belong, are also using a sample of convenience.

Virtually all samples are selected in part because of their availability. Even samples that include all of the units that exist at the time are samples of convenience to the extent that the theoretical population is all units that exist at all times. Studies collecting data on units for one year are not necessarily generalizable to the units for all years. To the extent that the year picked is a function of the availability of data, these are samples of convenience.

Of all the methods of selecting samples, samples of convenience are the least likely to reflect the population. They may, however, be representative of the theoretical population. With respect to the properties being studied, it is possible that students in an introductory class will be like citizens in general. The problem is that there is no way of knowing how representative a sample of convenience is likely to be.

Improving Samples of Convenience

There are many ways of increasing the extent to which a sample of convenience is representative of the population or strata of the population. These techniques make the selection less arbitrary than a sample picked completely for reasons of convenience. They also ensure that the researcher includes a variety of units in the sample and that some sources of bias in selection are reduced. The choice of units is removed at least somewhat from the control of the researcher, and this reduces the possibility that the researcher will select units that support his hypothesis.

Using All Available Units. One method of increasing representativeness is to include all of the theoretical population for a specific point in time, or all of the theoretical population for which there are data. This is frequently done when the population in existence at any time, or the population for which there is data, is relatively small. For example, this technique is generally used in studies of nations or states.

Even a sample that includes all units for which there are data may not be representative of all the units in the theoretical population. However, it is more likely to be representative than a smaller sample, and it is immune from the challenge that it was deliberately selected in order to make the hypothesis appear to be supported. Similarly, a sample that includes all nations in existence in 1975 is more likely to be representative of all nations than is a sample restricted to just some nations in 1975; no one evaluating that sample could claim that the sample was restricted to those areas of the world in which the hypothesis was most likely to be supported.

Varying the Time and Place for Selecting Units. Another method of increasing the degree to which the sample represents the population or the strata is to vary the time or place at which units are selected. This is generally done when the units are individuals. Varying the time or place of selection helps ensure that the sample will reflect any variation that exists in the population.

If populations were homogeneous, then a sample at any specific time and place would produce the same results as samples taken at other times and places. However, as indicated in our example of New Jersey counties and the gambling referendum, populations tend not to be homogeneous. Frequently, though, heterogeneous populations will include homogeneous pockets of one kind of unit or another. When that is the case, a sample of units selected at a single time or place is likely to be very unrepresentative of the whole population. We know of a large community sample done by telephone on weekday afternoons. Almost 80% of the people in the sample were women, and almost all of the men were 65 years old or older. Obviously that sample was not very representative of the community. It was unrepresentative because only certain types of individuals were available for inclusion in the sample on weekday afternoons. If the researchers had varied the days and times at which they phoned, they would have greatly increased the representativeness of the sample.

Quota Samples. A **quota sample** is a sample in which we select the units in the order in which they are found, but impose the constraint that only a certain number of each of specified groups will be selected. That is, if we wanted half of the sample to be male and the other half female, we might tell the interviewers to interview 50% men and 50% women. The quota could be set so that its proportion of the sample is equal the proportion of the group in the population, or it could be set to equal the size of the strata required to ensure large enough categories. Quotas are often used with other techniques. For example, interviewers could interview people in different places at different times and be required to interview a specified number of different types of people as well.

Using a quota sample does not ensure that the sample will be representative of the population within categories of the quota. For example, an appropriate number of men and women will be in the sample if gender is used as a criterion for the quota, but the men picked may not be representative of men in the population and the women picked may not be representative of the women.

Probability Samples

In the event that there is a complete list of the theoretical population, the researcher can select a very good sample by ensuring that each unit has a known probability of appearing in the sample. Samples of that type are called **probability samples**. A sample in which each unit had a one-in-ten chance of appearing in the sample would be a kind of probability sample.

Probability samples are the only kind of samples for which we can calculate the probability that the sample is unrepresentative of the theoretical population. Using a probability sample, we can make a statement like "There is a 95% probability that 52% of the population, $\pm$ 3%, favors John Doe for city council." Probability samples are especially useful for estimating unknown distributions of properties and for determining the likelihood that a relationship found in the sample will also be found in the population.

Random Samples. A **random sample** is a special kind of probability sample in which all of the units and all the combinations of units in the theoretical population have an equal chance of being selected for the sample. We may choose a random sample by numbering each unit in the population and then, using a random-number generator or a table of random digits, selecting the numbers to be included in the sample.

Using a table of random digits involves determining a starting point and proceeding in a predetermined way through the table. The researcher might choose a starting point by arbitrarily picking a row and column. Any method of proceeding can be chosen, as long as the researcher has no choice over the particular numbers that are used. For example, from the starting point, the researcher might take all the digits in the column, then move to the next column and take the digits in that column, and so on. The number of digits taken from the table to form a number must be equal to the number of digits in the largest number that must have a chance of being picked. If units numbering from 1 to 999 are to be sampled, the researcher would always pick three digits at a time. The one- and two-digit numbers are picked when the leading random digits are zeros. It is likely that there will be duplicate numbers generated with a random-digit table. For sampling purposes, those duplicates are used only once.

The brief random-number table below will serve to illustrate the previous discussion. (A larger table is presented in the appendix.) The circled digit was arbitrarily chosen as the starting point. The researcher needed 10 two-digit numbers, and she decided to select them by proceeding down the first two columns, then starting at the top of the next two columns, proceeding down them, and so on. Her sample included units numbered 51, 73, 94, 93, 80, 20, 11, 56, 45, and 78.

6	4	9	3	7	8
2	7	8	0	5	2
3	0	2	0	3	1
(5)	1	1	1	0	1
7	3	5	6	9	5
9	4	4	5	4	6

The random sample is seldom used, because it is usually difficult or impossible to select. We almost never have a complete inventory of units to be sampled. When such a list exists, it may be inaccessible or too long to be sampled easily. It is often impractical to observe objects as widely scattered as those produced by random sample. For example, if a random sample were taken of the population of the United States, the geographic distribution would be enormous. We would need interviewers in almost every state and a huge travel budget. For these kinds of reasons we modify the random-selection procedures to make them more practical.

Stratified Random Samples. Stratifying a random sample can have two purposes. It can allow the researcher to weight the strata differently than they occur in the population, or it can be used to ensure that each stratum is represented in the sample in the proportion it is in the population. We discussed above the advantages of using a weighted stratified sample. When the stratified sample is picked randomly within the strata it gives us a known probability that the sample will be representative of each stratum. When the proportion in the stratum in the sample equals the proportion in the stratum in the population, the probability that the sample will be representative of the population is greater than with a simple random sample.

In order to choose a stratified random sample we must have some way of identifying units of the population as belonging to a stratum. Suppose we are drawing a sample of registered voters. We could easily stratify the sample by precinct by randomly selecting names from each precinct and selecting an ap-

propriate number from each precinct. Or we could select a sample of cities stratified by region by creating a list of all cities in each of the regions. We could then
randomly pick a sample within each region.

Systematic Samples. A **systematic sample** is a slightly modified random sample
in which every *n*th unit is picked from a list. Suppose we wanted to sample one
tenth of the population; we would randomly pick one of the first ten units and
then pick every tenth unit thereafter. This would be very close to a random sample and would probably represent the population better than a random sample if
there was nothing about the way the list was constructed that would cause every
tenth unit to be different from the others. Though systematic sampling requires
that a list of units be available, it simplifies picking them from the list, particularly when the list is long and the objects are not sequentially numbered. Systematic samples are typically used in picking samples from phone books or directories.

Cluster Samples. A cluster sample is a modification of the random sample and is
generally used for selecting large samples scattered over a wide area. In a cluster
sample, identifiable groups of units (clusters) are first randomly chosen from
among all groups; units are then randomly chosen from within the clusters. For
example, in a cluster sample of the United States, the country would be divided
into areas, usually based on county or city boundaries. A random sample of
those areas would be drawn. Often 80 or so areas would be selected. Those areas
would be further subdivided into *chunks,* and some of those chunks would be
selected for each area. The housing units in each selected chunk would be
mapped. Households would be randomly selected from the maps. An interviewer would go to each selected household, find out how many people lived there,
and randomly select one for his interview.

  This procedure is not simple, but it has advantages over a random sample.
In the first place, no list exists with the names of all the people in the United
States. Any list that came close would not be accessible and would not have the
correct addresses of many people. Additionally, if a cluster sample is used, the
people to be interviewed would be concentrated in the 80 or so areas originally
sampled. This makes the job of interviewing much cheaper. We also find that
this kind of sample is a very good reflection of the population. The rate of error
can be calculated, just as it can for the true random sample, and the probability
of error is only slightly greater than for a true random sample.[2]

Random-Digit Dialing. Researchers are relying increasingly on the telephone
rather than the door-to-door interview for surveys of individuals and households. Phone interviews cost considerably less than door-to-door interviews, yet
the results are quite similar. To some extent, telephone interviews underrepresent lower-income families, who are less likely to have phones. In recent years,
however, the telephone has become inexpensive and common enough so that for
most purposes the underrepresentation is not significant.

  Generating phone numbers randomly is a common method of selecting households. The sample is relatively easy to pick, and doing so does not require a list of all existing telephone numbers. The procedure is to determine the area codes in the area to be sampled, and then the central-office codes within the area codes. The central-office codes are the first three digits of the seven-digit phone number. To construct a number, we randomly pick one of the area codes, then one of the central-office codes, and then a four-digit random number. The resulting number is placed in the sample. Not all numbers will be working numbers, and usually interviews are not conducted if the number is not a residence. These numbers are removed from the sample.[3]

This sample reflects the population even though the telephones are not equally distributed by central-office code. If one set of numbers has only 10% working numbers and another has 80% working numbers, randomly placing an equal number of calls to each will result in a sample containing about 10% completed calls to the first set and about 80% to the other.

Random-digit dialing has an advantage over sampling numbers from a list like the telephone book because it enables contact to be made with those who have unlisted numbers either by choice or because they have recently moved. In some communities, a substantial proportion of phones are not listed. Moreover, random-digit dialing does not require obtaining copies of all phone directories.

A major problem with random-digit dialing is the large number of calls that end up being made to nonexistent numbers, particularly where there is low population density and the set of numbers associated with a central-office code is very small. For this reason we often modify the procedure. For example, once we have found a working number by calling numbers produced according to the above procedure, we then sample an additional group of numbers (say three to five) within plus or minus 100 units around the working number. If the working number is 846-4321, for example, we might also select 846-4295, 864-4402, and 846-4278. The telephone company usually assigns new numbers in groups of sequential numbers, and thus the sample of numbers around the original usually has a high proportion of working numbers. This is a form of cluster sampling. Another technique is to sample numbers in the phone book and modify them before calling. A common procedure is to add a number such as five to each of the listed numbers. This also reduces the number of nonoperational numbers called, and has some of the advantages of random-digit dialing. But it requires that all of the phone books be available, and new banks of numbers will largely be left out.

When there is no answer, the number should be tried several more times at different times of day. Usually three or four tries are made to reach a number. Two calls in the evening, one in the morning, and another in the afternoon increase the likelihood of finding someone at home. Failure to use an adequate number of call-backs will result in the selection of a sample that overrepresents those who tend to be more available. This means that families in which only one member works or in which members are retired or unemployed are more likely to be selected.

Combinations and Alternatives

A combination of methods are often used in picking a sample. For example, it is common in selecting a sample for a national survey to use cluster sampling until the city block is selected, and then use a quota sample to select respondents from the block. A stratified sample can be picked by a systematic sample or by random-digit telephone-number selection. The important thing to understand is not the names of the different techniques, but that there are many different ways of selecting samples. Which one is best is a function of the kind of population being sampled, the hypotheses being tested, the method of data collection, and the resources available.

SUMMARY

To describe the research process we might make an analogy to a court case. The hypothesis is presented, and tested with some data. The research is then evaluated, first by the researcher and then by others. The others have to decide, based on the weight of the evidence, whether to accept or reject the hypothesis, or, as in Norwegian courts, to render a verdict of not proven. The sample upon which the study is based must be a major factor in the rendering of the decision. At the very least, a limited sample should suggest that additional evidence needs to be presented before an unqualified verdict is given. By now you should have some idea of the kinds of factors to consider in evaluating a sample, including a general knowledge of what some of the options are, and the basic weaknesses and strengths of each.

Endnotes

[1]Seymour Sudman, *Applied Sampling* (New York: Academic, 1976), p. 87.

[2]Martin Frankel, *Inference From Survey Samples: An Empirical Investigation* (Ann Arbor, Mich.: Institute for Social Research, 1971).

[3]Matthew Hauch and Michael Cox discuss procedures for random-digit dialing in "Locating a Sample by Random Digit Dialing" *Public Opinion Quarterly,* 38 (Summer 1974), 253–60.

LABORATORY EXERCISES

The purpose of this laboratory is to introduce you to several methods of picking samples and to allow you to see how the characteristics of the samples picked compare with each other and with the theoretical population.

Task 1. The theoretical population is 385 House members of the Ninety-fourth Congress who were eligible to vote on all roll calls.

   a. From the list of members at the end of the laboratory, draw a systematic sample of approximately 50. Indicate that a name has been selected by recording its identifying number. Compute the percentage from each region and party, and record in the table below.

   b. From the same list of House members, draw a random sample of 50. Record identifying numbers as above. Again compute the percentage from each region and party and record in the table below.

   c. From the same list, draw a stratified random sample of approximately 50. Stratify by region with no oversampling. Record identifying numbers, compute the percentages from each region and party and record in the table below.

   d. From the same list, draw a stratified random sample of approximately 50. Stratify so that each region has an equal number. Record numbers and compute percentages from each region and party. Compute the percentage from each party, using appropriate weights to make the percentages representative of the entire population.

Table of Results

Samples	Regions			Party	
	West	*South*	*North*	*Republican*	*Democrat*
a. Systematic					
b. Random					
c. Stratified random					
d. Stratified random weighted					

Task 2. Answer each of the following questions:

   a. Under what circumstances would sample *d* be the best sample (compared with samples *a, b,* and *c.*)?

   b. Evaluate samples *a, b,* and *c* in terms of how representative each is likely to be of each of the variables. Is there a difference between how representative it is likely to be of region compared with party? If so, why?

Data: Population of Members of House of Representatives, Ninety-fourth Congress

West OBS	Name	Party	West OBS	Name	Party
1	Adams	D	35	McCormack	D
2	Anderson	D	36	McFall	D
3	Armstrong	R	37	McKay	D
4	Aucoin	D	38	Melcher	D
5	Baucus	D	39	Miller	D
6	Bonker	D	40	Mineta	D
7	Brown	D	41	Mink	D
8	Burgener	R	42	Moorhead	R
9	Burton, J.	D	43	Moss	D
10	Burton, P.	D	44	Patterson	D
11	Clausen	R	45	Pritchard	R
12	Clawson	R	46	Rees	D
13	Conlan	R	47	Roncalio	D
14	Corman	D	48	Rousselot	R
15	Danielson	D	49	Roybal	D
16	Dellums	D	50	Ryan	D
17	Duncan	D	51	Santini	D
18	Evans	D	52	Schroeder	D
19	Foley	D	53	Sisk	D
20	Goldwater	R	54	Stark	D
21	Hannaford	D	55	Steiger	R
22	Hansen	R	56	Symms	R
23	Hawkins	D	57	Talcott	R
24	Hicks	D	58	Udall	D
25	Hinshaw	R	59	Ullman	D
26	Howe	D	60	Van Deerlin	D
27	Johnson, H.	D	61	Waxman	D
28	Johnson, J.	R	62	Weaver	D
29	Ketchum	R	63	Wiggins	R
30	Krebs	D	64	Wilson, C.	D
31	Leggett	D	65	Wilson, R.	R
32	Lujan	R	66	Wirth	D
33	Matsunaga	D	67	Young	R
34	McCloskey	R			

South OBS	Name	Party	South OBS	Name	Party
68	Alexander	D	77	Breaux	D
69	Andrews	D	78	Breckinridge	D
70	Archer	R	79	Brinkley	D
71	Bauman	D	80	Brooks	D
72	Beard	R	81	Broyhill	R
73	Bennett	D	82	Buchanan	R
74	Bevill	D	83	Burke	R
75	Boggs	D	84	Burleson	D
76	Bowen	D	85	Butler	R

Data (*Continued*)

OBS	South Name	Party	OBS	South Name	Party
86	Byron	D	134	Long, G.	D
87	Carter	R	135	Lott	R
88	Chappell	D	136	Mahon	D
89	Cochran	R	137	Mann	D
90	Daniel	D	138	Martin	R
91	Davis	D	139	Mazzoli	D
92	De la Garza	D	140	McDonald	D
93	Derrick	D	141	Milford	D
94	Dickinson	R	142	Mitchell	D
95	Duncan	R	143	Mollohan	D
96	Eckhardt	D	144	Montgomery	D
97	Edwards	R	145	Moore	R
98	English	D	146	Natcher	D
99	Evins	D	147	Neal	D
100	Fascell	D	148	Passman	D
101	Fisher	D	149	Perkins	D
102	Flowers	D	150	Pickle	D
103	Flynt	D	151	Poage	D
104	Ford	D	152	Risenhoover	D
105	Fountain	D	153	Roberts	D
106	Frey	R	154	Robinson	R
107	Fuqua	D	155	Rose	D
108	Gibbons	D	156	Sarbanes	D
109	Ginn	D	157	Satterfield	D
110	Gonzalez	D	158	Sikes	D
111	Gude	R	159	Slack	D
112	Haley	D	160	Synder	R
113	Hammerschmidt	R	161	Sellman	D
114	Harris	D	162	Spence	R
115	Hebert	D	163	Staggers	D
116	Hechler	D	164	Steed	D
117	Hefner	D	165	Steelman	R
118	Henderson	D	166	Stephens	D
119	Hightower	D	167	Stuckey	D
120	Holland	D	168	Taylor	D
121	Holt	R	169	Teague	D
122	Hubbard	D	170	Thornton	D
123	Jarman	D	171	Treen	R
124	Jenrette	D	172	Waggoner	D
125	Jones, E.	D	173	Wampler	R
126	Jones, R.	D	174	White	D
127	Jordan	D	175	Whitehurst	R
128	Kazen	D	176	Whitten	D
129	Kelly	R	177	Wilson	D
130	Landrum	D	178	Wright	D
131	Levitas	D	179	Young, A.	D
132	Lloyd	D	180	Young, C.	R
133	Long, C.	D	181	Young, J.	D

Data (*Continued*)

North			North		
OBS	*Name*	*Party*	*OBS*	*Name*	*Party*
182	Abdnor	R	230	Diggs	D
183	Abzug	D	231	Dingell	D
184	Addabbo	D	232	Dodd	D
185	Ambro	D	233	Downey	D
186	Anderson	R	234	Drinan	D
187	Andrews	R	235	Du Pont	R
188	Annunzio	D	236	Early	D
189	Ashbrook	R	237	Edgar	D
190	Ashley	D	238	Eilberg	D
191	Aspin	D	239	Emery	R
192	Badillo	D	240	Erlenborn	R
193	Baldus	D	241	Esch	R
194	Beard	D	242	Eshleman	R
195	Bedell	D	243	Evans	D
196	Beister	R	244	Fenwick	R
197	Bergland	R	245	Findley	R
198	Biaggi	D	246	Fish	R
199	Bingham	D	247	Fithian	D
200	Blanchard	D	248	Flood	D
201	Blouin	D	249	Florio	D
202	Boland	D	250	Ford	D
203	Bolling	D	251	Forsythe	R
204	Brademas	D	252	Fraser	D
205	Brodhead	D	253	Frenzel	R
206	Broomfield	R	254	Gaydos	D
207	Brown, C.	R	255	Giaimo	D
208	Brown, G.	R	256	Gilman	R
209	Burke	D	257	Goodling	R
210	Burlison	D	258	Grassley	R
211	Carney	D	259	Green	D
212	Carr	D	260	Guyer	R
213	Cederberg	R	261	Hagedorn	R
214	Chisholm	D	262	Hall	D
215	Clancy	R	263	Hamilton	D
216	Clay	D	264	Hanley	D
217	Cleveland	R	265	Harkin	D
218	Cohen	R	266	Harrington	D
219	Collins	D	267	Harsha	R
220	Conyers	D	268	Hayes	D
221	Cornell	D	269	Heinz	R
222	Cotter	D	270	Helstoski	D
223	Coughlin	R	271	Hillis	R
224	Crane	R	272	Holtzman	D
225	D'Amours	D	273	Horton	R
226	Daniels	D	274	Howard	D
227	Dent	D	275	Hughes	D
228	Derwinski	R	276	Hungate	D
229	Devine	R	277	Hutchinson	R

Data (*Continued*)

OBS	North Name	Party	OBS	North Name	Party
278	Hyde	R	326	Obey	D
279	Ichord	D	327	Ottinger	D
280	Jacobs	D	328	Patten	D
281	Jeffords	D	329	Pattison	D
282	Johnson	R	330	Peyser	R
283	Karth	D	331	Pressler	R
284	Kasten	R	332	Price	D
285	Kastenmeier	D	333	Quie	R
286	Kemp	R	334	Railsback	R
287	Keys	D	335	Randall	D
288	Kindness	R	336	Rangel	D
289	Koch	D	337	Reuss	D
290	La Falce	D	338	Richmond	D
291	Latta	R	339	Riegle	D
292	Lent	R	340	Rodino	D
293	Madden	D	341	Roe	D
294	Madigan	R	342	Rooney	D
295	McClory	R	343	Rosenthal	D
296	McCollister	R	344	Rostenkowski	D
297	McDade	R	345	Roush	D
298	McEwen	R	346	Ruppe	R
299	McHugh	D	347	Russo	D
300	Metcalf	D	348	Sarasin	R
301	Meyner	D	349	Scheuer	D
302	Mezvinsky	D	350	Schneebeli	R
303	Michel	R	351	Sebelius	R
304	Mikva	D	352	Seiberling	D
305	Miller	R	353	Sharp	D
306	Minish	D	354	Shipley	D
307	Mitchell	R	355	Shriver	R
308	Moakley	D	356	Shuster	R
309	Moffett	D	357	Simon	D
310	Moorhead	D	358	Skubitz	R
311	Morgan	D	359	Smith, N.	D
312	Mosher	R	360	Smith, V.	R
313	Mottl	D	361	Solarz	D
314	Murphy, J	D	362	St. Germain	D
315	Murphy, M.	D	363	Stanton, J. W.	R
316	Murtha	D	364	Stanton, J. V.	D
317	Myers, G.	R	365	Stokes	D
318	Myers, J.	R	366	Stratton	D
319	Nedzi	D	367	Studds	D
320	Nix	D	368	Sullivan	D
321	Nolan	D	369	Symington	D
322	Nowak	D	370	Thompson	D
323	O'Hara	D	371	Thone	R
324	O'Neill	D	372	Traxler	D
325	Oberstar	D	373	Tsongas	D

Data (*Continued*)

	North				North	
OBS	*Name*	*Party*	*OBS*	*Name*		*Party*
374	Van der Jagt	R	380	Wydler		R
375	Vander Veen	D	381	Wylie		R
376	Vanik	D	382	Yates		D
377	Vigorito	D	383	Yatron		D
378	Whalen	R	384	Zablocki		D
379	Wolff	D	385	Zeferetti		D

Source: *Roster of United States Congressional Officeholders and Biographical Characteristics of Members of the United States Congress, 1789–1980,* collected and made available by the Inter-University Consortium for Political and Social Research, University of Michigan, Ann Arbor, Michigan.

REVIEW QUESTIONS

1. Hypothesis: The higher the entrance requirements for a college, the higher the college's average grade-point ratio tends to be. Which of the following samples would be preferable for testing this hypothesis? Why?
   Sample A: a cluster sample of 400 colleges
   Sample B: a cluster sample of 3000 college students.

2. Hypothesis: Public-service employees from the Ivy League schools tend to have higher salaries than do public-service employees from other schools.
   Sample: 500 federal employees systematically chosen from United States government personnel lists.
   Evaluate how adequate the sample is for testing the hypothesis.

3. Hypothesis: As the tax rates of cities increase, the number of new businesses opening within city limits tends to decrease.
   a. What kind of units would be sampled?
   b. About how many of those units would be included in the sample?
   c. What would be a good way of selecting those units for the sample?

4. Hypothesis: The poorer a member of Congress's district, the more likely he or she is to vote against increased defense spending.
   Sample A: a systematic sample of all congressional districts in the United States
   Sample B: all members of Congress who voted against increased defense spending, 1960–1980
   What (if any) weaknesses are there in sample A?
   What (if any) weaknesses are there in sample B?

5. Use a random-number table to draw the samples requested in *a* through *d* from the population of Texans in the House of Representatives.

Population (Representatives From Texas; Margin Data Are Hypothetical)

Representative	Margin
S. Hall	High
Wilson	High
Collins	High
R. Hall	High
Mattox	High
Gramm	High
Archer	High
Fields	High
Brooks	High
Pickle	High
Leath	High
Wright	High
Hightower	High
Patman	High
De la Garza	High
White	High
Stenholm	Low
Leland	Low
Hance	Low
Gonzalez	Low
Loeffler	Low
Paul	Low
Kazan	Low
Frost	Low

a. Draw a systematic sample of eight representatives. List the representatives selected.

b. Draw a random sample of seven representatives. List the representatives selected.

c. Draw a stratified sample of six representatives, stratifying by margin of victory without oversampling either margin. List the representatives selected.

d. Draw a quota sample of ten representatives, oversampling those with a low margin so that the number in the sample equals those with a high margin. List the representatives selected.

CHAPTER FOUR

DEFINITION AND MEASUREMENT

Let us consider where we are in the research process. We have one or more hypotheses, each relating two properties of the units of analysis. Now we need to consider the properties in more detail. We need to be able to specify exactly what the properties are and then develop measures for them. That is what this chapter is about: defining and measuring properties.

DEFINING THE PROPERTIES

In order to tell others what the properties are (and perhaps in order to think about them herself), the researcher must attach a word or words to each property. The necessity of relying upon words creates many of the problems in verification of social science research. If we could arrange some kind of mind-to-mind hookup among scientists, there would be much less disagreement over which properties are interrelated. But we have no such hookup. Instead we must use a mind-to-word-to-mind hookup. Hence, the way we use words is very important in empirical research.

Unfortunately, words mean different things to different people. As a consequence, the researcher must define precisely what he means by a particular word. For example, many researchers have used the political ideology of legislators as a property in research. Some define ideology to be the way the legislator votes on issues; others define it to be the personal attitude of the legislator. Researchers also differ on the type of issues to be used to determine ideology: economic, social, foreign-policy, and so on. The choice of issues can greatly influence who is determined to be a liberal and who a conservative. Thus, knowing that a researcher plans to measure the political ideology of a member of Congress does not really tell us what he will be measuring. Is a conservative one who votes against school busing, or is she one who believes in free enterprise? The researcher must define what he means by a conservative or liberal.

In one way or another the researcher must make it clear precisely what the property is. Given the importance of definitions, it is odd that we often find research that uses terms without being explicit about what is meant. For example, the authors of an article discussing the property "quality of life" point out that "the literature is replete with references to the phrase 'quality of life' (QOL), but until recently, few writers have attempted to define the term."[1] The kind of confusion resulting from the inability or unwillingness to be precise in definition is detrimental to the development of social science.

Not every property needs to be explicitly defined. This applies, for example, to properties that are commonly understood, such as age and sex. Properties also do not need to be explicitly defined if the statement of the measurement procedure makes it clear what the definition of the property is. For example, a researcher might specify that a Republican is someone who classifies herself as a Republican when asked, "Do you consider yourself to be a Democrat, a Republican, an independent, or what?" The researcher would not need a separate statement of the definition in order to make clear what he means.

There are three things to consider when defining and using words:

1. The definition must be clear and specific.
2. The definition must be appropriate.
3. The word must be used consistently throughout the research.

Clarity of the Definition

It is obvious that the definition must be clearly stated and must allow the reader to understand precisely what the researcher has in mind when she uses the word. In practice, however, this is often difficult to accomplish. Words are almost always given meaning only by the use of other words. The only exception is when we can point to something or experience something directly and assign a word to the object or experience. When we use words to define other words, the imprecision in the meaning of the words used in the definition is a problem. Sometimes we may even have to define words in a definition before the definition itself is clear.

There are no firm rules to follow that will ensure clear definitions, nor are there tests that allow us to evaluate the clarity of definitions. Researchers must simply strive to maximize the communication, which means they must use extreme care in defining the properties.

Appropriateness of the Definition

The definition stated by the researcher must also be **appropriate.** An appropriate definition for a property is a definition that is consistent with the way the word is generally used by those viewing the research. The definitions of all properties should be appropriate. Since there is no association that officially defines terms in political science, the audience will likely accept a range of definitions for any property. However, there is a limit to such a range: Should you define wealth as "height in feet," your evidence will be judged inappropriate for verifying your hypothesis.

As researchers, we cannot determine absolutely what will be accepted as appropriate by our fellow scientists before we have presented our study to them. However, we can get a feeling for what their reaction is likely to be by noting what the scientific community has previously been willing to accept as appropriate. We can usually determine that by a survey of the literature on the property.

Occasionally a researcher finds it necessary to invent new terms to describe a property that he has observed. An advantage of this is that the new term will not have different meanings for different people. The disadvantage is that it increases the amount of jargon in the discipline, which makes it difficult for people to read and understand what is being said. Since appropriateness is an evaluation of how well the researcher's usage of a term fits with normal usage of the term, a totally new term can be considered neither appropriate nor inappropriate.

Researchers may find no satisfactory definition of a term that is in common usage. If that is the case, they offer a new definition for the word. New definitions of this type may be judged inappropriate if the new meaning of the word is far from what the old meanings were.

Consistency in the Use of Words and Definitions

Misunderstanding will occur if the researcher discusses the same property defined in different ways. This often occurs when the researcher cites other studies. Although all of the studies may have used the same word for a property, and all may have used an appropriate definition, not all may have used the same definition. For example, in the article on quality of life noted above, the authors argue that there are several very different ways in which the phrase has been used. A researcher assuming that all research on the quality of life was talking about the same property would be misled.

HOW THE PROPERTIES ARE MEASURED

After defining a property, the researcher must develop a procedure for determining how much of a property each unit has or to which category of a property each unit belongs. The procedure used is called the *measure,* or *operational definition,* of the property. For example, exactly how do we determine who identifies with the Republican party, with the Democratic party, with some other party, or with no party? How do we go about finding out the amount of unemployment in each country?

The Need for Measurement

Like definition, measurement often appears deceptively easy. We are all used to measuring things with instruments and in units that have wide acceptance. We measure height with a ruler calibrated in inches, weight with a scale calibrated in pounds. If our hypothesis relates height and weight, we can present the height and weight of each individual without having to explain in detail how our ruler or scale was constructed or define precisely an inch or a pound.

The properties we study in political science are frequently used in everyday conversation, but they rarely have commonly accepted measures. We all use terms like *power, status, liberalism,* and *integration.* But what is our power ruler? Our scale for measuring status or liberalism? What are the accepted units for calibrating integration?

If you were relating height and weight, you wouldn't have to go into great detail about why you considered one man 70 inches tall and another 72 inches tall. Nor would you have to explain why you concluded that the first man weighed 170 pounds and the second 200. If you are relating status and power, however, you *do* have to give a detailed explanation of what would cause you to conclude that one man was very powerful, and another only moderately powerful. You will have to explain on what basis one man might get a status rating of 10, and another only 5.

Categorization

Putting the tasks of measurement more generally, the researcher has to give the decision rules that she will follow in separating units according to the level or amount of the property that is present. This is called **categorization,** and it is essential to all measurement. Basically, we must specify the characteristic or characteristics of the unit that will cause us to put it in one category and not in another.

Suppose you have defined wealth as individual net worth. You might decide that you will measure net worth by asking a group of individuals what each estimates his or her net worth to be. Alternatively, you might ask a key informant (say, a banker) to estimate the net worth of various individuals in town. Or you might run a credit check on each individual, and so on.

You must choose among these alternatives, and tell the audience what your choice is. But even that does not finish your task, for you must also indicate how many categories of wealth you will distinguish, and how you will determine which unit is in which category.

For example, if you have chosen to ask respondents what their net worth is, how will you classify the responses? Will you simply sort them out according to estimated dollar value—$10,000, $50,000, $50,001, and so on? Or will you combine those worth $250,000+ into a "very wealthy" category; treat those with $100,000–$249,999 as "wealthy"; and so on? The boundary lines between categories must be clear.

There are three general considerations in defining the categories of the measure. First, the boundary lines between the categories must be clear: There should be no ambiguity about what distinguishes one category from the next. Second, the categories must be mutually exclusive. That is, units must not be able to fit into more than one of the categories. Finally, the categories must be exhaustive, in that all units of analysis must be placed in one of them.

We often do not have enough information to classify a unit on a particular measure. It is common for people to refuse to answer some of the questions on a survey. Some nations do not report all of the statistics we need. Legislators are absent and do not vote on some of the roll calls we may be analyzing. We say that the data for these units are *missing*. We usually do not wish to throw the unit out of the sample if we have data on it for other variables in the analysis. Rather, we want to indicate that the information was missing on this particular variable. To do this we establish a category labeled "no information available." Units placed in this category can be ignored in later analysis of the variable in question.

Levels of Measurement and the Assignment of Values

Measuring something almost always involves assigning numbers to the units of analysis in the sample. We call the numbers assigned to each category the *values* of a variable. For example, suppose we compute the percentage of questions on an examination answered correctly as a measure of how much each student knew. Each score is the value of the variable measuring how well each student did on the test. Another example would be coding people with a low sense of political efficacy as 1, people with a moderate sense of efficacy 2, and people with a high sense of efficacy as 3. A third example would be, when measuring party identification, to assign a 1 to those classified as Democrats, a 2 to Republicans, and a 3 to those not identifying with either of the two parties.

We can distinguish three different general types of measures, or variables: interval, ordinal, and nominal. These **levels of measurement** constitute one of the most important factors determining what kind of analysis we can use when dealing with a set of variables. We will be discussing levels of measurement throughout the rest of the book.

Interval-Level Variables. When we are measuring quantitative variables, the numbers we record sometimes stand for the actual amount of the property that each unit is observed to have. These are **interval-level** variables. In a study of causes of coups, one variable used to explain the occurrence of a coup could be the number of months that had passed since the last election. The values recorded for the variable would be the actual number of months since the last election.

We call these variables *interval* because it is possible to determine the size of the interval between each of the units in the analysis. The distance between 1 and 2 is the same distance as that between 2 and 3 and that between 3 and 4.

Ordinal-Level Variables. When we measure variables the numbers can also stand for only the *relative* rather than the actual amount of the property each unit has. In that case, the numbers indicate which units have more and which have less of a property. We call measures that indicate only relative amount of a property **ordinal-level** variables. An example would be a researcher asking a legal expert to rank a series of court decisions with respect to the quality of legal reasoning used. Such a ranking would produce numbers indicating where each case was relative to the others.

Ordinal variables differ from interval variables in that we do not determine how much of a property a unit has, only whether it has more than, less than, or the same amount as another unit. We cannot determine the distance between the units, as we could with interval-level variables. In the example of the measure of the quality of legal reasoning we could determine which decisions were better and which were worse with respect to the property; we could not determine the amount of the property or how much more of it one decision had relative to another.

We may choose to use numbers indicating relative amounts of the property even when the actual amounts are available. If we were measuring wealth, we might choose to classify people as very wealthy, wealthy, average, poor, or very poor instead of recording their actual net worth. Those categories would indicate only the relative and not the absolute wealth of each unit. We would then use numbers that indicated the relative order of the categories. For example,

1 = very poor
2 = poor
3 = average
4 = wealthy
5 = very wealthy

The higher the number, the greater the relative wealth.

Nominal-Level Variables. Variables that distinguish differences between units of analysis but do not indicate either the actual or relative amount of a property are called **nominal-level** variables. Nominal variables are the qualitative variables we discussed earlier. Nominal variables include sex, religion, job classification, and so on. When the property to be measured is nominal-level the numbers we assign do not convey either actual or relative amounts of the property. Numbers are assigned arbitrarily, and are used only to distinguish among units that fall into different categories of the property. There is no theoretical reason why we need to assign numbers to nominal-level variables at all. For example, we could record sex simply as either male or female. As a practical matter, however, we almost always use numbers to represent different categories of qualitative variables. They take less space to record and are generally easier than words to computer-analyze.

CRITERIA FOR EVALUATING MEASURES

A clear description of how the properties are measured is a necessary but not sufficient condition for acceptance of a measure. The **reliability** and the **validity** of the measure must also be examined before the measure can be accepted. Reliability and validity have specific meanings in social science and we will consider each carefully.

Reliability

When we say that measures must be *reliable,* we mean that they must yield the same results when applied to the same units under the same circumstances, regardless of who does the measuring. The measure states the procedures by which one can tell how much of a property is exhibited by each unit. If, by following those procedures, others would categorize units differently than the researcher has, the measure is unreliable. If, for example, you would classify a respondent as very wealthy and another scientist, *using your measurement procedures,* would classify that respondent as moderately wealthy, then your measure shows some unreliability.

Determining Reliability

A major source of unreliability is vagueness. All too often in the political science literature, measurement procedures are not described or are only vaguely noted. Data sources are not listed, not available, or inadequately cited. Fellow scientists cannot tell how the original researcher obtained his results, nor can they replicate (repeat) the work to check its accuracy. When researchers make it impossible for us to replicate their work, they are essentially asking us to take their word that the world is as they say it is. Though they may be correct, we can hardly rely upon it. If we were willing to take everyone's word for what the world is like, there would hardly be a need for empirical science.

Replication is not the only test for reliability. Some measurements cannot be replicated, for reasons other than unreliability—cost, time, and so forth. The test of reliability must be whether it seems reasonable that other scientists measuring the same properties of the same units would have come up with the same values that the researcher did.

Occasionally, clear measurement procedures will nevertheless be unreliable because following the outlined procedure will lead different people to different conclusions regarding the level or amount of a property that is present. This is more likely to happen as the procedure calls for more judgment on the part of the researcher. For instance, if the procedures require a panel of coders to count the number of biased statements in a newspaper article, they will likely make somewhat different counts. If the measure requires instead that the coders simply count the number of times the terms *redneck, bigot,* or *demagogue* appear, there will be very little room for judgment and all of the coders will probably get the same count.

Reliability can be increased by the presence of clear and detailed instructions. Those instructions that leave the least room for researcher judgment (that is, those that are objective rather than subjective) will prove to be the most reliable.

Validity

Valid measures are those that will measure a property as it was defined. This is best explained by an example of a measure. Suppose you defined a member of Congress's support for the president as the extent to which he or she acts in Congress to see that bills that the president favors are passed. A valid measure of this would be the index of presidential support reported in the *Congressional Quarterly Almanac.* This index determines what the president supports by analyzing his public statements and the bills that reach the voting stage. It then computes the percentage of times each representative voted in a manner consistent with the president's wishes.

Given the definition of presidential support, it would not be valid to search the *New York Times* and *Washington Post* to determine which members of Congress had made public announcements that they supported the president and to classify those who had as supportive and those who had not as not supportive. There would probably be some relationship between the actual voting record and the public announcement, but the two measures need not be the same. A measure based on public announcements would not measure public support as it had been defined; hence it would not be valid.

Where the measure is not valid, the reader is forced to conclude that either the definition of the property or the measure is not relevant to testing the hypothesis.

In cases where the properties are not explicitly defined, we must determine validity by evaluating the measure on the basis of commonly accepted definitions of the property or definitions of the property used by other researchers who have apparently studied it. For example, if a researcher were measuring po-

litical alienation in order to test a hypothesis, she would have cited several previous studies on the subject. If the researcher provided no definition for political
alienation, we could determine the validity of the measure by using the definitions provided in the cited literature.

Determining Validity

Validity of measures is dependent upon acceptance by the scientific community in general. A researcher cannot definitively judge such acceptance before
the fact. But again, we can estimate acceptance by surveying the literature to
discover measures used by others. If we can find another case in which a property has been defined as we have defined it, we can choose the same measure as
was used in that case. If we are presenting a new definition, or are unhappy with
previously used measures, we can develop a new measure and ask colleagues to
evaluate whether it is valid.

To the extent that a measure is unreliable, it cannot be valid. A measure
that does not classify the same units in the same way cannot consistently be measuring what we are claiming it is measuring. It should also be noted that just
because a measure is reliable does not mean it is valid. We might have a very
reliable method of measuring how tall a person is, but if we claimed it was also a
measure of the person's political ideology, it would clearly not be valid.

Validating Indirect Measures

Measurement may be direct or indirect. Indirect measurement is required
whenever a property cannot be observed and must be inferred on the basis of
other properties that can be observed. This is the case when the property to be
measured is an attitude or belief. Beliefs and attitudes cannot be directly observed; they must be indirectly measured through observation of some behavior,
usually the response to a questionnaire.

Indirect measures may also be used for properties where direct observation
is possible but is either inconvenient or prohibitively expensive. For example,
you might determine whether a person voted by asking him whether or not he
voted rather than by stationing yourself at the polling place to see for yourself.
Direct observation of the voting booth would have been possible, but inconvenient. Inferring whether the individual voted on the basis of his response to your
question is an indirect measure—perhaps less valid but certainly more conve-
nient.

Indirect measures are often more difficult to validate than direct measures.
It can be argued that the indirect measure being applied really does not measure
what a direct measure would. When no direct measure is possible, it may be argued that the property supposedly being measured does not even exist.

Direct observation is preferable to indirect observation, just as eyewitness
reports are preferable to circumstantial evidence. However, the nature of the

property or the cost of direct observation may make such observation impossible. If it is necessary to rely on indirect observation, it is particularly important for the researcher to present evidence that establishes the validity of her measure.

One of the most common ways to demonstrate the validity of indirect measures is to present a logical argument as to why the indirect measure should be an adequate substitute for a more direct one. This kind of demonstration is limited in that it does not really confirm that the measures are in fact related.

Sometimes we can apply a direct measure and an indirect measure to the same units to see if they classify the units in the same way. An example of this kind of validation is the use of official voter lists to validate responses to surveys asking a respondent to report whether he or she voted. Official lists of voters are available in most locations and are a much more direct indicator of whether or not a person voted in an election than asking the person. A study of voting behavior in the 1976 election found that turnout among the national sample was 72% according to the responses to a survey attempting to determine who voted, and 61% according to the actual voting records. About 13% of the survey sample misreported whether or not they voted. Twelve percent reported voting when they had not, while only 1% said they did not vote when they did.[2] When we find that the less direct measure does not produce the same classification as the more direct measure, we have to decide whether the less direct measure is sufficiently valid to be used in research.

When we have no direct measure with which to validate an indirect measure, it is often useful to develop two or more indirect measures of the same property and compare how they classify the units. The greater the similarity in the way these different measures classify the units, the more likely they are to be valid. For example, a researcher measuring the liberalism of members of Congress has no direct measure available, but he can find several political organizations that publish liberalism ratings for them. If those several ratings tend to classify the same members as liberal and the same members as conservative, it is likely that all of the measures are valid. If the ratings differ markedly, then it is less likely that any one of the measures is valid.

SUMMARY

Definitions and measures can never be perfect. Definitions will almost always leave some ambiguity as to exactly what is meant by a word. Both the reliability and the validity of a measure are matters of degree rather than absolutes. To some extent all measures are unreliable and invalid. When doing research, make your definitions as clear and precise as possible and your measures as reliable and valid as possible given your time and resources. When you are evaluating research, the final test is whether the problems with definition and measurement are sufficient to cause you to doubt the conclusions of the researcher.

In this chapter we have considered general issues of definition and measurement. In the next two chapters we look in more detail at how we go about constructing measures and how we try to maximize reliability and validity in specific situations.

Endnotes

[1]Zielger, J. A. and Britton, C. R., "A Comparative Analysis of Socioeconomic Variations in Measuring the Quality of Life," *Social Science Quarterly,* 62, no. 2 (June 1981), 303.
[2]Michael Traugott and John Katosh, "Response Validity in Surveys of Voting Behavior," *Public Opinion Quarterly,* 4, no. 3 (Fall 1979), 359–377.

LABORATORY EXERCISES

The purpose of this laboratory is to give you some experience in evaluating measures that are found in research and in developing some measures of your own.

Task 1. At the end of this laboratory are selections from three different articles that develop measures that are similar to one another. In this task you will evaluate the definitions and measures used. The first selection is from Philips Cutright's "National Political Development: Measurement and Analysis," *American Sociological Review,* 28 (April 1963), 253–64. The second selection is from Deane Neubauer's "Some Conditions of Democracy," *American Political Science Review,* 61 (December 1967), 1002–9. The third selection is from Kenneth Bollen's "Issues in the Comparative Measurement of Political Democracy," *American Sociological Review,* 45 (June 1980), 370–90. After carefully reading the three articles, answer the following questions:

   a. Cutright wants to measure the degree of "political development" that a nation has. What is his definition of the phrase?
   b. Neubauer argues that Cutright is not really measuring what he says he is measuring. Is Neubauer's criticism based on the appropriateness or consistency of the definition, or the reliability of Cutright's measure, or on the validity of his measure?
   c. Compare what Bollen wants to measure with what Cutright and Neubauer want to measure. In what ways are they the same and in what ways are

Country Ranks on the Three Measures

Country	Cutright	Neubauer	Bollen
Austria	15	18	13
Belgium	11	6	1
Britain	1	1	11
Canada	1	6	1
Chile	1	19	1
Denmark	9	11	1
Finland	15	3	13
France	11	2	20
India	23	21	19
Ireland	1	20	16
Israel	19	12	16
Italy	17	14	13
Japan	19	7	11
Luxembourg	11	8	1
Mexico	17	8	1
Netherlands	11	5	1
New Zealand	1	10	1
Norway	9	9	1
Sweden	1	4	1
Switzerland	1	22	1
United States	1	16	16
Venezuela	22	17	23
West Germany	19	13	21

Scores were rounded before being assigned a rank. When more than one country is assigned the same rank, the next country down is assigned a rank that reflects its actual position and not the rank immediately below the same-ranked countries.

they different?

d. Why does Neubauer want to develop a measure different from Cutright's?

e. How appropriate are the definitions used by the three researchers?

f. How reliable are the measures used by the three researchers?

g. How valid are the measures used by the three researchers?

h. Below is a list of countries and their ranks on each of the three measures. The articles ranked other countries also but we have included only those which can be ranked on all three measures. What can you conclude about the degree to which the different measures actually measure the same thing?

Task 2. Develop a definition and measure for one or more properties assigned by your instructor.

SELECTIONS FROM ARTICLES

Selection 1

In the first part of this paper we develop an index of political development. The index of political development is operationally defined. The concept that guided construction of the index can be stated simply—a politically developed nation has more complex and specialized national political institutions than a less politically developed nation. Degree of political development can be measured and each nation can be placed on a continuum of development, which will allow it to be compared with any other nation in the world. Operationally we bank heavily on the role played by political parties in national political life in measuring political development.[1]

The following items were selected and given the weights indicated. The time period covered by the data is 1940 through 1960. The score each nation received for the first year was added to the score it received the following year to get a cumulative total score.

A scheme for scoring the nations (in which high scores mean high development) should penalize each nation for political instability which represents "backsliding" and reward it for achieving or retaining more complex political forms of organization. Points for any one year were awarded in the following manner.

1. Legislative Branch of Government.
   Two points for each year in which a parliament existed in which the lower or the only chamber contained representatives of two or more political parties and the minority party or parties had at least 30 percent of all seats. One point for each year in which a parliament existed whose members were the representatives of one or more political parties, but where the "30 percent rule" was violated. No points for each year no parliament existed or for years when either of the above types of parliaments was abolished or discarded by executive power. Parliaments whose members are not members of political parties are given a zero. Parliaments that are not self-governing bodies (e.g., the mock parliaments of colonial governments) are given a zero.

2. Executive Branch of Government.
   One point for each year the nation was ruled by a chief executive who was in office by virtue of direct vote in an open election where he faced compe-

---

[1]The index is, of course, heavily dependent upon available data. The selection among alternative items for the index was guided by the coherent interpretation of Max Weber's political sociology as given by Reinhard Bendix, *Max Weber: An Intellectual Portrait,* Garden City: Doubleday, 1960.
The primary source for the materials used in this study was the *Political Handbook of the World: Parliaments, Parties and Press,* published annually for the Council on Foreign Relations, New York: Harper and Brothers, from 1940 through 1961. Needed supplementary checks were secured by reference to the *Encyclopedia Britannica* and other reference works.

tition or was selected by a political party in a multi-party system, as defined by the conditions necessary to get 2 points on the legislative branch indicator above. If the parliament ceased being a multi-party parliament because of executive action, the chief executive stopped getting points. One half point each year the chief executive was not selected by virtue of his hereditary status but was selected by criteria other than those necessary to attain one point as given above. Colonial governments receive one half point per year. No points if the nation was governed by a hereditary ruler.

It is possible for a nation to acquire no points, one half or 1 point depending on the selection of the chief executive. The combined index has a range of zero to 3 points per year. Over the 21 year period of our study it would be possible for a nation to have a total raw score between zero and 63 points.

Selection 2

[Cutright's] index does not measure "political development" in Cutright's definition of the term. It measures "degree of democraticness" by which is meant the extent to which nations institute and maintain overtime multiple party political systems and "open elections." The use of Cutright's index is directly equivalent to asserting that those nations which are characterized by the institutions of liberal democracy, are those which are most highly developed politically. Given another set of normative assumptions one might wish to agree that "most highly developed" means "most democratic," but one cannot, utilizing Cutright's definition of the term "political development," easily equate development with democracy. To cite the most obvious example, many modern states are characterized by political institutions of considerable complexity, but this fact is not related to the existence of a set of democratic political institutions. The Communist countries most clearly fit this category. . . .

In order to suggest the effect which continued socio-economic development has upon democratic development, it is necessary to have an index which goes beyond Cutright's, one which is capable of measuring variation within the sub-sample of "most democratic" countries which are largely undifferentiated on Cutright's index.

We have devised an index of democratic development expressly for this purpose. This index, derived from definitional and empirical constructs of Dahl and Downs, concentrates mainly on electoral features of democratic regimes. Explicitly, the index is composed of four indicators which measure the relative amount of *electoral equality* and *competition* present in a given political system. The rationale behind the index construction is rather simple. The most characteristic feature of democratic regimes is the election of key governmental personnel. As suggested in the introduction, this is the mechanism whereby citizens give some indication of which preferences they wish scheduled for governmental decision. The form of elections alone, however, does not guarantee their democratic substance. Democratic elections are those in which opposition groups are given some opportunity to contest office with ruling groups. Two key indicators of a country's tolerance of electoral opposition groups are the existence of actual electoral competition and the existence of multiple sources of public information. The indicators chosen for the index reflect these considerations. They are:

a. Percent of the adult population eligible to vote. This indicator is basic to the concept of "democraticness." The variation between nations on this measure indicates the percentage of the population which is excluded from the suffrage for whatever reasons (sex, race, residence, literacy, etc.). . . .

b. Equality of representation. The notion of one man, one vote is basic to modern concepts of democracy. The implication of this norm goes beyond the exclusion of plural voting. It demands that votes be given equal weight in the choice of candidates. We will make use of a measure which calculates the "mean range of distortion" in equating votes with seats in legislatures. The computation is arrived at by determining which parties are most over-represented in the assignment of seats and which are most under-represented. The two are combined to obtain a range of distortion and the mean for all elections studied is then computed.

c. Information equality. An important condition in Dahl's model, but one which is absent from Downs is: "All individuals possess identical information about the alternatives." Clearly the task of measuring this directly is overwhelming. As an indicator of this condition, we have made use of a measure of the degree to which multiple sources of information are available to citizens of a given country. The measure focuses upon newspapers under the assumption that, if there is considerable "pluralism" in this sphere of mass communications, there is a positive probability that it will exist in other areas of communication. The indicator also attempts to measure the degree to which pluralistic ownership of the press exists. Since adequate data of this form exist only for large cities, the indicator is explicitly concerned with the pattern of newspaper ownership in capital cities. In order to provide for greater comparability among the sample countries, one must also build into the measure some control for the size of the capital city. The formula:

$$\text{number of separately owned papers} \times \frac{\text{average circulation}}{\text{size of capital}}$$

is utilized to derive a coefficient that suggests the relative number and circulation of newspapers in capital cities.

d. Competition. Electoral competition by political parties is meaningful only if the nature of that competition is such that the alternation in office of competing sets of leaders is probable as well as possible. The measure should reward those countries which come most close to providing the electorate with this alternative. Two measures are utilized.

1. Percent of the time period in which the dominant party held office. . . .
2. Mean percentage of the vote received by the winning party (parties). This indicator actually measures the closeness of the competition. . . .

A sample of twenty-three democratic countries was selected and scored on the above indicators. The scores were then combined into an index of democratic performance.[2]

Selection 3

It is these *differences* in the political power held by the elite, relative to the nonelite, that helps identify how democratic a nation is. I define *political democracy* as *the extent to which the political power of the elite is minimized and that of the nonelite is maximized.* Identifying the differences in political power is extremely difficult. The major difficulty is that there is no widely accepted unit of measure for political power. Unlike in a study of the distribution of income, the number of "dollar-like" units of political power held by the various groups in a country cannot be evaluated. The approach to measurement, in this case, must be more indirect. . . .

In the theoretical definition of political democracy, the two most important aspects were political liberties and popular sovereignty (as represented in electoral processes). Most characteristics attributed to political democracy may be classified under one or the other of these two general concepts. For instance, the fairness of elections, the proportion of the most important government positions that are elected rather than appointed, and the type of electoral system (proportionate vs. other) are indicators of popular sovereignty. The extents of free speech, free press, and the freedom to organize opposition parties or groups are indicators of political liberties. Thus, at a minimum, a measure of political democracy should include indicators of both political liberties and of popular sovereignty.

The revised index of political democracy (hereafter, POLDEM) has indicators of both of these concepts. Table 1 lists these indicators, their sources, and several technical notes on their use. A brief description of these measures follows. A more detailed description is in the original sources and in Bollen (1979).

---

[2]In order to avoid unnecessary complications in comparing these results with those obtained by Cutright, the democratic performance index was constructed in a manner analogous to that used by Cutright to construct the political development index. In fact, to enhance overall comparability between the two studies, his scoring procedure was utilized on all the data. The data for the independent variables (the indexes of communication, urbanization, education and agricultural employment) were obtained by consulting the sources cited by Cutright. The individual scores for each indicator were T-scored, combined (by adding T-scores) into the appropriate indexes and those T-scored. [T-scoring is a method of changing the variable so that when combined with other variables it has an equal impact on the combined measure. It is nearly identical with Z-scoring, which is discussed in Chapters 5 and 8.]

The three indicators of political liberties are: (1) press freedom, (2) freedom of group opposition, and (3) government sanctions. Freedom of the press is ranked on a nine-point scale that measures the degree of control normally exercised by any official agency which has the power to interfere with the dissemination and discussion of the news (Nixon, 1960:17). Freedom of group opposition measures the degree to which organized opposition is allowed. It is scored on a four-point scale, ranging from a low of no parties or all but dominant party and its satellites excluded, to a high of no parties excluded.

The third indicator of political liberties is government sanctions. Government sanctions are actions taken by the government which curtail the political activities of one or more groups of the population. The sanctions include censorship of the mass media, instituting a curfew, banning or harassing political parties, and the arrest of opposition party members. This indicator is based on the number of such events.

The three measures of popular sovereignty, as listed in Table 1, are (1) fairness of elections, (2) executive selection, and (3) legislative selection. Fairness of elections scales the degree to which elections are relatively free from corruption and coercion. The scoring of this variable is based on whether or not alternative choices exist, and on whether or not the elections are administered by a nonpar-

TABLE 1 Six Components of the 1965 and 1960 Revised Index of Political Democracy

Variable	Symbol	Source	Notes
Press Freedom	Y_1	Nixon (1965; 1960)	—
Freedom of Group Opposition	Y_2	Banks (1971: segment 10, field o)	1
Government Sanctions	Y_5	Taylor and Hudson (1971)	1
Fairness of Elections	Y_4	Taylor and Hudson (1971)	2
Executive Selection	Y_5	Banks (1971: segment 2, field j)	1, 2, 3, 4
Legislative Selection	Y_6	Banks (1971: segment 2, field p; segment 10, field l)	1, 2, 4

Notes:

1. For Y_2, Y_3, Y_5, and Y_6, the average scores for 1964–1966 and 1959–1961 are used for the 1965 and 1960 measures, respectively. If the indicators are not available for the full three-year period, the average scores, over those years with data, are used.

2. If no elections were held from 1956–1964 (or 1961–1967) a country is scored zero for 1960 (or 1965) on variables Y_4–Y_6. Election information is from Taylor and Hudson (1971; 1972). No election information after 1967 is available from this source.

3. The "indirect election" category of Banks is combined with the "elective."

4. Trinidad and Tobago, Jamaica, and Uganda's 1960 rank, and Y_5 and Y_6, are derived from 1962 data, because earlier data are not available.

tisan administration. Also considered are whether or not the elections are rigged and if the results of the elections are binding on all parties. The four-point scale ranges from a low of no elections, to a high of relatively free and competitive elections.

The executive selection variable indicates whether the chief executive of a country is elected, or not. The legislative selection variable determines whether the legislative body is elected but, in addition, considers the effectiveness of the legislative body.[3] The lowest score is given to countries with no elections or a nonelective legislative body, while the highest score is given to legislative bodies that are both elected and an effective power in determining national policies.

Each of the six components was linearly transformed to range from a low of 0 to a high of 100.

REVIEW QUESTIONS

1. Property: wealth of nations
   Measure: total gross national product
   a. Is this measure likely to be reliable? Why?
   b. What might increase its reliability?
   c. Is it likely to be valid? Why?
   d. What might increase its validity?

2. Property: support for the Equal Rights Amendment
   Measure: In a door-to-door survey, ask each respondent, "Do you feel that women and men are equal, and that therefore the ERA should be passed?"
   a. Is this measure likely to be reliable? Why?
   b. What might increase its reliability?
   c. Is it likely to be valid? Why?
   d. What might increase its validity?

3. Property: education level (for individuals)
   Measure: In a telephone survey, ask each respondent, "What is the highest educational degree you have received?" Code responses as follows: 1, high school or lower; 2, associate's degree; 3, bachelor's degree; 4, master's degree; 5, Ph.D.
   a. Is this measure likely to be reliable? Why?
   b. What might increase its reliability?
   c. Is it likely to be valid? Why?
   d. What might increase its validity?

---

[3]The elective/nonelective legislature variable is scored 1 or 0. This is then multiplied by the effectiveness of the legislative body. The scores are multiplied so that, for example, elected "puppet" legislatures do not score as high as those that are both elected and effective, on the assumption that the former are not as important to political democracy as the latter.

4. Property: professionalism of city government

   Definition: Cities with city-manager forms of government are professional; other forms of government are unprofessional.

   Measure: the form of government, as given in the "Profiles of Individual Cities" table, which includes all United States cities with a population greater than 10,000, in the *Municipal Yearbook*, published annually.

   a. Is this definition likely to be appropriate? Why?
   b. Is this measure likely to be reliable? Why?
   c. What might increase its reliability?
   d. Is it likely to be valid? Why?
   e. What might increase its validity?

CHAPTER FIVE

DATA COLLECTION

This chapter and the next are really extensions of Chapter 4. In that chapter we discussed definitions and measurement in general terms. Now we look at specific techniques. In this chapter we examine measurement techniques that are used primarily in data collection other than surveys. In Chapter 6 we consider data collection in survey research.

We will not try to discuss all possible data-collection techniques. Our goal is to introduce some of the general types of data collection and some of the factors that may influence the reliability and validity of the properties being measured. In addition, we want to discuss some of the sources of data that may provide measures or information needed to construct measures.

The activity of classifying the units of analysis on the measures needed for analysis is referred to as **data collection.** There are two general types of data collection. In one type the researchers observe behavior, either directly or indirectly, and they code and record the measures based on the information they gather. This type of data collection is sometimes called **primary-data collection.** In the second type of data collection the researcher uses information that has been collected by someone else and published or otherwise made available. This type of data collection is called **secondary-data collection** or **archival-data collection.**

COLLECTING PRIMARY DATA

Observation and Participant Observation

Because of the cost of direct observation and because many things we study in political science cannot be directly observed, relatively little direct observation is used. Perhaps even when we could use it, we are so accustomed to using survey techniques or other indirect indicators that we do so without seriously considering the alternatives. But some direct observation is done, and we shall consider the particular problems it presents for the researchers.

Observation as a method of measurement consists of the researcher watching units and categorizing and coding their properties. An example of observation used in political science is the analysis of interactions in the General Assembly of the United Nations conducted by researchers who sat in the visitors' balcony and observed the representatives. They counted the number of conversations between representatives of different countries and the number and length of public speeches by representatives. Some of the difficulties of doing this rather than relying on published roll calls or similar data are obvious. The direct observation took many more hours than indirect observation would have required. To do the observation, the researchers had to be in New York, whereas analysis of secondary sources could have been done elsewhere. Direct observation was also more expensive than other methods would have been.

One of the major problems with observation is that it is often difficult to get access to the place where the units are to be observed. A few years ago a group of researchers studying jury behavior obtained permission to tape-record jury deliberations without the jury's knowledge. The jury room is generally considered a place for private deliberations, and when word of the practice leaked, a controversy ensued that ended that part of the project. The researchers had to be content with simulated juries. Limited access frustrates much direct observation.

One way to gain access to observation is to become a participant in the process. A **participant observer** is a researcher who observes while being a member of the group he or she is observing. The participant-observer method is commonly used in studying Congress. The American Political Science Association has a program for sending scholars to work for senators and representatives. While participating as staff members, these scholars make observations about Congress and the staff.

The major problem for observers, once they have access, is to avoid influencing the units they are observing. The people in the balcony of the United Nations might have gone unnoticed by the people they were observing, but in most cases the presence of the observers is obvious. This may cause those being observed to behave more like they think the observers would want them to behave.

A final problem with observation is that much of it is unreliable. Observers often do not record their observations systematically. What they report may sometimes be nothing more than impressions about behavior. Such impressions might easily be different if reported by another observer. This problem can be overcome if the researcher carefully determines what he or she is trying to measure and the procedures for measuring it. The procedures for making observations should be no less well defined than those for making a survey.

Content Analysis

Although the ability to observe other behavior is severely limited, the spoken and written communications of units are frequently available for unlimited examination. Research using measures based on spoken or written communications is called **content analysis.**

The measures we use in content analysis must be as reliable and valid as the measures we use in other types of research. We achieve reliability and validity by developing a systematic procedure for observing the communications. For example, we might count the proportion of self-references in speeches.

Counting the proportion of times that certain words appear is the simplest form of content analysis. More complex analysis may involve counting words only if they appear in a certain context, or it may involve counting phrases. The simpler the analysis, the more reliable it tends to be (that is, the more likely different researchers are to get the same count). The more complex the analysis, the more valid it tends to be (that is, the more likely the count is to reflect the property the researcher is measuring).

Indirect Observation

Thus far we have discussed ways in which the researcher directly observes the behavior he or she wishes to measure. Of course direct observation is often impossible or too expensive, which makes indirect observation necessary. The primary form of indirect observation is probably the survey. Surveys are so prevalent and there are so many special considerations to take into account when using them that we have devoted all of the next chapter to them. But although surveys are used so much, they are not necessarily the preferred method of collecting data. It is our general observation that political science as a discipline relies too much on surveys; we should try to use methods of data collection other than surveys when possible. We discuss some of these other methods below.

USING ARCHIVAL DATA

There are many kinds of archival data and many different sources of them. Some archival data have been collected by researchers for a specific research project and then made available to others. The Inter-University Consortium for Political and Social Research (ICPSR) collects and disseminates data commonly used by social scientists. They have well over 2000 sets of data in their archives. The data is usually provided on magnetic tape that can be processed by computers. The vast majority of these data sets were produced by researchers collecting data for a special project. After they had completed their research, the data were made available through the consortium.

Archival data are sometimes gathered by organizations that disseminate data for use by a large number of researchers with different interests. The Center for Political Studies, for example, has conducted long surveys before and after each presidential election since 1952 and surveys after each off-year election. The purpose of these surveys is not primarily to gather data for a particular research project, but rather to collect a lot of data relevant to a large community of researchers. Similarly, the National Opinion Research Corporation has conducted the General Social Survey since 1972 (every year until 1978, every other year since then). That survey produces about 500 variables on a sample of Americans. It too is a resource for all researchers and not a survey designed for a specific research project.

Perhaps the major producer of data used by American social scientists is the United States Bureau of the Census. Not only does it collect and disseminate information on population characteristics of communities and areas in the decennial census, it constantly collects demographic data on individuals in the annual Current Population Surveys, on governments in the periodic Census of Governments, and on housing, farms, and manufacturing in other data-collection activities. Although collected primarily for use by government and business planners, the data represent an important resource for people doing social science research.

A somewhat different kind of data is produced by individuals and organizations as part of routine record keeping. One example of this kind of data collection is the voting statistics produced by a state office, usually the secretary of state. These data may sometimes be used as prepared, but often researchers will need to modify them, recode them, or combine them with other data in order to test hypotheses.

A second example of this kind of data collection is the records of the disposition of criminal cases, which are kept as a normal part of the legal process. A researcher might use these records to measure properties such as length of sentence or severity of crime. One of our students once used such records to test the hypothesis that people who could afford their own lawyer in criminal cases received lighter sentences than those who had a court-appointed attorney.

Some archival data consist of collections of data from original records that have been published or otherwise processed so as to be more available or more useful to researchers. Collections of election returns, compilations of roll-call votes in the United States House and Senate, and collections of social and economic indicators published by the United Nations are examples of archives based on data collection that were not part of a specific research project.

Reliability of Archival Collections

If we remember that our measures are reliable only when others can replicate our measurement procedure and get the same results, then it will often be easy for us to obtain reliability with archival data. If we want to measure the size of cities in the United States, we can simply cite the specific census report and table from which we obtained the information. Anyone going back to the same source would measure city size exactly as we did. The reliability of archival data can be easily checked because these data, unlike data collected by observation or surveys, usually remain available unchanged.

Reliability may be a problem, however, if the original producers of the archival record used measures that were not reliable. For example, some of the data on different countries found in data archives are based on "expert judgments" or estimates; often the basis on which such judgments were made is not clear. Any reliability problem that would have confronted a researcher who was gathering the data himself, without being able to use the archival record, is a reliability problem for the researcher who is using the archive.

With some archival data, ensuring reliability requires more than a citation. The student who looked at records of court cases had to specify how he identified the cases, how he coded the information, what he did when the data for a case were not recorded, and so on. As with any other statement of a reliable measure, we must give the details of the procedure to ensure that it can be replicated.

Validity of Archival Data

There are two general decisions we must make in order to evaluate the validity of archival data. The first is whether the archive is likely to be accurate. The second, assuming the information in the archive is accurate, is whether the information is a valid measure of the property the researcher is measuring.

Evaluating the validity of data in an archive is exactly like evaluating a measure that a researcher might have used when she collected the data herself. To the extent that the methods of measurement were not reliable, the reported measures are not valid either. Archival data may be invalid for many reasons. Often they are based on reports from officials who may not have specific data. Sometimes there may be incentives to misreport data. For example, the *Uniform Crime Reports* published by the FBI give data on crime rates in different categories, broken down by city and state. The validity of those figures has often been questioned because of the many ways in which they can be presented by the local police either to make things look good (crime rate decreasing, or going up at a low rate) or bad (crime rate increasing at a high rate).

Census data are widely respected and used, but there has always been the problem of undercounting some groups. Further, census data are based on surveys that have all of the validity problems of surveys in general (we will consider these problems in the next chapter).

The important rule to remember is that just because it is printed does not necessarily make it correct. Archival data are based on some kind of observation, direct or indirect. Therefore, any validity problems with the original data collection are validity problems for any researcher who relies on the data.

There is an additional validity problem in using archival data: In measuring a property we are often forced to use data that may not be as good an indicator of the property as we could have devised if we had controlled the way in which the data were collected. Unable to construct the ideal measure, we use an indicator that we think should be related. For example, a researcher wanted to determine the influence of presidential coattails on United States House election outcomes. To do this he needed to measure the percentage of vote each candidate got and the party of the candidate. He also needed the percentage of voters in each district who identified with the Republican and Democratic parties. Since there is no direct measure of party identities available, he averaged the vote for the parties in the districts over United States Senate and House races held in previous years. The election statistics were fairly valid measures of what the vote was in those elections, but the use of them to determine the percentage at party identifiers in the district may not have been valid.

Sources of Archival Data

Retrieving Information About the United States Government. The greatest source of information about the behavior of the United States government is the government itself. The U.S. Government Printing Office is the largest publisher in the United States. It publishes information on the operations of the government and data that might be useful in those operations.

Since there are thousands of government publications, your first step in finding specific information should be to consult the *Monthly Catalog of U.S. Government Publications,* which indexes all government publications. The *Monthly Catalog* will lead you to publications by Congress, the executive branch, and the independent government agencies. If you are interested just in congressional publications and documents, the nongovernmental *Congressional Information Service Index* is quite useful.

Perhaps the most useful governmental publications are

Congressional Record—Includes remarks made in the House and Senate plus insertions.

Congressional Reports, Documents, and Hearings—Contain testimony, background information, and recommendations regarding subjects before House and Senate committees.

Federal Budget—Contains presidential spending and revenue recommendations along with data on past spending and revenue.

Department of State Bulletin—The most comprehensive source on United States foreign policy.

U.S. Government Organization Manual—Describes and gives addresses for all United States government organizations. Also lists top personnel in those organizations.

Nongovernment sources of information are important supplements to governmental reports on the activities of the government. Among these are

Congressional Quarterly Weekly—Generally more useful than the *Congressional Record* in reporting congressional activities. Annual congressional summaries appear in the *Congressional Quarterly Almanac.*

> *Supreme Court Reporter, Federal Reporter, and Federal Supplement*—Report Supreme Court, United States Court of Appeals, and Federal District Court Opinions; cross-indexed with summaries.

Retrieving Information About United States Government Officials. The most useful government publication containing biographical data on United States officials in the *Congressional Directory.* Its coverage is restricted to the House and Senate.

Of more general use to researchers are several nongovernmental publications that contain biographical data and/or report voting behavior of officials. Nearly indispensable are

> *Congressional Quarterly Almanac*—Reports House and Senate votes by members of Congress; also includes summary measures of several properties for each member: his or her liberalism, party support, and so forth.
>
> *Almanac of American Politics*—Contains biographical sketches on all members of Congress and governors. Also summarizes characteristics and history of the states and congressional districts. Reports position of members of Congress on key votes, and certain pressure groups' ratings for each member.
>
> *Members of Congress Since 1789*—Contains brief biographical information on all members of Congress. Includes age, religion, occupation, sex, and race.
>
> *Biographical Dictionary of the Federal Judiciary*—Contains biographical data on all who have served on federal courts.
>
> *The First Hundred Justices*—Contains biographical data on Supreme Court justices and statistical data on their decisions.

In addition there are many *Who's Who* publications that include biographical information about public officials.

Retrieving Information About State and Local Governments. As was the case with the federal government, much useful information about state and local governments is published by those governments themselves. You can locate specific items by using the index to the *Monthly Checklists of State Publications.* State almanacs, bluebooks, registers, manuals, and the like will provide much useful information, especially regarding governmental structure. State house and senate journals will generally report on legislative behavior. A very good source of comparative state data is the *Book of the States.*

City directories will report structural information for local areas. A nongovernment publication, *The Municipal Yearbook,* reports recent statistics for individual cities and guides to where more data may be found.

Retrieving Demographic and Other Statistics About the United States. You will frequently want to relate government activities or the activities of government officials to other properties of geographic areas, particularly of characteristics of the population of those areas. A number of federal agencies, but especially the Bureau of the Census, gather such information.

All statistics released by the federal government are indexed in the *American Statistics Index*. The general index to census publications is the *Catalog of U.S. Census Publications*. Specific censuses include

Census of Population—Presents data on population and characteristics of the population (sex, race, occupation, education, income, and so on) for virtually all legally defined geographic areas.

Census of Housing—Data on numbers, characteristics, and quality of housing in almost all geographic areas of the country.

Census of Government—A detailed collection of data from local governmental units. Includes data on type of government, number of employees, budgets, debt, and so on.

Historical Statistics of the United States—A series of volumes comparing census data collected at different times from the colonial period to the present.

Census of Agriculture (Business, and *Manufacturing)*—Major special-purpose census reports containing detailed data on the indicated subjects.

Statistical Abstract of the U.S.—Summarizes much census information as well as other data.

If you are working with congressional districts, counties, cities, or other local areas, you will find a valuable guide to statistical information in the *Directory of Federal Statistics for Local Areas: A Guide to Sources*. The Census Bureau publishes two statistical abstracts organized to facilitate the study of local areas: the *County and City Data Book* and the *Congressional District Data Book*.

Retrieving Information About the Voting Behavior and Opinions of United States Citizens. When the unit of analysis is the individual, you must either collect the necessary information yourself or turn to a data achieve. Two of the most accessible archives for political scientists are the Inter-University Consortium for Political and Social Research and the Roper Public Opinion Center, mentioned above.

For a complete list of the data available from the ICPSR, see the *Guide to Resources and Services* for the current year. This guide is published by the Institute for Social Research, University of Michigan, Ann Arbor, Michigan.

Data on groups are more widely available than data on individuals. Published sources of group data include

Guide to U.S. Elections—Published by *Congressional Quarterly;* a complete set of data on presidential, Senate, House and governors' races since 1824. It has actual returns and data on nominations for these offices.

America Votes—Includes data on national races and primaries for those races since 1952.

Gallup Opinion Index—Contains opinions on political, social, and economics issues.

Public Opinion Quarterly—A journal that includes a section entitled "The Polls," which contains data on opinions in the United States and other countries.

Apart from these published sources, data archives can supply group-level data already stored on cards or tape. The extensive research processing that has already been done by the archives will save you a substantial amount of work.

Retrieving Data on Other Nations. You can go to national publications like those for the United States government to gather similar data for other nations that collect it. However, this is a very laborious process, especially when library facilities are limited. The most useful place to begin searching for data on other nations is the subject index to *Sources of International Statistics.* There are also collections of cross-national data that may greatly ease your task. Several are published by the United Nations, the most useful being the

Statistical Yearbook—Summarizes demographic, economic, and educational data reported by nations to the United Nations.

The most useful published sources of cross-national data collected by individuals are

Charles Taylor and David Jodice, *World Handbook of Political and Social Indications, Third Edition*—studies over time of more than 75 properties for almost all the countries of the world.

Rudolph Rummel, *Dimensions of Nations*—An analysis of 276 properties of 82 nations.

Useful cross-national information can also be found in the *World Tables, Book of World Rankings, World Almanac,* the *Worldmark Encyclopedia of Nations,* and the *Statesman's Yearbook.* There are even some reports on public opinion in other nations. Perhaps the most useful are those by Gallup in Canada and Britain, and the multinational reports by the United States Information Agency's research and reference service.

Retrieving Information About Events. The dates and frequency of occurrence of some type of behavior may be an important property. The most frequently used source for such data is the *New York Times Index.* Other resources include the index to *Keesing's Contemporary Archives* (London), *Facts-on-File,* and *Deadline Date on World Affairs.*

COMPOUND MEASURES

The measures we have considered up to this point have used a single indicator of a property. Here we discuss **compound measures,** which are combinations of several variables used to measure a single property. Compound measures have three advantages over simple measures of properties:

1. When the property is defined as having several different aspects, having several variables enables you to measure them all.
2. When the property is being measured indirectly, increasing the number of variables decreases the chances of misclassifying a unit.
3. Using a combination of variables usually enables you to discriminate smaller differences in the level or amount of a property than would be possible if you used just one variable.

Suppose, for example, that we were interested in measuring several students' knowledge of research methodology. Using a single variable, we could ask each student a single question and infer from the answers how much each student knew about methodology. Correct answers would indicate knowledgeable students and incorrect answers, unknowledgeable students. We might even infer from a partially correct answer that the student was partially knowledgeable.

Using a compound measure, we could observe the behavior of each student on 20 or 30 questions. We could determine for each question whether the student had responded correctly. We might then measure how knowledgeable each student was by the number of correct responses that he made.

What have we gained by asking each student more questions? First, we can cover several aspects of methodology. Knowledge of methodology would generally be defined as knowledge of many different skills and the ability to combine them (explaining, designing, testing, and so forth). No single question could check knowledge in all of those areas.

Second, the compound measure reduces the chance of misclassifying students. On a single exam question many error factors may operate to misclassify some students. A student might misread the question or make some error irrelevant to the property we are measuring. Or a student with no knowledge of what is being asked might make a good guess and answer correctly. If a series of questions are asked, the effect of the error factors will probably be limited to just a few of the questions, and the overall classification will be approximately correct.

Third, we can better discriminate the level of knowledge of each student. With a single question we might distinguish three categories of knowledge: knowledgeable, partially knowledgeable, unknowledgeable. With 20 or 30 questions we might distinguish 30 or more categories of knowledge.

Criteria for Good Compound Measures

Like any other measure, a compound measure must be reliable and valid. Since a compound measure is a combination of two or more other measures, the reliability and validity of those component measures influences the reliability and validity of the compound measure. A compound measure created from unreliable or invalid indicators must itself be unreliable or invalid. Thus, the first step in determining the validity of a compound measure is to evaluate its parts. Other criteria must then be considered: independence, coverage, discrimination, and homogeneity. As you will see, you can use some of these in evaluating single-indicator measures as well.

Independence. Measures, whether or not they are parts of a compound measure, need to be **independent** of each other. That is, classification of a unit on one variable should not cause the unit to be classified in a particular way on the other variable. If in order to answer one test question correctly a student had to answer a previous question correctly, the two questions would not be independent. Independence is a major problem in survey analysis, and we will discuss it in considerably more detail in the next chapter.

Coverage. Compound measures must consist of indicators that **cover** in a balanced way all of the relevant aspects of what is being measured. An examination that covers the material presented in only one lecture is not likely to be a valid indicator of what was learned over several weeks in a course. Similarly, if a researcher wanted to measure the willingness of senators to vote to increase government expenditures, he or she would not want to look at votes on appropriations for only one kind of expenditure. A combined measure that looked only at willingness to expend money on farm programs would not likely be accepted as a valid measure of general willingness to increase government expenditures. Rather, spending in a variety of areas (welfare, defense, education, transportation, and so on) should be reflected in the final measure.

Determining that a measure covers all of the relevant aspects of the property being measured is easier than deciding whether the coverage is balanced. Some appropriations may have many more votes taken on them than others. Should the measure of willingness to increase appropriations reflect to a greater extent the issues on which a greater number of votes were taken? Some issues may involve fewer votes but more money. Should a balanced measure reflect those votes that involve more money to a greater extent than those involving less money? Perhaps votes to increase spending in all issue areas should be weighted equally. We will consider this issue again when we take up various methods of weighting the indicators used in a compound measure.

Discrimination. A compound measure must be able to classify a reasonable percentage of the units into each of several different categories. The ability of a measure to classify units into several categories is called **discrimination.** Precisely what is a reasonable percentage of units in each category varies with the property, the size of the sample, and the requirements of the research design. However, a test that gives 99% of the students Cs clearly does not discriminate among students sufficiently to be of much use to the professor. Similarly, measures that classify 99% of all senators as middle-of-the-road are not of much use to the researcher.

The researcher should attempt to measure the whole range of a property and to discriminate as finely as possible along that range. She generally makes finer discriminations by adding more indicators to her measure. However, quality, availability, and cost put a limit on the number of indicators that a researcher can reasonably use.

When several indicators classify all units nearly identically, it is not necessary to use more than one of the indicators. The additional indicators do not increase the ability of the researcher to discriminate.

Homogeneity. The indicators used to create a compound measure must usually classify units in a **homogeneous** fashion. By *homogeneous* we mean that units classified in one way by one of the indicators also tend to be classified in the same way by the others. When a compound measure is made up of variables that are all related to one another in this way, we say that the compound measure is homogeneous. Homogeneity is especially important when the researcher is attempting to infer the level or amount of a property that cannot be directly measured.

If one or more of the indicators does not classify units in the same way as the others do, it can be argued that those particular indicators are not measuring the same property that the other indicators measure. Returning to our test example, suppose we found that people who scored high on the test were more likely to miss one question than those who scored low. This would suggest that the question was not measuring the property of methodological knowledge. Suppose two tests were given to 60 students, and on each test one third received grades of 80 or more, one third grades of 60 to 79, and one third grades of less than 59. Table 5–1 indicates how well each third did on each of the six test questions making up each test.

The grading for test A is the most homogeneous. The students in the top third did better on every question than those in the middle third, and those in the middle always did better than those in the lower third. On test B, students in the lower groups did as well or better than those in the upper groups on questions 2 and 4. If those questions were discarded, the grading would be more homogeneous. Had this happened on an exam, there are many professors who would eliminate or reword questions 2 and 4 if they were planning to use test B again.

Homogeneity is not an absolute requirement for compound measures, as

TABLE 5-1 Percentage in Each Grade Level Answering Questions Correctly

	Test A *Grade Level*			Test B *Grade Level*		
	80+	60–79	59 —	80+	60–79	59 —
Question 1	80	60	30	90	70	30
2	90	75	40	60	60	60
3	70	55	30	80	50	20
4	80	75	50	50	55	60
5	90	70	60	85	75	55
6	80	60	40	80	60	40

are independence, coverage, and discrimination. Occasionally a researcher may want to measure a property that has several unrelated aspects. Volume is a property often measured by a combination of the unrelated aspects of length, height, and width. But in general, political scientists expect that the unobservable property they are trying to measure will have several observable consequences, all of which will point to roughly the same conclusion regarding how much of the property is present. Say we wished to measure support for civil liberties. It is reasonable to assume that there are many roll-call votes, court cases, or questionnaire responses from which we might infer degree of support. We cannot examine all possible votes, cases, or responses. But this is not a problem in most cases, because we assume that the inferences we would make on the basis of one set of votes, cases, or responses would be very much the same inferences we would make on the basis of another. This is another way of saying that we expect homogeneity in compound measures of support for civil liberties. If such homogeneity is not present in a particular set of indicators, the researcher will frequently drop one or more of the indicators, sometimes replacing them with others, in an attempt to increase homogeneity and clarify the inferences he or she is getting.

Methods of Creating Compound Measures Used Mainly in Nonsurvey Research

There are several different ways that compound measures can be created from individual indicators. Most of them involve adding or averaging values on several indicators. When using interview data we often create *scales,* compound measures created from a series of questions. Scales can be created with data other than that from surveys. Roll-call votes and judicial decisions are often scaled. Since scales are used primarily with survey data, we defer discussing them until the next chapter. In this section we consider the problem of combining indicators that may be measured in different units into a compound measure.

Standardized Scores (Z-scores) Suppose we wanted a measure of how well developed communications were in each country. We define well-developed communications as the facilities for individuals to communicate with each other and the availability of mass communication. We decide that the following variables, available in the *World Handbook of Social and Political Indicators,* reflect these factors:

telephones per 1000 people
number of domestic letters per capita per year
number of newspapers per 1000 people
number of radios per 1000 people
numbers of televisions per 1000 people
movie attendance per capita per year
literacy rate

The problem is how to create a single compound measure that reflects all of these equally. The units in which they are measured are quite different. A researcher cannot simply add the number of telephones, the number of letters, the percentage of those who are literate, and so on and obtain a meaningful figure.

There is an additional problem. Even if the different indicators are measured in the same kind of units, unless the distributions of the units are the same on all of the indicators, some of the indicators, when added together, will influence the final measure to a greater extent than the others. Consider a simple example. A class had two examinations that made up the final grade in the course. On one test scores were evenly distributed between 70 and 80 but on the other the scores were evenly distributed between 50 and 100. It is clear that the final distribution of scores in the course will be primarily a function of the test on which the scores differ to a greater degree. The general principle is that indicators whose scores differ greatly will be counted more heavily in the final measure than indicators whose scores differ less.

In order to deal with these two problems, we transform the individual indicators into **z-scores,** or **standardized scores.** These scores are measures of the original property in terms of a standard unit of measure that is comparable across indicators of all different properties. They can therefore be added or averaged together to produce a score that is a meaningful reflection of all of the indicators. Standard scores also transform the data in such a way that the scores are spread out in the same way on each of the indicators. Therefore, each indicator influences the compound measure to the same degree. The computation of standard scores will be discussed in Chapter 8.

Factor Scores. Series of analytic techniques called **factor analyses** also allow us to combine different types of units into single compound measures. A detailed discussion of these techniques is well beyond the scope of this book, but we can indicate what they do in a very general way. You will probably run across measures produced by factor analysis as you read social science literature, for its techniques are quite popular.

Factor analysis provides weights for the indicators used in a compound measure. The weights are determined by how closely associated the indicators are, given criteria determined by the method of factor analysis used. More closely associated indicators are weighted more highly, and less closely associated ones less. Factor analysis can also indicate when we need more than one compound measure in order to reflect the individual indicators. When more than one compound measure is to be formed, factor analysis provides a set of weights for each compound measure. Indicators weighted highly in computing one of the compound measures will generally be weighted low in computing the others.

SUMMARY

There are innumerable ways of measuring properties. Often the researcher must be quite inventive in order to find an acceptable measure of properties that cannot be easily observed. In this chapter we have discussed the general types of data collection and some of the things we must consider in developing reliable, valid measures, particularly when we are using archival data. We also introduced the idea of compound measures, measures that are combinations of other measures. Compound measures are necessary when we wish to produce valid measures of certain properties, and they can reduce the measurement error involved when we are using only a single indicator. The topics considered in this chapter will be discussed again in the next chapter in the context of survey-data collection.

LABORATORY EXERCISES

The purpose of this laboratory is to introduce you to some sources of non-survey data and to give you some experience in creating a simple compound measure.

Task 1. In this task you will gather data on members of Congress and their districts. Your instructor will assign a state and district numbers. Use information from the Ninety-seventh Congress, first session (1981). Collect data and record the following items:

congressional-district number
Congressional Quarterly Conservative Coalition Score

years of senority (number of consecutive years of service)

urbanization of district (percentage of district living in a central city)

willingness to raise congressional income:

Congressional Quarterly rollcall 194: to establish a cost-of-living adjustment to income and eliminate limit on business deductions

Congressional Quarterly rollcall 264: to raise the limit on outside income.

Task 2. In this task you will gather data on nations. Your instructor will assign you a short list of nations on which to gather the data. Find and record each of the following pieces of information:

life expectancy (in number of years; record 99 if not available).

gross national product per capita (in number of dollars; record 99999 if not available).

literacy (percentage of the population who are literate; record 999 if not available).

food supply (calories per capita; record 9999 if not available)

number of terrorist acts, 1981 (999 if not available)

Task 3. Create a simple index of the two roll calls collected in Task 1. Code a vote favoring an increase as 1 and a vote not favoring it as O. Sum the two scores for each member of Congress. If the member was not present on either of the two votes, assign him or her a missing data value of 9 on the index.

REVIEW QUESTIONS

1. Match the best data source with the information needed.

   Information Needed
   a. Vote of each House member on whether to extend sugar quotas for another year (1980 vote)
   b. amount of money spent by each candidate for the Senate, 1976
   c. age at which each senator was first elected to the Senate
   d. vote for the president, by party, for each county in Nebraska
   e. median family income, by city, for United States cities
   f. whether a city has a mayoral or city-manager form of government
   g. inequality in landholdings, by country, 1965
   h. spending on education, as a percentage of total government budget, by country, 1975

i. number of visits by Reagan cabinet members to foreign countries, by country, 1981

Data Sources (each may be used any number of times)
p. *U.N. Statistical Yearbook*
q. *County and City Data Book*
r. *Municipal Yearbook*
s. *America Votes*
t. *Congressional Directory*
u. *Almanac of American Politics*
v. *Biographical Dictionary of the Federal Judiciary*
w. *New York Times Index*
x. *Congressional Quarterly Almanac*
y. *World Handbook of Political and Social Indicators*
z. *Congressional District Data Book*

2. What is the purpose of using z-scores in computing a compound measure?

3. The following are five countries classified on a compound measure of degree of centralization of management:

County	Measure A	Measure B
1	27	15
2	3	5
3	23	15
4	10	5
5	7	5

Assuming the measures were otherwise similar in reliability and validity, which would be the better measure? Why?

4. Design a good measure of the extent of development of transportation in countries that reflects all of the different transportation systems.

5. Design a good measure of the effectiveness of legislators in the legislature. In .what ways could you demonstrate the reliability and validity of the measure?

CHAPTER SIX

USING SURVEYS IN MEASUREMENT

Probably the most common way in which measurement is done is with surveys. A **survey** is any collection of data in which people are asked to respond to questions. There are different methods for obtaining responses, among them personal interviews, interviews conducted over the telephone, and paper-and-pencil interviews. In paper-and-pencil interviews respondents are asked to fill out a questionnaire. This is often done in a group setting, such as a class of students or a meeting of an organization. A very common form of the paper-and-pencil survey is the mail survey, where respondents are contacted by mail and return the questionnaire by mail.

Surveys are directed at different types of respondents. **Mass surveys** use the general population as the sample. **Elite surveys** involve interviewing people who are defined by their position as being important in some way.

Surveys may be designed to measure characteristics of different units of analysis. Since it is an individual who responds to a questionnaire, surveys are used most often to collect data on the individual as the unit of analysis. Thus, we use surveys to measure attitudes and behavior of people. But we often use data collected by survey to measure characteristics of other units. For example, we use census data, which is produced through surveys of individuals, to produce measures of characteristics of cities, counties, states, or other areas. Or we ask individuals to report information about other units of analysis through a survey. For example, members of a research project collected data on hospital policies on abortion by surveying hospital administrators and asking what the policy of their hospital was.

In this chapter we deal with measurement methods that use surveys. We first consider a major problem common to almost all surveys: getting people to respond. Then we consider the particular problems of reliability and validity that are involved in the construction of survey questions and questionnaires and in the gathering of data. Finally we consider techniques used in the construction of a measure of a single property from several different questions.

RESPONSES TO SURVEYS

The difficulty of getting people to respond depends on the kind of people being surveyed, the subject matter, and the method used for the survey. The percentage of individuals in the initial sample who respond to the survey is called the **response rate**. Ideally, we would like to have a response rate close to 100%. The best response rate is usually achieved through personal interviews. In mass surveys, a typical response rate used to be 85% or so of the sample. Now it is usual to have a response rate of 60% or less even for personal interviews. Telephone response rates may actually be a little better than personal interviews when the questionnaire is short. However, since it is easier to hang up on an interviewer than order him out the door, the number of completed telephone interviews is usually less than the number of personal interviews for a long questionnaire. Mail surveys typically have the lowest response rate. Achieving a 50% rate is considered adequate in most research, since it is rare that people do much better.

Lost Responses

Two problems are created when individuals in the sample are not surveyed. First, the loss of responses may reduce the sample so much that it is no longer large enough to test the hypotheses. This is particularly true where the sample is necessarily small to begin with. For example, a survey of current state senators in Texas could produce a maximum of 30 interviews. If 50% do not respond, the 15 interviews obtained would be too few for most analyses.

The second problem is usually more serious. The sample drawn may have reflected the population but the sample actually surveyed may not have. Some types of respondents are less likely to respond than others, and some may be more difficult to contact than others. For example, more mobile people and people who work long hours are generally more difficult to contact, and unless care is taken survey samples will underrepresent such individuals. The tendency for some groups to be underrepresented in the sample will make the sample unrepresentative of the theoretical population and may invalidate the test of the hypothesis.

Researchers often present data showing that nonresponses have not made their sample unrepresentative. One way of doing this is showing that the distribution of a property for the resulting sample is like the known distribution of a property for the whole population. For example, you may know from existing data that a community is about 50% female, 15% nonwhite, and 40% college-educated. If a sample of that community has approximately 50% females, 15% nonwhites, and 40% college-educated, it can be argued that nonresponses did not cause the sample to be unrepresentative of *those* properties. This increases the likelihood that it is representative of other properties. However, a sample representative of some properties is not necessarily representative of others.

Another way to demonstrate that refusals probably did not decrease representativeness is to compare the distributions of properties of respondents and nonrespondents. This requires that some information be known about those who did not respond. This is most likely to be the case with an elite sample. Suppose you wanted to show that refusals by some legislators probably did not make your sample unrepresentative. You could indicate that the distribution of known properties such as party, seniority, leadership and committee positions, and type of constitutency was similar for those who responded and those who did not.

Maximizing the Response Rate

A variety of things can be done to increase the response rate of a survey. We can divide such techniques into three classes: maximizing the opportunity to respond, minimizing the cost of responding, and providing incentives to respond.

Maximizing the Opportunities to Respond. There are several ways to make certain that a person in the sample has sufficient opportunity to respond. Repeated attempts to contact the people in the sample is one. Surveys in which people are interviewed personally require that interviewers make several attempts to contact a respondent before giving up. Often attempts are made by phone to make an appointment at an appropriate time. In well-executed telephone surveys numbers are called back at least three times, often more, at different times of the day, and on different days of the week. Only after several tries is a person dropped from the sample.

The most effective mail procedure involves sending everyone in the sample a cover letter and questionnaire. A week or two later a postcard is sent thanking those who have responded and urging those who have not to please send the questionnaire back. Three or four weeks after the first questionnaire another letter is sent to those who have not responded. If no response has been received after six weeks, a certified letter is sent, with another copy of the questionnaire enclosed. Some researchers using this method claim that response rates of 80% to 90% are common.[1]

Minimizing the Costs of Responding. The costs of responding can be minimized in a number of ways. A major consideration is to keep the questionnaire short. This is particularly the case with mail surveys, where the potential respondent may well be discouraged by a fat questionnaire even before finding out what it is about. Long telephone interviews are easily terminated. Even personal interviews, the usual method for very long interviews, are much easier to obtain if the interviewer can promise the respondent to take only a "few minutes" of his or her time rather than an hour or two.

Questionnaires should be easy to read and responses easy to make. Making the questionnaire a neat little booklet with plenty of white space is considered useful. Prominent blocks where responses are to be indicated and multiple-choice questions rather than questions requiring the respondent to write an answer make responding easier and quicker.

Questionnaires in a mail survey must be accompanied by a stamped envelope addressed to the researcher. Although you lose postage on envelopes that are not returned, such envelopes are preferable to business-reply envelopes, which communicate to the potential respondent that you expect many people not to return the questionnaire.

Assurances of confidentiality, keeping secret information on an individual, or anonymity, may be necessary if respondents feel that their answers might lead to embarrassment or worse. For example, surveys of drug use usually require some of the respondents to admit illegal activity. Questionnaires asking students to evaluate professors are perceived to be potentially dangerous to the student and anonymity is usually guaranteed.

There are practical, ethical, and legal issues involved in the question of confidentiality. A researcher should never say that responses to a survey are anonymous when they are not. Hidden identification numbers and other ploys for identifying respondents without their knowledge are clearly not ethical. It is necessary to be candid and explain in the cover letter that identification numbers are used only to determine who has returned the questionnaire.

When confidentiality is assured, the researcher has an obligation to make certain the data are protected. Care must be taken that there is limited access to information that might be used to determine which responses came from which respondent. Courts can subpoena confidential questionnaires and data, and many researchers destroy any information that might be used to determine who answered the questionnaires as soon as that information is no longer needed.

Finally, data containing codes that would even indirectly allow an individual respondent to be identified should not be published or made available to other researchers. Perhaps an extreme example is the General Social Survey, which does not code the state of the respondent on the chance that knowing the state and the other information in the survey might make it possible to identify the respondent.

Providing Incentives to Respond. Most people like to express opinions and be listened to, particularly if they think that what they are being asked is important and that it is important that the researcher really talk to them. The importance of their contribution must be communicated to them.

Central to establishing the feeling that the respondent is important to the researchers is making the interaction as personal as possible. In phone and personal surveys the interviewers must develop rapport with the respondents. Mail surveys should include a cover letter that is obviously typed and addressed specifically to the person being interviewed and that is signed by hand. Automatic typewriters are often used to produce such letters, but they should still appear to be personal letters.

The cover letter should indicate the importance of the research. Organizations that are likely to be respected by members of the sample may be asked to endorse the research. A survey of doctors might be supported by the American Medical Association, and informing doctors of this could encourage many to participate.

In some cases respondents are paid, usually a token amount of money. A useful technique is to send the person 50 cents or a dollar with the questionnaire. This produces a greater response than promising payment in exchange for completing the questionnaire. Because of the increasing difficulty in getting people to respond to surveys, we may eventually have to pay more money to respondents. Otherwise, response rates may drop below the point where surveys can be used to gather data. Although payment is likely to increase the response rate, it will do so disproportionately among those for whom the payment is most valuable, and the resulting sample may not reflect the population.

THE RELIABILITY OF SURVEY RESPONSES

Measurement that uses surveys presents peculiar reliability problems because the respondent is likely to react to the questioner as well as to the questions. Respondents may give different interviewers different answers to the same questions. For example, a study found that white respondents were more likely to indicate racial prejudice when interviewed by whites than when interviewed by blacks.[2] The presence of the interviewer is likely to inhibit responses of which the person thinks the *interviewer* will disapprove. Some interviewers may not be able to instill the same confidence in the respondent than others can. For example, we might expect a researcher from a government agency to get different responses on a question dealing with marijuana than a researcher associated with a university. The answers that interviewers get may vary with race, sex, age, social class, sponsoring agency, and other properties, as well as with the subject matter of the questions and the characteristics of the person being interviewed.

Another possible cause of unreliability in surveys is differences in the way that interviewers ask the questions. The wording of questions determines to a great extent the kind of answers a respondent gives. Minor variations in wording, or even in voice inflection, may influence the respondent. Related to this is the problem of reporting the answers to the questions. This is particularly a problem with questions that do not have multiple-choice responses. The interviewer must write down what the respondent says. The responses often will not be reported verbatim, and what is written down may vary with the interviewer.

There are ways to increase the reliability of survey responses collected by interviewers:

1. Interviewers should be trained to use identical procedures.
2. They should put the respondents at ease, but interact as little as possible.

3. The questions should be asked in the same way, in the same order, and under the same conditions (for example, always in private).

4. Recording of responses should be simple and identical for all interviewers.

Reliability problems due to differences among interviewers are greater in personal interviews, where interaction between the interviewer and the respondent that could influence responses is greatest. Less interaction occurs in telephone interviews, although even there differences in tone of voice, sex of interviewer, or accent may cause reliability problems. Mail surveys are usually the most reliable, but there is no control over the circumstances in which the questionnaire is filled out and other factors that may limit reliability.

CONSTRUCTING VALID QUESTIONS

Asking questions of individuals creates a series of validity problems. Some respondents may not understand the question, or different respondents may interpret the question differently than others do. Respondents may make errors in reporting information or give misleading responses, either deliberately or not.

Any long, involved question is likely to be misunderstood, particularly if it is presented orally. In fact, it has been suggested that any question containing more than 15 words is likely to be misunderstood.[3] Consider the following question that was used in a public-opinion poll conducted by Louis Harris:

> In order to cut down on federal spending, to keep inflation in check, and to avoid a 15% rise in taxes, President Nixon wants to cut back some social programs started under Democratic Presidents, which he feels have been failures. Some Democrats in Congress believe that the President is wrong and wants to undo social programs badly needed by the poor and disadvantaged. Democratic Senators also say they will not spend more than the ceiling they and the President have agreed on, so no tax increase or greater inflation will result. If you had to say, who do you think is more right on this disagreement over cutting back social programs—President Nixon or the Democrats in Congress?[4]

It is difficult to imagine how typical respondents could make sense of such a question. Not only is it long, it is somewhat confusing as well. It is difficult to know the meaning of the respondent's answer or even what property the question is intended to measure.

Compound questions can cause validity problems. These are questions that really ask more than one question at the same time. Responses are usually ambiguous. Consider this question asked of judges:

> Agree or disagree? "The job of changing the law should be left to appellate judges and legislators."[5]

If the judge responded no, did he or she think that neither appellate judges nor legislators should make laws? Only the legislators and not the judges? Only the judges and not the legislators? There are several possible interpretations of the response.

There is considerable evidence that even slight changes in the wording of a question can influence the way in which people respond to it. It is often difficult to determine what the most valid question is. Consider these questions:

> People who don't earn their own living are not entitled to have the taxpayers support them in comfort. (agree or disagree)
>
> A country has an obligation to see that its less fortunate citizens are given a decent standard of living. (agree or disagree)

A sample of respondents were asked both of these questions two weeks apart as a way of measuring support for welfare programs. On the basis of the first question, half the sample was classified as supporting welfare. With the second question, 88% were classified as supporting welfare. Neither of the questions presents the subject neutrally; one biases responses one way, the other in the opposite way.

Although the differences between these two questions are obvious, major differences in classification may result from subtle differences in questions. For example, a number of researchers pointed to a dramatic increase in the consistency of the American electorate on political issues beginning with the 1964 election. Recent research has demonstrated that the change was a function of changing the wording of the questions from asking respondents to place themselves on a five-point scale to asking them to place themselves on a seven-point scale in indicating their position on an issue.[6]

Here is another question that may misclassify people due to the way in which it is worded. It was included in a questionnaire as one of a series of questions used to measure "willingness to punish people who violate conventional values."

> Agree or disagree? Sex crimes, such as rape and attacks on children, deserve more than mere imprisonment; such criminals ought to be publicly whipped, or worse.[7]

Respondents who are willing to punish violaters may still be unwilling to consider public whipping seriously. They may consider whipping to be ridiculous these days. Would responses to that question be measuring "willingness to punish" or "willingness to consider ridiculous alternatives"? There is some evidence that the less educated are more likely than the better educated to agree with seemingly ridiculous alternatives. Therefore, the question may even be measuring level of education.

It is not always clear how to word questions so as to get the most valid responses. **Loading** questions (that is, wording them so as to encourage a particular response) is likely to decrease validity. Asking silly questions is also likely to decrease validity.

Validity problems arise from the general subject matter of questions as well as from the specific wording chosen. For example, less valid responses may be expected when the subject matter is touchy. "How many times did the committee meet last week?" is likely to give more valid responses than is "How many times did you have sex last week?"

Less valid responses are also expected when questions are subjective—that is, when they call for a judgment by the respondent. "Are you tolerant?" is likely to get less valid responses than is "How many children live in this house?" The researcher can increase validity by avoiding touchy subjects and by asking objective rather than subjective questions. However, that may mean avoiding the most interesting and important research questions.

Validity problems may arise from the context in which questions are asked. Valid answers are most likely when the respondent can remain anonymous. If anonymity cannot be guaranteed, the researcher should at least assure the confidentiality of the responses. If confidentiality cannot be maintained, respondents may give answers that they want to have heard even if they are invalid.

Even when the researcher has devised short, simple, sensible, objective, neutral, and confidential questions, he is not assured of a valid measure. The validity of responses ultimately depends upon the truthfulness and knowledge of the respondent. Although most respondents probably respond honestly, we know that some do not. Some may be embarrassed by the truth. Some may want to boast a bit. Others may simply enjoy messing up surveys. Even some who respond truthfully may be mistaken. They may have convinced themselves that they voted for Kennedy when in fact they voted for Nixon. They may think they are tolerant when in practice they are bigoted.

Clearly, it is difficult to develop valid measures based on questions. Once seemingly valid questions have been written, they should be *pretested*—that is, given to a small number of people, whose response to each question is then observed. It is often useful to discuss the questions with these respondents after they have answered them. This may point out ambiguities or unexpected interpretations. Although it is not necessary to have a large number of respondents for a pretest, those selected should be similar to the respondents who will ultimately be getting the questions. Other college students may respond to the questions much the way you would but very differently from the way blue-collar workers would.

The validity of questions can also be evaluated with the methods for validating indirect measures discussed in Chapter 5. Comparing classifications of respondents based on a question with a more direct measure or with other questions that are supposed to measure the same thing can help demonstrate validity. Using questions that have been used in surveys that have a proven record of utility and acceptance is usually better than constructing new questions.

In general, anything that contributes to clear writing will result in more valid questions. Questions containing double negatives or words that are beyond the vocabulary of the respondent will create problems. Remember that in most samples a large percentage of respondents can read and understand at only about the sixth-grade level. Questions must be carefully worded so as to be understood by the least capable person being interviewed.

VALIDITY OF THE QUESTIONNAIRE

Asking valid questions is only one factor in the validity of measures done by survey. The construction of the entire questionnaire—how the questions are related to each other—affects the validity of the responses. The environment in which the survey is conducted and the behavior of the interviewers are also critical factors, as we have seen.

Validity of the Questionnaire

As we noted above, the questionnaire should be easy to fill out. This is not always possible, however, with questionnaires containing *branching* questions— questions that cause the respondent to answer one set of questions rather than another. For example, you might ask a person if she is employed. If not, you might ask a series of questions probing why. If she is employed, you might ask instead a series of questions about the job. Unclear branching instructions may lead to invalid responses to inappropriate questions.

Another serious problem is that some questions may influence the responses to other questions on the same questionnaire. For example, it has been found that if a respondent is first asked his parents' party identification and then his own, he is more likely to say that they differ than if he is asked his own party first and his parents' second.[8]

The researcher should pretest several different question sequences in order to determine if there is a validity problem. If question order appears to influence responses, the researcher can increase validity by (1) separating questions dealing with the same subject, (2) asking open-ended questions before asking forced-choice questions, and (3) randomly altering the order of questions that appear to influence the responses to each other.

By separating the questions that might influence each other, the respondent is less likely to remember the response to the first question and therefore is less likely to be influenced by it. When respondents are given a set of responses to a question and then asked an open-ended question on the same topic, many of them answer the open-ended question in terms of the forced-choice response already provided by the researcher. Random rotation of the questions eliminates any systematic effect of one question on another, since half of the sample is influenced one way and half the other.

Another problem arises when a series of questions are asked in the same form; this encourages respondents to mark them all the same way, regardless of the substance of the questions. The tendency for people to respond to a set of questions in a patterned way that has little to do with the substance of the questions is called a **response set.** For example, many people will agree with a set of statements that they do not understand, rather than saying they have no opinion or indicating that they disagree. We will consider ways of limiting the response-set problem in the next section.

USING MULTIPLE QUESTIONS TO MEASURE A PROPERTY

It is often desirable to use a series of questions to measure a property. As we noted in the last chapter, multiple indicators may be necessary when we are measuring a single property. The property may have several different aspects, the determination of which requires more than one question. A measure of socio-economic status might require questions on income, race, education, and other aspects. Or a series of questions might be a useful way of determining how much of a property a person has. For example, the following series of questions has been used to measure degree of support for legalized abortion:

> Now, please tell me whether or not you think it should be possible for a pregnant woman to obtain a legal abortion
> A. If the woman's own health is seriously endangered by the pregnancy?
> B. If there is a strong chance of serious defect in the baby?
> C. If the family has a very low income and cannot afford any more children?
> D. If she is married and does not want any more children?[9]

This series of questions allows us to divide respondents into categories of degrees of support based on which of the questions (if any) they gave proabortion responses to.

Another reason for using multiple questions is to reduce the likely measurement error. If we use several different questions to measure the same thing, the classification based on all of the questions considered together will be more accurate than a classification based on any one of them.

SCALING: TECHNIQUES FOR COMBINING INDICATORS

A variety of techniques exist for combining responses to questions into a single measure. We refer to these methods as **scaling.** In this section we introduce some of the commonly used methods of scaling questions.

Counting Responses

The simplest method of combining questions is to count the number of times that a person has responded in a specified way to a series of questions. We might ask people to indicate whether or not they had watched each of a list of news-related television programs. We could determine a measure of watching news programs by counting the number of questions to which each person had responded yes, indicating they had watched the show.

A small modification of the counting technique for creating compound measures is to use the percentage of the questions that the person answered in the prescribed manner. This is most useful when we want to base a measure on questions that have not been answered by every respondent. For example, not all respondents might have been able to receive all of the news programs we wanted to ask about. In that case we should record the percentage of the shows that they could receive that they watched, rather than the total number of shows watched.

Averaging Responses

Counting responses or computing the percentage of responses for a category is used to combine indicators when the responses can be considered as falling into only two categories, each indicating the presence or the absence of the property being measured. Often we use indicators having more than two categories and indicate how much of a property they have. So that the compound measure will reflect all of the information available, we usually average the value of each indicator used in the measure over all of the indicators.[10] For example, three indicators might be code 1 for low, code 2 for medium, and code 3 for high. If a respondent gave two lows and a high, we would average two 1's and a 2 for a score of 1.33.

Likert Scaling. The most common use of the technique of averaging responses to create a compound measure is called **Likert Scaling.** In Likert scaling the researcher presents each respondent with a set of statements and asks her how strongly she agrees or disagrees with each statement. The researcher gives each response a number indicating the degree of agreement with each statement. The response categories are *strongly agree, agree, neutral, disagree,* or *strongly disagree.* The responses are coded 1, 2, 3, 4, or 5. The high number must always indicate that more of the property being measured is present. Depending on the wording of the statement, the high number may be assigned to the *strongly agree* response or the *strongly disagree* response. Suppose you were using these two statements to measure political efficacy:

> People like me don't have any say about what the government does.
> Strongly agree . . . strongly disagree
> Public officials generally care a lot about what people like me think.
> Strongly agree . . . strongly disagree

If higher scores indicate higher efficacy, the 5 would be assigned to the *strongly disagree* response on the first question (with 1 assigned to *strongly agree* and the other numbers assigned in order to the middle categories). The 5 would be assigned to the *strongly agree* response on the second question because, unlike the case of the first question, agreeing with that statement indicates higher efficacy.

Weighting Questions and Selecting Questions

When we count or average responses, each question counts equally. That is, no one question influences the final measure more than any other. But it may be the case that a response to one question reflects more of the property being measured than a response to another question. Arguably, the questions that reflect more of the property should be counted more heavily in the measure. For example, agreeing to abortion when a mother's life is in danger might indicate far less support for legal abortion than agreeing to abortion when a married person simply desires no more children. A measure of support for legal abortion might be more valid if it weighted the question on abortion when desired more heavily than the other questions. The problem is that it is difficult to know how to weight the questions.

Thurstone Scaling. One technique for weighting questions is to use a panel of judges to evaluate statements and assign weights to them. Respondents indicate whether or not they agree with the statements, and we then use the average weights assigned by the judges to compute their scale scores. This technique is called **Thurstone scaling.**

The procedure for developing a Thurstone scale involves submitting to a panel of judges a large number of statements that the researcher thinks may indicate different levels or amounts of the property to be measured. The judges are asked to sort the statements into categories, ranging from lowest amount of the property present to highest amount present, and to form the categories in such a way that they divide the range of the property into equal intervals.

For example, if you wished to construct a Thurstone scale for measuring support for civil liberties, you might present to a panel of judges a series of statements like these:

1. The government should jail those who distribute pornography.
2. X-rated movies should not be shown in public theaters.
3. Black Panthers should be allowed to speak in our schools.
4. Communists should be prohibited from holding public office.
5. There should be no restrictions on the rights of homosexuals.

The judges would classify these statements from 1 (most opposed to civil liberties) to 9 (most in favor of civil liberties). A classification of 2 would be

TABLE 6–1   Judges' Evaluations of Five
Civil-Liberties Items

Statement No.	Mean Evaluation Score	Variability
1	1	0
2	3	3
3	7	1
4	2	1
5	8	3

slightly more in favor than a classification of 1, and a 9 slightly more favorable than an 8. The difference in degree between 1 and 2 should be the same as the difference between 8 and 9. To determine the weight to be given for agreement with each statement, we compute the average weight assigned to the statement by the judges. The average weights for the evaluations of the questions in our example are presented in Table 6–1.

Not only does Thurstone scaling provide a criterion for weighting the questions, it also provides a basis for judging the validity of the questions. When the judges disagree on how the statement should be weighted, this indicates that the question does not appear to clearly reflect the property being measured. There are easily computed measures of how much variability there is in the evaluations of the judges. (We will consider measures of variability in Chapter 8.) In the variability column in Table 6–1 the numbers larger than 1 indicate a relatively great amount of disagreement among the judges. In our example we would eliminate statements 2 and 5 from the measure of support for civil liberties because of the high level of variability of the judges' weighting of these items. Statements 1, 3, and 4 would constitute the Thurstone scale. An agree response to 1 would be weighted 1, agreeing to 3 would be weighted 7, and agreeing to 4 would be weighted 2.

We determine the score for each individual on the Thurstone scale by averaging the weights for all of the statements with which he or she agrees. In our example, if a respondent agreed only with statements 1 and 3, we would average the weights assigned by the judges to those items (1 and 7). This would yield a scale score of 4 for that person.

If a Thurstone scale is to be constructed, the statements should have a range of different weights. If agreeing always meant the same thing, some people would disagree with all of the statements and no scale score could be determined.

Guttman Scaling. Another technique for weighting questions is **Guttman scaling.** Although the applications of Guttman scaling are not limited to survey measurement, the technique is frequently used in creating a measure from several questions.

Guttman scaling is appropriate when the questions can be *dichotomized*—that is, responded to as one of two categories (such as yes or no). The questions must measure the same property. Usually they also require a distribution of responses ranging from a large part of the sample answering one way to a large part of the sample answering the opposite way. For example, four statements agreed to by 80%, 60%, 40%, and 20% of the sample would be more likely to form a Guttman scale than the same four statements each receiving about 50% agreement. Finally, the responses to the statements must fit a certain pattern (which we discuss below). If they do not fit that pattern, the items might still be combined, but not by the Guttman scaling technique.

In using Guttman scaling the researcher first orders the items by the distribution of responses on one of the categories. Let us consider the four statements on abortion listed earlier in this chapter. The respondent could either agree that abortion should be legal in each situation or not. The statements appear in the order of the number of positive responses in a national survey. That is, item A— abortion should be legal if the mother's life is endangered—had 90% of the respondents agreeing with it. Item D, abortion should be allowed for a married person who wants no more children—had the fewest people agreeing with it (49%).

Table 6–2 shows the expected pattern of responses to these questions, assuming a Guttman scale can be formed. Across the top of the table are the four statements. Down the side are hypothetical respondents who are behaving as we would expect if the items form a Guttman scale. Each person's response to each statement is indicated in the column under the statement. As is usually the case, a favorable response is indicated by a 1 and a negative response by a 0.

Person 1 agrees to legal abortion under all the conditions; person 5 agrees under no circumstances. When a person does not agree or disagree with all of the items, we expect the ones they do agree with to fit this pattern. If they agree with only one of the five, they will agree with the "easiest" one to agree with, the one that most people agree with. A person who agrees abortion should be legal in only one of the cases is most likely to agree that it should be legal in cases where the mother's life is in danger. It seems implausible that someone would think that a married person who simply did not want any more children should be legally allowed to have an abortion, but not someone who had financial or health problems or whose baby was likely to have a serious defect. Ideally, in a

TABLE 6–2 Ideal Scale
Pattern for Abortion
Statements

	Statement			
Person	*A*	*B*	*C*	*D*
1	1	1	1	1
2	1	1	1	0
3	1	1	0	0
4	1	0	0	0
5	0	0	0	0

table set up like Table 6–2 no row should have a zero to the left of a one. If there is such a case, it would suggest that the person responded inconsistently to the items.

When people behave inconsistently with what should be the perfect pattern of responses, we consider that an error. If too many errors are made (usually if 10+% of the responses are in error), we decide that the statements do not form a Guttman scale. Sometimes we may find that one or more of the statements are causing most of the errors. Removing these items from the scale may produce an acceptable scale. In the national survey, 97% of the responses fit the scale pattern shown in Table 6–2.

The score for each individual is equal to the highest numbered column in which he has a one. If the person has a one in the fourth column (which means he responds positively to statement D), we assign him a score of 4 on the measure. When an individual does not conform to the perfect scale pattern, we essentially ignore his "error" and code him according to the "hardest" item he responded positively to. Suppose someone said he thought abortion should be legally available in all of the cases except when a mother's life is in danger. We would assign that person a score of 4. We ignore the one response that did not fit the pattern.[11]

Guttman scales have advantages over other types of scales. They provide a method for dealing with errors and missing data. They also communicate more information. If we do not have a Guttman scale, saying someone agreed with three of five statements tells us nothing about which three statements they were. A Guttman scale, however, communicates which items the person agreed with.

COMPOUND MEASURES IN SURVEYS: SUMMARY

Using compound measures in surveys can improve the validity of our measures in a number of ways. What we have done here is to introduce you to a few of the common ways that compound measures are formed and some basic considerations in constructing them. You will encounter other scaling and weighting techniques used in research. All of them try to accomplish the same thing: to combine individual indicators that either measure different things about a single property, or are different measures of the same property. The purpose is to create a single measure that is more valid than any measure based on a single indicator.

Endnotes

[1]Don Dillman, *Mail and Telephone Surveys: The Total Design Method* (New York: John Wiley, 1978), p. 21.

[2]Shirley Hatchett and Howard Schuman, "White Respondents and Race-of-Interviewer Effects," *Public Opinion Quarterly,* (Winter 1975–76), pp. 523–28.

[3]James Payne, "Will Mr. Harris Ever Learn?" *National Review,* 26 (June 21, 1974), 701–2.

[4]Louis Harris and Associates, Inc., *The Harris Yearbook of Public Opinion, 1973: The Compendium of Current American Attitudes* (New York: Louis Harris and Associates, Inc: 1976), p. 213.

[5]Austin Sarat, "Judging in Trial Courts: An Exploratory Study," *Journal of Politics,* 39 (May 1977), 394.

[6]George Bishop, Alfred Tuchfarber, and Robert Oldendick, "Change in the Structure of American Political Attitudes: The Nagging Question of Question Wording," *American Journal of Political Science,* 22 (May 1978), 250–269.

[7]T. W. Adorno et al., *The Authoritarian Personality* (New York: John Wiley, 1964).

[8]Daniel H. Willick and Richard Ashley, "Survey Question Order and the Political Preferences of College Students and Their Parents," *Public Opinion Quarterly,* Summer 1971, pp. 189–99.

[9]James A. Davis, *General Social Survey Cumulative File, 1972–80,* ICPSR edition (Ann Arbor, Mich: Inter-University Consortium for Political and Social Research, 1981), pp. 204–07.

[10]The scores are generally averaged together even though the responses are usually coded on an ordinal scale, which makes an average inappropriate. It is assumed that the numbers on a scale are about the same distance apart and can therefore be treated as interval.

[11]The preceding discussion of Guttman scaling has simplified the technique somewhat. The percentage of correct responses can be misleading, so we usually use a Goodman test or other statistic to determine if the statements scale. In determining scale scores of respondents with errors, we sometimes modify the method suggested here.

LABORATORY EXERCISES

The purpose of this laboratory is to give you experience in constructing questions and questionnaires for survey data collection. In addition you will use survey data to construct indexes.

Task 1. Write questions and construct a questionnaire for a survey of citizens 18 years or older to be used to obtain the following information:

a. Whether or not the person intends to vote in the next election. (Assume a general election will be a month or less away when the interviews are done.)
b. The party identification of the person.
c. The income of the person.
d. The occupation of the person.
e. The attitude of the person towards increasing penalties for driving while intoxicated.

f. Who the person will vote for for the office of governor in the election (candidates are Milton Spivick, Democrat; Harold Wallace, Republican; James Conrad, Independent; Janice Spath, Socialist Worker.)

Assume the survey will be conducted on the telephone. Be sure to include a statement of introduction and any questions you must ask in order to make certain the respondent belongs in the sample.

Task 2. In this task you will create a compound measure using a Thurstone scale. The scale will measure support for civil liberties. The class will act as a panel of experts who evaluate the following list of statements and provide a basis for determining which items should be eliminated from the scale. (The list is adapted from Lois Noble and Ransom Noble, "A Study of the Attitudes of College Students Towards Civil Rights," *Journal of Social Pathology,* 42 (1954), 289–97.)

Evaluate each statement as to the amount of support for civil liberties indicated by agreement with it. Assign each statement a score of 1 to 9, with 1 indicating that agreement means the least amount of support for civil liberties and 9 indicating that agreement means the most support for civil liberties.

a. Communists should have the same right to make public speeches as the members of other political parties.

b. Government authorities should be allowed to ban books and movies that they consider harmful to the public interest.

c. In public schools, time should not be set aside for prayers.

d. State universities would be justified in limiting enrollment by members of racial and religious groups in proportion to their percentage of the state's population.

e. Communists should not be allowed to hold government jobs.

f. Personal ability alone should determine an applicant's right to a job regardless of sex, race, religion, or national origin.

g. Only citizens literate in the English language should be allowed to vote.

h. Residents of a neighborhood should be entitled to prevent members of any particular racial or religious group from living there.

i. Trade unions should not be entitled to restrict their membership on the grounds of color, sex, religion, or national origin.

j. Parochial schools should be included in government financial aid to education.

k. Homosexuals should be allowed to teach in schools and colleges.

l. Tests of government employees' loyalty should be required only in jobs where national security is involved.

m. Under no circumstances should reporters have to reveal the sources of news.

n. Movies, plays, and books should be suppressed if they present an offensive characterization of a particular ethnic or religious group.

o. Law-enforcement officials should have the right to listen in on private conversations whenever it is necessary in their judgment for carrying on their work.

p. Private housing developments that receive state assistance should not have the right to refuse tenants on the basis of color, religion, or national origin.

q. Teachers should not be required to sign special non-communist-loyalty oaths.

r. Government employees accused of disloyalty should have the right to know their accusers and to cross-examine them.

s. "Gay liberation" parades should be banned.

t. Fraternities and sororities are justified in using race, religion, or national origin as qualifications for membership.

After each person in the class has finished the evaluation, determine what the average evaluation for each item is. Also, after eliminating the highest and lowest evaluation for each statement, determine what the range of the evaluations is for each item. (The range is the difference between the highest evaluation score and the lowest, after the extremes have been eliminated.)

Based on the evaluations, which items should be retained for the questionnaire? (Assume no more than five statements can be used.)

Ask three students (outside of class) whether they agree, disagree, or are neutral with respect to each of the five statements that are retained. Record their responses and determine their Thurstone scale score.

Task 3. The statements below can be used to form a Likert scale that measures pacifism. (The statements are adapted from Snell Putney, "Some Factors Associated with Student Acceptance or Rejection of War," *American Sociological Review,* 27 (1962), 655–67).

a. The United States must be willing to run any risk of war that may be necessary to prevent the spread of communism.

b. If disarmament negotiations are not successful, the United States should begin a gradual program of unilateral disarmament—that is, disarming whether other countries do so or not.

c. Pacifist demonstrations, such as picketing missile bases and holding peace walks, are harmful to the best interests of the American people.

d. The United States has no moral right to carry its struggle against communism to the point of risking the destruction of the human race.

e. It is contrary to my moral principles to participate in war and kill other people.

f. Pacifism is simply not a practical philosophy in the world today.

Assuming that the most pacifist response gets the highest value, indicate what code each of the responses to each of the statements should be given. The responses are *strongly agree, agree, undecided, disagree,* and *strongly disagree.*

Determine the Likert scale score for an individual who responded to the statement as follows:

1 strongly disagree

2 strongly disagree

3 strongly agree

4 agree

5 undecided

6 agree

What would the scale score be for this individual if for some reason she did not respond to item 2?

REVIEW QUESTIONS

1. Property: Extent of individual support for United States military supremacy.
   Definition: degree to which the individual favors increased military spending by the United States.
   Measure: In a mail survey, ask each respondent, "Agree or disagree: Since other countries, such as the Soviet Union, place heavy emphasis upon military strength, the United States should do the same." Code responses as follows: 1, agree; 2, neutral; 3, disagree.
   a. Is this definition likely to be appropriate? Why?
   b. Is this measure likely to be reliable? Why?
   c. What might increase its reliability?
   d. Is it likely to be valid? Why?

2. Use the information below to answer questions a through d. Property: extent to which individual feels he is politically efficacious (*efficacious* means being able to produce a desired effect.)
   Indicators: extent of agreement or disagreement with the following statements:

   A. My congressman pays attention to my letters to his office.   SA <u>A</u> ? D SD

   B. The vote is a powerful political tool.   SA A ? D <u>SD</u>

   C. My local city council does not care about my opinion.   SA <u>A</u> ? D SD

    D. Politicians pay no attention to public-opin-   SA A <u>?</u> D SD
       ion surveys.

    a. Suppose that an SA (strongly agree) response to statement A is coded 5 (strongest feelings of efficacy). How would the underlined responses to the items be coded?
    b. Assume that all four statements were used to form a Likert scale. What would the score be for an individual giving the underlined responses above?
    c. A panel of judges rated statements A–D from 1 (weakest feelings of efficacy) to 9 (strongest feelings), as follows:

Statement	Average Rating	Range of Ratings
A	7	6–7
B	8	6–9
C	4	4–5
D	2	2–4

    Suppose you wanted to develop a Thurstone scale from three of these statements. Which statement would you not use, based on the judges' ratings? Why that one?
    d. Use the three remaining statements to form the Thurstone Scale. What would be the score for an individual giving the underlined responses shown above? (Compute to one decimal place; do not consider strength of agreement.)

3. Response rates for mail surveys are likely to be enhanced by what methods?
4. Comparing phone, mail, and face-to-face surveys, which would
    a. have the lowest response rate?
    b. be the most reliable?
    c. be the least reliable?
    d. be the most expensive per respondent?
5. What would generally be considered an acceptable minimum response rate for a mail questionnaire?
6. Which of the following two sets of items would be more likely to form a good Guttman scale? Why?

Set 1			Set 2		
Item 1	Yes: 29%	No: 71%	Item 1	Yes: 56%	No: 44%
Item 2	Yes: 60%	No: 40%	Item 2	Yes: 63%	No: 37%
Item 3	Yes: 75%	No: 25%	Item 3	Yes: 49%	No: 51%
Item 4	Yes: 43%	No: 57%	Item 4	Yes: 45%	No: 55%

7. A Guttman scale was formed from five variables. Order the columns properly and then assign each unit an appropriate scale score.

Units	Variables				
	A	**B**	**C**	**D**	**E**
u	1	1	1	1	0
v	0	1	1	1	1
w	1	0	1	1	0
x	1	1	1	1	0
y	1	0	0	1	0
z	1	0	0	1	0

CHAPTER SEVEN

AUTOMATED DATA PROCESSING

Automation has transformed social science analysis during the last 25 years. The use of computers and related equipment has made possible great increases in the types of analysis that can routinely be done by a researcher having few resources. Massive sets of data can be manipulated with ease. Techniques that could be used only with much effort and training can now be used routinely with little or no effort. In addition, new techniques have been developed that can only be performed on computers.

Much of this is positive. New research strategies are available to help us explore more complex research questions. More research can be done since the cost of analyzing the data has been reduced. We no longer have to emphasize computational formulas for statistics in introductory courses like this. Since you will seldom carry out the computation of a statistic yourself, it is no longer necessary to know the shortcuts to computing it. We can spend more time learning what a technique actually does.

There are, however, some negative aspects to the automation of data processing. Although it can be reasonably argued that a knowledge of computational methods is not always necessary to an understanding of a statistical technique, when the researcher must do the computation it tends to ensure that she does understand it. Modern computer programs allow a person to execute the most complex statistical methods with virtually no understanding of them. This can lead to misapplication of techniques. Another problem with removing the task of computation from the researchers is that the researcher is not as "close" to the data as when the manipulations must be done manually. It is possible for the researcher to do analysis by machine without discovering critical characteristics of the data that would be obvious if she were analyzing it manually. At the same time, the ease with which data can be explored with automated data-processing techniques should make it possible for a researcher to look more thoroughly at the data than she could without it.

Perhaps the greatest potential abuse of automated data processing is caused by the ease with which it can analyze data. It is very tempting to have the computer look at all possible relationships without thinking through the analysis in advance. The biggest danger in this is the increasing likelihood of finding chance relationships and imputing significance to them.

The problems caused by automated data processing can be overcome if the researcher plans the analysis carefully, makes certain that he fully understands the techniques being used, and evaluates the data completely. The advantages of automated data processing are enormous, and it is necessary to learn to use the techniques well.

A problem in discussing automated data processing is that there are so many different ways in which it can be done. To instruct someone in how to perform automated data processing requires specific information about the computer and programs available. There are, however, some general considerations that can be discussed without reference to particular machines or programs. We can examine the types of facilities used in automated data processing. We can also look at some considerations that apply generally to automated data processing.

FACILITIES FOR AUTOMATED DATA PROCESSING

There are many different kinds of facilities for automated data processing. In order to discuss them, we first need to distinguish between hardware and software. **Hardware** is the actual equipment; **software** refers to the languages and programs that control the hardware. From the user's point of view, the software is often more important than the hardware. The same program may operate on several different kinds of machines, and even though the machines may operate quite differently, the differences in the hardware do not affect how the program is used or what the results are.

The Machines: Hardware

Computers. The most important machine in data processing is the **computer.** Any automated device that does calculations can be considered a computer. The devices range from multimillion-dollar machines that do millions of computations a second to hand-held calculators. The larger the machine, the more it is able to do. However, it would be very rare that a social science researcher would need all of the power of a very large machine. Large computers are usually processing many different jobs at the same time. Smaller machines may be able to do the same work, but process fewer jobs. Small personal computers can now do analysis that would have required very large computers a few years ago. In the years ahead we will depend less on large central computers and more on smaller processers.

Unit-Record Devices and Terminals. Other machines are involved in automated data processing. They are not computers, but are usually required for the operation of the computer. Keypunches, verifiers, card reproducers, card interpreters, and counter-sorters are the major pieces of noncomputer equipment seen in the typical data-processing center. These machines all deal with the standard computer card and are generally called **unit-record devices.** The keypunches punch the holes in the cards that allow the machine to read them. The verifier allows punched cards to be checked for accuracy. The reproducer duplicates a stack of cards, either exactly like the original cards or with the data rearranged. The interpreter prints the symbols that the codes stand for across the top of the card so that they can be easily read by a human. Counter-sorters sort cards into stacks based on the codes in a specified column. They can separate or order a deck of cards.

A few years ago researchers used these devices in the absence of computers to tabulate large sets of data. Any tabulation that could be done with a computer could be done with a counter-sorter. But now counter-sorters and even duplicators have been replaced by more elaborate machines that do the operations more quickly and reliably. The keypunch, however, is still the main way of preparing data and control statements for entry into the computer, and usually will be found in large numbers around a computer center.

Often, instead of communicating with the computer through punched cards, we use terminals. Some of these terminals look like typewriters, and among these many are teletypewriters similar to the ones used to communicate wire stories to and from newspapers. Others are like standard electric typewriters with some additional features. It is also common to see a terminal that uses a television screen rather than paper. Some terminals are wired directly into the computer; others are connected to it through standard telephones. Increasingly, the control of computers is carried on through terminals rather than by instructions punched on cards. Eventually, the familiar punch card may be virtually obsolete.

Interactive and Batch Computers. A distinction of importance to the user is whether the computer is operated interactively or by batch processing. In **batch processing,** the user submits all the instructions to the machine at one time, usually on punched cards. The machine reads the cards, performs the requested activities, and returns the printed output to the user. **Interactive processing** requires the user to enter commands one at a time. The machine processes one instruction, reports the result to the user, and waits for the next command. The calculator is a simple interactive device.

The interaction between a user and a large computer with appropriate software can be conversational. The computer can ask questions in ordinary language and the user can respond in ordinary language. This allows a user to control the machine with very little knowledge of what he is doing. It is usually easier to learn to operate the machine through interactive processing than through batch processing.

One of the advantages of the small personal computers is their ability to interact with the user. Interaction with a central computer tends to be limited to typing in commands and receiving printed messages back, usually at a relatively slow speed. Small computers dedicated to a single user can instantly fill up a screen with information, either printed or graphic. Input devices such as light pens, screens that respond to the touch of a finger, and a "mouse" that the user can push around on a table and thereby move a pointer on the screen are available. These kinds of features allow small, single-user machines to be more "user friendly" in interacting with the user.

In addition to allowing easy control of the machine, interactive data processing has the advantage of informing the user immediately when an error has been made. If a command is not understood by the machine, a statement indicating the problem and requesting a new command is given. Also, since the results of a command are returned immediately, responses indicating a problem with the analysis can cause the user to make changes before continuing. With batch processing, the researcher submits the job and must wait anywhere from a few minutes to a few hours for it to return. Only when it is returned can errors be corrected. Even if an early statement contains an error that will cause the subsequent analysis to be incorrectly done, the machine may go ahead and do the remaining steps anyway, wasting resources in the process.

Interactive computing has some disadvantages as well. It encourages the researcher to make up analysis as she goes. Unplanned wandering through the data is very easy to do in interactive computing and has all the problems of any unplanned research. Also, interactive computing requires greater machine resources than batch computing for the same amount of work. Finally, some operations, such as large-scale data entry, are difficult to perform interactively. Data entry is a major problem with even the most sophisticated calculators. The data must be entered each time the machine is used, and it must be entered by hand. Most computers can store data that have been entered, so they have to be entered only once. Some machines have both batch and interactive capabilities. This makes it possible to enter data under the batch system, store it, and use it interactively.

Controlling the Machine

Software. A computer requires thousands of detailed instructions to do the most simple task. Fortunately, instructions can be stored by the machine such that all we have to do is tell it which stored set of instructions to execute rather than having to give it every instruction each time we want something done. A **program** is a set of instructions for a particular task. When we want something done, we tell the machine to find the program we need in order to do the task, and provide some additional instructions that indicate exactly what we want done. The machine then executes the stored instructions. The ability to call up stored programs is what makes computers so easy to use. If we all had to learn the languages that a computer can understand directly and use one of them to tell it how to do something, it would usually be faster to do the data analysis by hand. Fortunately, there are thousands of available programs. The biggest problem may be finding the one that is needed.

A few years ago the most common kind of software consisted of individual programs written for specific tasks. If a researcher wanted to do descriptive statistics (like computing averages), he used one program; to compute a table, he used another. Usually the programs had little in common with one another. Learning to use one program did not enable the researcher to use another. In recent years, however, programs for specific tasks have been grouped together into *packages* or *systems of programs.* With these packages it is possible to do almost all the different kinds of analysis that a researcher could need. Since the programs are packaged together, they are easy to find. They also use a similar method of communication with the user, no matter what analysis is being done. Essentially the researcher needs to provide the same instructions in order to do descriptive statistics on the data as to do more complex analysis.

A major advantage of large packages of computer programs is that several of them have become commonly used on different kinds of computers. This means that knowledge learned in one environment will not be lost if the researcher moves or a new computer is installed. It also means that errors in the programs are likely to be detected since so many different people use them.

One count a few years ago suggested that there were in excess of thirty fairly large packages of programs for statistical analysis.[1] The oldest and probably the most widely available program system for statistical analysis is the BMD package.[2] It has been updated and improved over the years and contains programs for techniques not generally available elsewhere. One of the most commonly used systems is probably the Statistical Package for the Social Sciences (SPSS).[3] This package of programs can be used on almost all large scale computers. It is well documented and includes a relatively easy-to-read manual and a student-user's manual. Also very popular are OSIRIS, DATA–TEXT, and SAS.[4]

Packages of programs for statistical analysis on personal computers are available, and a few reasonably good ones are beginning to appear. But few of them make good use of the strengths of the machines, and in general software for statistical analysis is not well developed. It will probably improve before long, but statistical packages will probably always lag behind business, word-processing, and game software for personal computers.

One of the characteristics of program packages is that although the user must give the machine information about her own unique job, the program allows the use of relatively simple statements. For example, if we wanted to tell

SPSS to compute a variety of tables and other indicators describing a variable, we would enter the following statement:

FREQUENCIES   GENERAL=RELIGION
STATISTICS   ALL

Although learning the statements that control the program package takes a little time, once learned they can be used without constant recourse to the reference manual. Also, a lot of analysis can be done with a very simple statement. Consider this SPSS statement:

FREQUENCIES   GENERAL=ALL
STATISTICS   ALL

This statement would produce descriptive statistics on all variables on a file of data. Since a file may have up to 500 variables, that single instruction can make the machine do a large quantity of work.

ANALYZING DATA WITH AUTOMATED EQUIPMENT

Let us consider some strategies for using automated data-processing equipment. The first step for the researcher is to find out what specific resources are available and learn to use them. In designing a research project one may have to consider the limitations of the sources available. If the only system available is interactive and data must be entered on a terminal, the researcher may want to leave the large surveys to someone else. If the data processing is very expensive and the resources are limited, smaller projects should be undertaken. If locally available software is not adequate for the analysis, it may be possible to obtain the necessary software from somewhere else at a nominal cost, provided enough time is available. Otherwise it may be necessary to plan projects not requiring these capabilities. Though social science should perhaps proceed without these impediments, they must be considered.

Let us turn now to the process of making data available to the machine and then to the process of analyzing the data. We will discuss considerations that will be useful no matter what machinery and software are being used. Specific techniques must be learned from manuals for the packages.

Designing Data for Entry into the Computer

Data should be collected and recorded in a way that will make it easy to enter it into the computer. Precisely how this is done depends on the way the machine handles data entry. As we indicated above, the most common form of data entry is the computer card.

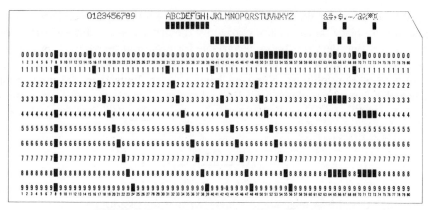

FIGURE 7–1 The Standard Computer Card

The Computer Card. To indicate how information is written on a computer card, we have presented a sample card in Figure 7–1. Notice that there are 80 columns on the card. Each column will contain one or more holes, the location of which represent a particular character (number, letter, or symbol) to the machine. For the convenience of the person using the cards, the character is usually printed at the top of the card. Notice that only 80 columns of single characters can be recorded on a single card.

Let us consider how the number 0 is coded on the card. Looking at the 15th column of the card, you should see ten rows of numbers, from 0 to 9. The number 0 has been punched out to indicate the number 0, and has been printed above the column, at the top of the card. We code the other digits in like manner, by punching out the corresponding row number. There are two rows above the rows printed on the card. The one nearest the top produces a + or &, depending on the keypunch. The lower one produces a −. The letters and other symbols are produced by combinations of punches. The letter *A,* for instance, is coded with a punch in the topmost row and another in the 1 row.

Formatting Data for Machine Reading. Data will almost always be entered one unit of analysis at a time, and the variables will be in the same order for each unit. Suppose we were collecting data for all states on three variables: median family income, percentage living in a city, and median years of education. We would first enter into the computer the data for Alabama for income, central city, and education, then the same data in same order for Alaska, and so on for rest of the states. This suggests that the best way to collect data is to put all the information about one unit in a single place and to list the variables in the same sequence for each unit.

The machine will expect the data to be entered in either of two ways. **Free-format entry** allows each code or number to be punched or typed so that it is separated from the next item by spaces or commas. The number of digits for a variable need not be the same from one unit to another. The numbers can be typed in any place on the line or card; only the order matters. **Fixed-format entry** requires that data for the same variable for each unit be recorded in exactly the same place on the line or card and be justified right (aligned on the right-hand side of the column). Numbers having fewer digits than the number of spaces that have been allowed fill the rightmost columns; the left ones remain blank or are filled with zeros. For example, the number 74 is justified right in a four-column space as follows:

$$\boxed{\,|\,|\,7\,|\,4\,|}$$

Consider the example of the three variables being collected for the states. Here is the data for Alabama and Alaska written for free-format entry:

7263,26,10.8
12441,0,12.5

Here is the same data written for fixed-format entry:

7263   26   108
12441   0   125

The spaces between the fixed-formatted numbers are optional. The decimal point has been omitted, since the machines can be told how many places there are to the right of the decimal.

If the data are to be entered free-format, we can simply record them on ledger sheets, using rows as units and columns as the variables. If a fixed-format entry is used, we should record the data on forms that indicate specific spaces. Figure 7–2 consists of a coding form set up for entry of the state data. Notice

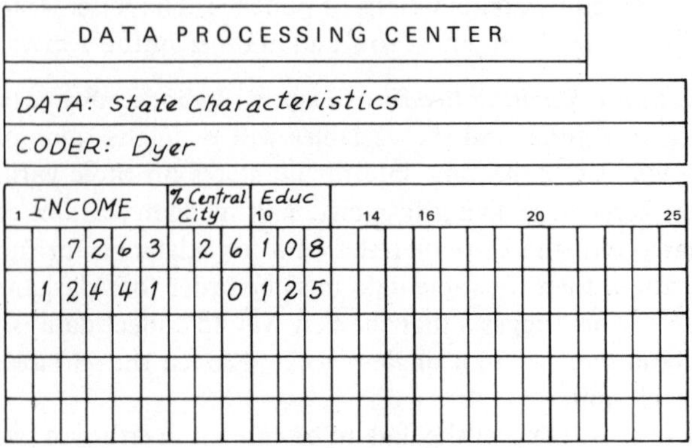

FIGURE 7–2   A Portion of a Standard Coding Form for Computer Cards

that each variable is found in exactly the same columns. The number of spaces allowed for a variable is determined by the number of digits in the largest num- ber to be recorded. There is no requirement that the numbers be separated by spaces or commas as there is in free-format entry. If data must be entered in a fixed format, they should be recorded directly onto a proper coding form that has the card columns indicated on it. This is the only way to ensure that the numbers are punched in the correct columns.

Data entered through an interactive system are more likely to be entered free-format; when entered on cards in batch mode, they are likely to be entered fixed-format. The important thing is that the data be prepared according to the requirements of the systems available.

Data for a single unit of analysis may require more than one card. Programs allow as many cards per unit of analysis to be read as needed to record the information. In either fixed or free format, a new card must be used for the start of the data for a new unit of analysis. In the case of fixed-format entry, each unit must have the same number of cards.

All cards should have an identification number punched on them. This allows for easy location of the cards for correction and also provides a way of determining which cards are missing in cases of lost cards. (Machines occasionally mangle cards, and they can be dropped.) When there is more than one card per unit of analysis, there should be an identification number on each card as well as a sequence number indicating which of the two cards comes first. If one card is out of order when there is more than one card per unit of analysis, the entire deck will be misread.

Coding the Data. The codes we use to record the data are an important consideration. As we observed in Chapter 4, we use numbers to stand for categories of a property. For example, we might code a 1 for Democrats, a 2 for Republicans, and a 3 for all others. When it is appropriate, we can record the value of the variable directly—the amount a respondent earned, or his age, for example.

If we are going to be using automated data processing in analyzing data, there are several things we should consider in selecting codes. The first is to keep as many different categories of the measure as could possibly be useful rather than combining categories. For example, if region of the country is a variable, we might consider South as one category, and non-South as another. Alternatively, we might divide the country into five different regions and have a code for each. The advantage of the latter procedure is that we can easily have the machine combine the categories so as to yield a South/non-South comparison, but if the categories have been combined into South and non-South codes, it is impossible to break them down into a five-region distribution. Although the hypothesis for which you are collecting the data may need only the South/non-South distinction, you may be led to explore other possibilities, or other researchers may wish to use the data for different purposes. We can take advantage of the case with which most programs manipulate data to avoid restricting later use of the data by the categories we use in coding the data.

A second consideration is to use codes that limit the number of digits required to record the data. For example, if there are ten different categories, use codes from 0 to 9 rather than from 1 to 10; the extra digit takes up more room on a computer card. For the same reason, it may be desirable to record a variable in hundreds or thousands rather than in units if the additional accuracy is not needed. For example, you might code the median income for cities in thousands of dollars rather than in single dollars. Thus, if a city's median income were $10,900, it would be coded as 11 rather than 10900. Of course, the savings in space and entry time costs are accompanied by a loss in accuracy. On the other hand, many variables are not so accurate that the loss will be significant. Unit-record devices can effectively handle only one card for each unit of analysis, which makes it particularly important to get as much data as possible on a single card. Minimizing the size of the codes is not as important when we are using modern computers.

Another consideration is to use only numeric codes for variables. Most computer programs are not designed to deal with alphabetical codes, and those that are usually do so awkwardly. However, fixed-format input can be made to ignore certain columns, and thus we can use alphabetic characters to identify a unit as long as this identification does not need to be read by the machine. For example, we might punch MAINE on the card containing data on Maine, TEXAS on the Texas card, and so on, so that the card for each state can be identified easily. The machine can be told to skip over these names when it reads the data.

The coding of missing data deserves special comment. Most programs can deal with missing data, usually by causing the case with the missing data on the variable of interest to be deleted from the analysis. In order to program the computer to do this, we must indicate to it what value or values are to be considered missing. The missing-data code should be a single number that cannot be confused with any legitimate code. It is usually helpful if the code is as far away from a legitimate code as possible. For example, if 1 is yes and 2 is no, the no-answer code could be 9. If income is being recorded in units, a -999 might make a good missing-data code. Making the code as different from the others as possible has the advantage not only of making confusion between the code and real data less likely, but of highlighting instances where the program is not removing the missing data correctly. It is usually easy to see that the analysis is wrong when missing data are included when the codes used are extreme.

Though it is commonly done, blanks should usually not be used to indicate missing data. Many machines and programs cannot distinguish between blanks and zeros. If a zero is a legitimate code and a blank is missing data, the real data and the missing data cannot be distinguished. Occasionally, however, a program requires missing data to be coded as blanks.

Analyzing the Data

We indicated early in the chapter that there were several ways that automated data analysis could lead the researcher astray. The problems arise from the apparent ease in asking the machine to do things and the fact that the researcher does not need to get involved with the data during the computation. There are rules, however, that if followed can make automated data processing useful and remove the risk of these problems.

One rule is to understand exactly what the machine and the programs are doing. If a researcher does not understand the technique, he or she should not use it, even if the results look good. A major problem is that most programs have default options that allow the researcher to use a technique in which critical choices are made by the program if the researcher does not make a choice. Some of the options may be inappropriate for the data being analyzed, and the careless researcher may not even be aware that the choice was made. The documentation of the program must be read carefully; the formulas used in the programs should be noted and understood. If the analysis begins to indicate quite unexpected things, check the computer programs and the instructions used to run them before trying to develop novel explanations for the bizarre behavior of the data. This may save a lot of wasted time and effort.

It is common to use the computer program to modify the data. Though easily done, such modification can often be a source of undetected errors. One common problem is for codes designating missing data to be modified in a data transformation and no longer be recognized as missing by the program. Suppose you were dividing the amount of bonded indebtedness (DEBT) in cities by the population (POP) in order to get the amount of debt per person (DEBTPOP). Suppose the missing data was coded -999 (the figures are in thousands of dollars). A statement to do the computation would look like this in SPSS:

```
COMPUTE     DEBTPOP=DEBT/POP
```

Unless another statement were present to tell the program to set DEBTPOP to a missing value if either DEBT or POP were missing, in the subsequent analysis DEBTPOP would be a large minus figure for some cities.

A good rule is that whenever transformations are done, statistics or frequency distributions of the transformed data be done routinely. Glancing at the minimum value of a large negative number found in the distribution of DEBTPOP would immediately alert the researcher to a problem.

Another rule is to ask only for what you need in order to test the hypotheses. Just because it is easy to ask for a lot of computation does not mean it should be done. For one thing, unnecessary analysis costs money. It also leads to unhypothesized exploration of the data, which, as we have already argued, is far less useful than proceeding through carefully written hypotheses. Asking for quantities of analysis also means that the researcher can end up with so much unnecessary output that interpretation becomes difficult. A dozen well chosen tables will be easier to consider than 200.

The ease of asking for computations leads to one further rule: Be careful. An innocuous statement like

CROSSTABS   TABLES=RACE BY EDUCATION BY AGE BY INCOME

could easily cause 50,000 worthless tables to be produced.

Finally, care should be taken to document the work so that several months from the time the computer work was done the procedures will be clear. Most programs allow the researcher to label tables and to insert comments into the instructions to the machine. It is surprising how often a researcher will return to work completed earlier only to find it impossible to determine exactly what was done. Even if the program will not allow documentation, the researcher should take the time to write comments on the results.

SUMMARY

Automated data processing has made possible a revolution in social science analysis. A student can analyze large sets of data and use techniques that a few years ago would have been available only to well-funded researchers.

It is well worth the effort to learn to use automated data processing. Automated data processing has become an important part of many occupations and is beginning to find a place in the home. It is a skill with wide-ranging applications.

Endnotes

[1]Edwin Coover, et al., "Design of an Optimally Compatable Social Data Analysis System: The First Steps," *Social Science Information,* 13 (June 1974), see 105–46.

[2]W. J. Dixon, ed., *BMD: Biomedical Computer Programs* (Berkeley and Los Angeles: University of California Press, 1970); W. J. Dixon, ed., *BMD: Biomedical Computer Programs, X-Series Supplement* (Berkeley and Los Angeles: University of California Press, 1970).

[3]Norman Nie, et al., *SPSS: Statistical Package for the Social Sciences* (New York: McGraw-Hill, 1975).

[4]*OSIRIS III: An Integrated Collection of Computer Programs for the Management and Analysis of Social Science Data,* Vols. 1–6 (Ann Arbor, Mich.: Institute for Social Research, 1973); David Armour and Arthur Couch, *The DATA–TEXT Primer* (Glencoe, Ill.:Free Press, 1972); *SAS76: Statistical Analysis System* (Chapel Hill: University of North Carolina, 1976).

LABORATORY EXERCISES

The purpose of this laboratory is to familiarize you with methods of preparing data for computer processing and, if facilities are available, to demonstrate the method of entering data for machine processing.

Task 1. In the laboratory exercises for Chapter 5 you collected some data on members of Congress and on nations. Using a standard computer coding form, prepare the data on members of Congress and their districts for fixed-format data entry. On another form, prepare the data on nations for free-format entry.

Task 2. Following instructions given by your instructor, prepare the data coded above so that it can be read by the computer for analysis.

REVIEW QUESTIONS

1. Code the following data exactly as you would for fixed-format entry into a computer terminal.

Units	Pop. Rank	Per-Capita Federal Aid	Unemployment Rate
Brownsville	1	314.56	15.5
Austin	2	1010.00	3.0
Dallas	3	54.83	4.6
Houston	4	255.42	5.8

2. Which of the following types of data are best suited for free-format data entry? Why?
   a. 25 items of economic data for countries
   b. responses to 25 survey questions.
3. Packages of computer programs make analysis of data quite easy, but what are the problems created by this ease of analysis?

CHAPTER EIGHT

PRESENTATION OF PROPERTIES

Once we have measured the properties, we must display the information so that it is readily understandable. Occasionally we can do this by listing the values for each unit on the variable, often ordering the units according to the values. For example, we could present data on size of welfare payments by state by listing the states from least payments to most and by placing the corresponding amount beside each state. The reader could quickly get a picture of what the distribution looked like and could also find the relative position and amount paid in any specific state. This is usually not a satisfactory method of data presentation if there is a large number of units, or if exact comparisons need to be made of two or more distributions. We could not easily tell much about a distribution of a variable for 1000 units if the data were just listed. Even when the number of units is small, we cannot determine something like whether AFDC payments by states are tending to increase or not just by looking at the numbers for each state. To present data in a useful way, we have to summarize them. This chapter is about using visual methods and simple statistics to summarize measures.

DECIDING WHAT TO DO

A variety of different statistics and methods are used to summarize data. The nature of the data and the features of the distribution that the researcher wants to present are the primary considerations in determining the method to use. The space available for the presentation can also be a factor. Visual presentations may communicate a great deal of information, but they require a relatively large amount of space compared with summary statistics.

The Nature of the Data

The nature of the data influences both the type of visual presentation and the statistics that can be used effectively. The major consideration is the level of measurement of the property. We first discussed those levels in Chapter 4, and we review them briefly here.

Nominal-level measures do nothing more than separate the units into different categories. Nominal-level measures cannot indicate that one category has more or less of the property than another category. Religious affiliation is an example of a property measured at the nominal level. A typical measure of religious affiliation might separate people into four categories: Jewish, Catholic, Protestant, and other. One category does not indicate more religious affiliation than another category; it simply indicates that the units in that category are different than those in other categories.

Measures that distinguish among different categories of a property and also order the categories according to the amount of the property are classified as *ordinal-level measures.* For example, judges might be asked to rate candidates for public office as having a high, medium, or low amount of television appeal. This would be an ordinal measure. The measure not only separates the candidates into different categories, it also indicates the order of the categories. The candidates in the high category have more television appeal than those in the medium category, and those in the medium category have more than those in the low.

Interval-level measures distinguish categories that can be ordered and indicate the distance between them. Income, measured in actual dollars earned, is an interval measure. The measure distinguishes between people who earn different amounts of money. It also orders them from high to low income, *and* it tells us how far apart they are. Suppose we have three persons. One earns $5000, another $5500, and the third $6000. You can say that the person earning $5000 is different from the other two—that she earns the least—and that the amount she earns is $500 closer to that earned by the second person than to that earned by the third.

Understanding the differences among the different levels of measurement is very important because the level of measurement not only determines which of the statistics can be used for describing variables but also determines the choices of statistics when we are studying relationships. Analyzing relationships is the ultimate activity in testing hypotheses, and we devote Chapters 9 through 14 to that subject. Levels of measurement will thus be a matter of concern to us throughout most of the remainder of this book.

What We Want to Communicate

What we want to communicate about a distribution is the final consideration in determining the method to be used in summarizing the data. Visual presentations usually allow the greatest amount of information to be communicated, but as we indicated above, they tend to be cumbersome to present, and precise comparisons between them are difficult to make. For these reasons we often use summary statistics to communicate information about the shape of the distribution. Two types are commonly used. **Indicators of central tendency** are statistics that reflect a middle or central or most common value in a distribution. **Indicators of dispersion** indicate the extent to which the units of analysis are spread out or concentrated together.

SUMMARIZING PROPERTIES

In the following sections we discuss the methods of summarizing measures for each of the levels of measurement. We first discuss the use of simple tables in presentations, and finally appropriate measures of central tendency and dispersion.

Summarizing Nominal-Level Measures

Summarizing nominal data is relatively simple, providing there are not a large number of different categories. The most basic analysis—to count the number of units falling into each category—is called a **frequency distribution.** Let us consider the religious-affiliation variable again. A frequency distribution for a sample might look like Table 8-1.

This would indicate that in the sample of 1366 people there were 314 Catholics, 870 Protestants, 40 Jews, and 142 in the others-or-none category.

To simplify the presentation, we commonly eliminate those units for which there is no information about the property. Those who refused to announce their religious preference were excluded from the frequency distribution in Table 8-1. It is also common to combine categories, particularly when the number of units in each is very small. We have combined all of those who expressed no religious preference and those who had some religious preference other than Protestant, Catholic, or Jewish into a single others-or-none category. Furthermore, all Protestants have been lumped into a single category rather than separated into the hundreds of Protestant denominations that can be found.

Instead of reporting just frequencies, we usually present percentages. By dividing the number of units in each category by the total number of units, we find the percentage in each category. A list of those percentages is called a **percentage distribution.** Percentage distributions facilitate comparisons between

TABLE 8-1   Frequency Distribution of Religious Affiliation

Catholics	Protestants	Jews	Others or None
314	870	40	142

Source: Center for Political Studies' 1980 Presidential Election Study; provided by the Inter-University Consortium for Political and Social Research.

TABLE 8–2 Percentage Distribution of Religious Affiliation (With Frequencies)

Catholics	Protestants	Jews	Others or None
23%	64%	3%	10%
(314)	(870)	(40)	(142)

samples of different size. Also, since the theoretical population is usually larger than the sample, using percentages makes it easier to understand the size of the category in the theoretical population. A table presenting percentages might look like Table 8–2.

We usually indicate the frequency as well as the percentage in the same table. This enables readers to see how many units the percentages are based on, and gives them a better idea of the general applicability of the table.

A visual representation of data is very useful. The most popular way to represent nominal data is with a **bar graph** (sometimes called a histogram). A bar graph is nothing more than a series of bars, one for each category of the variable. The height of each bar corresponds to either the number of units or the percentage of units in the category. Figure 8–1 is a bar graph of our data on religious affiliation.

Other visual presentations can be used. A bar graph can be presented horizontally rather than vertically. Bars are sometimes superimposed on top of each other for easy comparison. Pie charts, where a circle is divided into segments, are also used. The size of each segment is proportional to the number of units in the category. In all of these, distance or area on the paper represents the size of the category.

The indicator of central tendency for nominal measures is the **mode.** The mode is the category in which the most units are contained. Thus, the central tendency is the most common category. For example, the mode for religious affiliation is Protestant.

Special measures of dispersion are not commonly used for nominal-level

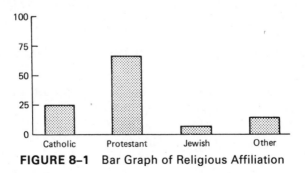

FIGURE 8–1   Bar Graph of Religious Affiliation

measures. It is usually enough to indicate the percentage of cases found in the modal category. If the percentage in the modal category is high, the dispersion is low. For example, we found 66% of the sample to be Protestants, which indicates fairly low dispersion compared with the 25% we would have found if the distribution had had the greatest possible dispersion.

Summarizing Ordinal-Level Measures

Ordinal-level measures can be summarized in the same way that nominal-level measures can, with frequency and percentage distributions, bar graphs, and modes. The **median** is an additional indicator of the central tendency appropriate for ordinal measures; it is the middle category of a distribution. It is the middle in the sense that if all of the units are ordered from high to low on the property, the median is the category to which the middle unit belongs.

If each unit is uniquely ranked—that is, if it is not tied with any other unit—then the median will fall between the middle two scores in the case of an even number of units. In the case of an odd number of units, it will fall on the middle score. There are problems with what to do with the median when there are a large number of tied cases around the midpoint.

Let us consider an example of ordinal data obtained from responses to the statement "It is more important for a wife to help her husband's career than to have one herself." Respondents were asked to indicate strong agreement, agreement, disagreement, or strong disagreement with the statement. Since there are only four categories, many respondents were tied at the same rank. The distribution is presented in Table 8–3.

There were 1472 respondents in the sample, so the middle is between the 736th and 737th persons. This is somewhere in the *agree* category.[1]

There are ways of indicating dispersion of ordinal measures. The simplest, but often the most misleading, is the **range.** The range indicates the highest and lowest categories in which the units of analysis are found. In the example of an ordinal distribution given above, the range would be from *strongly agree* to *strongly disagree.* Range can be a bad indicator since only one unit in an outlying category will cause the range to seem as great as if all units were in the extreme

TABLE 8–3 Response to Wife Helping Husband's Career

Strongly Agree	Agree	Disagree	Strongly Disagree
14%	43%	36%	7%
(205)	(636)	(534)	(97)

Source: NORC General Social Survey, 1980.

categories. A more useful indicator of dispersion for ordinal measures is the **interquartile range.** This measure indicates the high and low categories of the middle 50% of the units. It is called interquartile because the end points are a quartile (one quarter of the units) above and below the median. The simplest way to find the interquartile range is to eliminate the top 25% and the bottom 25% of the scores; the range of the remaining scores is the interquartile range. In the distribution above, 25% of the cases is 368. Removing 368 cases from the *agree* side of the scale puts that end of the interquartile range in the *agree* category. The other end is located in the *disagree* category. Hence, the interquartile range is from *agree* to *disagree.*

Summarizing Interval-Level Measures

Interval-level measures can be summarized in ways similar to nominal- and ordinal-level measures. However, interval measures usually distinguish so many different categories that a frequency or percentage distribution would be very large and meaningless. One way to avoid this is to recategorize an interval variable so that each category represents a range of values of the original variable. Suppose we had a measure of income. A frequency distribution would require thousands of categories, one for every unique amount of money everyone in the sample earned. Instead, we might recategorize the variable so that each category represented a $1000 division. Thus, everyone earning $0 to $1000 would be in one category, those earning $1001 to $2000 in another, and so on. A frequency distribution and a bar graph would then be useful. What we have done by recategorizing the interval measure is to transform it into an ordinal measure. We no longer can determine the distances between the units as we could before the transformation.

The large number of categories created by interval-level measures makes a bar graph with a separate bar for each category an inappropriate way of visually presenting the data. Interval variables are usually displayed on a **line graph,** in which a continuous line represents the distribution. An example of a line-graph distribution is presented in Figure 8–2.

We produce a line graph by dividing the variable into a number of equally spaced categories. There is no easy way to state how many categories produce the best representation of the distribution. The number depends on the number of cases in the sample and the shape of the distribution. Too many cases will obscure the general shape of the distribution and too few will hide significant smaller features of the distribution. The number of cases falling into each category is determined, and the graph is constructed like a bar graph. Instead of constructing bars, though, we place a dot at the midpoint of the first category at the place representing the number of observations found in the category. We follow the same procedure for all categories until the number in each is represented by

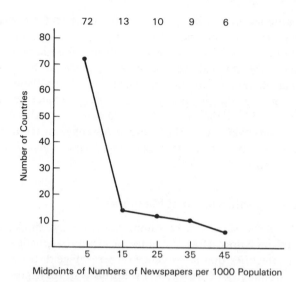

FIGURE 8–2   Line Graph of the Distribution of
Numbers of Newspapers per 1000 Population
in Countries, 1965

Source: From data in the *World Handbook of Social and Political Indicators II*, collected by Charles Lewis Taylor and Michael C. Hudson. Made available by the Inter-University Consortium for Political
and Social Research.

a dot above the midpoint. We then connect the dots with a line, which indicates
the distribution is considered continuous. Sometimes we smooth the line as well.

We created the line graph in Figure 8–2 by dividing the continuous distribution into five even categories. The first ranged from 0 to 10, the second from
10.01 to 20, the third from 20.01 to 30, the fourth from 30.01 to 40, and the fifth
from 40.01 to 50. We then determined the frequencies for each category. The
first category had 72 observations, the second had 13, the third had 10, the
fourth had 9, and the last had 6. We prepared the graph by placing at the bottom five equally spaced marks representing the midpoints of the five categories.
The midpoints were labeled. The side of the graph was divided into intervals
representing the number of cases. In the first category, a dot was placed above
the midpoint 5 at the place where the line on the side indicated about 72 cases. A
dot was placed above midpoint 15 at the location indicating 13, and so on for the
rest of the categories. The dots were then connected.

When we measure the central tendency of interval-level data, the mode is
usually not useful because of the large number of unique categories. The median,
however, is a very good measure of central tendency for interval data. In addition, the **mean,** or average, is a useful indicator of central tendency. The mean is
the sum of the values of each of the units divided by the number of units.

Let us consider an example. Table 8–4 presents the average salaries for teachers in the New England states:

TABLE 8–4

State	Average Teacher Salary, 1978–1979
Conn.	15,235
Maine	12,328
Mass.	16,125
New Hamp.	11,825
Rhode Island	16,698
Vermont	11,786

Source: *The Book of the States 1980–1981* (Lexington, Ky.: Council of State Governments, 1980), p. 358.

To determine the median, we rank the values (salaries) from lowest to highest:

> 11,786
> 11,825
> 12,328
> 15,235
> 16,125
> 16,698

Then we find the middle value. Since we have an even number of cases, the middle number is between 12,328 and 15,235. The usual procedure is to find the difference between the two numbers surrounding the middle, divide the difference by 2, and add the result to the lower value. In this case the difference between the numbers is 2907. Dividing this figure by 2 produces 1453.5, and adding this to the lower value of 12,328 produces a median of 13,781.5.

We compute the mean by summing the values and dividing by the number of values. In our example the sum is 83,997; dividing it by 6 produces a mean of 13,999.5.

The mean and the median are sometimes very similar, but can be quite different. Suppose we have a village inhabited by 101 people: one lord plus 100 vassals. Suppose further that the lord makes $5 million a year and each vassal $5000 a year. The average income would be $54,455.44. Not bad, but you still might not want to move there unless you were going to take over the lord's job. The median is a better measure in cases like this (and often even in less dramatic cases). The median income would have been $5,000 in this example—a much better indicator for most purposes.

The mean is much more sensitive than the median to the presence of a small number of values relatively different from the others, as long as these extreme values fall at one end or the other of the distribution. If the mean and median lead you to essentially the same conclusion about the location of the central tendency, it does not matter which you report. But when they are different, it is often desirable to report both.

Indicators of dispersion for interval-level data involve measuring how far from the mean the values of all the units are. The **mean deviation** is the average difference between each value and the mean. To compute it, we first must find the mean of a set of values. We then find the differences between the mean and each of the values. Ignoring the signs of the differences, we compute the mean deviation by dividing the sum of the differences by the number of units. It will be large if the dispersion is large, small if it is small.

Let us compute the mean deviation for the data on teachers' salaries. We subtract the mean of 13,999.5 from each of the six values for the states and find the differences.

Salary		Mean of Salaries		Difference
15,235	−	13,999.5	=	1,235.5
12,328	−	13,999.5	=	−1,671.5
16,125	−	13,999.5	=	2,125.5
11,825	−	13,999.5	=	−2,174.5
16,698	−	13,999.5	=	2,698.5
11,786	−	13,999.5	=	−2,213.5

Ignoring the signs and summing the differences gives a total of 12,119. Dividing by the number of states (6) produces a mean deviation of 2,019.8.

The mean deviation is not the usually reported indicator of interval dispersion. The standard deviation and variance are more common. The **variance** is computed like the mean deviation except that the differences between the mean and each value are squared before being averaged. That is, we multiply each difference by itself before adding them together and dividing by the number of values. The sum of the squared differences from the mean is often referred to as the **sum of squares.** The sum of squares will be used in statistical techniques discussed in later chapters. We squared the differences between the salaries and the mean for our example:

$$
\begin{aligned}
&1,526,460.25 \\
&2,793,912.25 \\
&4,517,750.25 \\
&4,728,450.25 \\
&7,281,902.25 \\
&4,899,582.25
\end{aligned}
$$

The sum of these squared differences is 25,748,057.5, and dividing by 6 gives us a variance of 4,291,342.917.

The **standard deviation** is simply the square root of the variance. Whereas the variance is reported in average squared units of the original values, the standard deviation is reported in the same kind of units as the original values, which makes it easier to interpret. The square root of the variance in our example is 2071.56.[2]

Computing Standardized Scores (Z-scores). When we discussed creating compound measures in Chapter 5, we suggested that when measures with greater variation were combined with measures of lesser variation, the combined measure reflected to a greater extent the measures having the greater variation. We can now state this idea more precisely. When one measure has a greater standard deviation than another, the one with the greater standard deviation will influence the combined measure more than the one with less standard deviation will.

We indicated that we could cause the indicators to count equally in the final measure by transforming them into standardized scores, or z-scores. We had to leave until now a discussion of how that is done. We compute a z-score for each unit by subtracting the mean from the value of the unit and dividing the difference by the standard deviation. After this transformation, the mean will always be 0 and the standard deviation will always be 1. Therefore, after indicators have been z-scored they can be combined with the assurance that no one of them will contribute to the combined measure more than any other.

Let us compute the z-scores for the teachers' salaries in the six New England states. We use the difference between the mean of 13,999.5 and the average salary in each state. We divide that difference by the standard deviation of 2071.55 and obtain the following z-scores. We have computed the mean and standard deviation on them to demonstrate that the former is 0 and the latter 1.

	Z-score	Squared Difference Between Mean and Z-score
	.60	.36
	−.81	.65
	1.03	1.05
	−1.05	1.10
	1.30	1.70
	−1.07	1.14
sum =	0	sum of squares = 6.00
mean =	0	standard deviation = 1.00

Summary of Methods Used to Describe Distributions

We indicate in Table 8-5 appropriate methods of presentation for each of the levels of measurement we have discussed. Xs designate the most appropriate

TABLE 8–5 Appropriate Descriptive Techniques for Different
Levels of Measurement

	Level of Measurement		
	Nominal	*Ordinal*	*Interval*
Visual			
Bar graphs	X	X	X
Line graphs			X
Central Tendency			
Mode	X	?	?
Median		X	X
Mean			X
Dispersion			
Number in most numerous category	X	?	?
Range and interquartile range		X	X
Variance and standard deviation			X

techniques. A question mark indicates that the technique is permissible but not generally useful.

THE SHAPE OF THE DISTRIBUTION

When we look at the visual displays of the distribution we see a picture of how units of analysis are spread across the values of the measure. We often refer to that picture as the shape of the distribution. Using the indicators of dispersion that we discussed above, we can say whether the shape of the distribution is spread out or clustered together. We can also indicate the central points of the distribution. But we often go further in describing the shape. We talk about the number of modes that a distribution has. We can indicate whether the distribution is symmetrical or not and if it is not symmetrical, how it is skewed. We often indicate how well the distribution corresponds to a particular bell-shaped distribution known as a normal distribution.

These qualities of shape apply only to relative measures—that is, ordinal and interval measures. Since the order of the categories in nominal measures is arbitrary, the shape of the distribution is arbitrary.

Number of Modes

We defined the mode as that category of the measure having the most units in it. In describing the shape of distributions we must enlarge that definition a little. We consider a modal category to be one that has significantly more cases than the other categories, provided that the modal categories are separated from each other by categories having substantially smaller number of units in them. We would call Figure 8–3 a **bimodal** (two modes) **distribution,** because

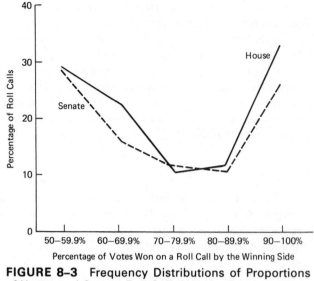

FIGURE 8–3 Frequency Distributions of Proportions of House and Senate Roll Calls Won by Percentages in Specified Ranges, 1972

Source: David R. Mayhew, *Congress: The Electoral Connection* (New Haven: Yale University Press, 1974), p. 113.

both ends of the distribution have substantially more units than the middle does. We call it bimodal even though the number of units in each of the two end categories is not identical. It is clear, though, that most roll-call votes tend to be taken when the margin is small or when the vote is nearly unanimous.

A unimodal distribution has but a single mode. Some distributions may have three or more modes. Distributions in which the cases are distributed more or less evenly across the range of categories may have no modal areas. We call these **uniform distributions.**

Symmetrical and Skewed Distributions

A distribution whose values are distributed equally on each side of the midpoint is called a **symmetrical distribution.** The distribution in Figure 8-4 is one example of a symmetrical distribution. Distributions that are not symmetrical are called **skewed distributions.** A skewed distribution has cases that are further from the median in one direction than in the other. The distribution of numbers of newspapers per thousand population that was shown in Figure 8-2 is an example of a skewed distribution.

One of the indications that a distribution is skewed is that the mean and median are substantially different. In the case of the distribution of newspapers per thousands, the mean was 110.74 and the median was 47.

When the outlying cases are lower than the midpoint of the distribution we say the distribution is **left-skewed** or **negatively skewed.** When the outlying cases are higher than the midpoint we call the distribution **right-skewed** or **positively skewed.** The difference between the mean and the median indicates the direction of the skew. When the mean is greater than the median the distribution is positively skewed; when the mean is lower than the median the distribution is negatively skewed. In the example of newspapers per thousands, the mean was well above the median, confirming the picture presented by the line graph of a strongly positively skewed distribution.

Bell-Shaped Distributions

When a distribution is symmetrical and unimodal it often looks like the distribution in Figure 8–4. We say that such a distribution is **bell-shaped.** Depending on some additional distributional requirements, a bell-shaped distribution may be a **normal distribution** (see Glossary).

SUMMARY

Being able to describe a distribution is an important part of research. When we look at associations among properties, we are usually comparing the distribution of a measure among one group of units with the distribution of the measure among another. Simply looking at a distribution of a single measure may be useful to us. We may want to find out how salaries are distributed, or how the class did on a test, or what the religious preferences of a group are. We can answer many questions just by looking at the distribution of measures.

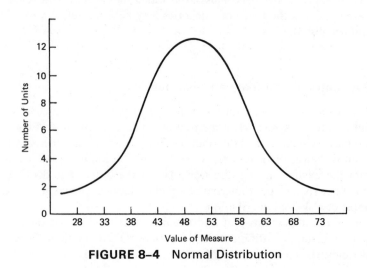

FIGURE 8–4   Normal Distribution

Endnotes

[1] In a case like this we sometimes interpolate in order to indicate where in the category the middle person would be. But this interpolation violates the characteristics of the ordinal measure.

[2] We usually compute the standard deviation and variance by dividing by $n-1$ instead of by n. This formula is the definitional one and is applicable when populations rather than samples are analyzed. The reason is that the $n-1$ calculation produces an unbiased estimate of the variance and the standard deviation in the population. The difference is trivial when n is large.

LABORATORY EXERCISES

The purpose of this laboratory is to give you experience in describing distributions.

Task 1. In this task you are asked to determine frequency distributions, draw bar or line graphs, and compute appropriate descriptive statistics. You will then interpret what the analysis tells you about the distributions. You will be assigned three variables to analyze from the data below.

a. For each of the assigned variables, present the frequency and percentage distributions.
b. Construct a bar or line graph (whichever is most appropriate) for each distribution.
c. Indicate (when appropriate) the general shape of each distribution.
d. Compute appropriate indicators of central tendency.
e. Compute appropriate measures of dispersion.

Data

	Nominal				Ordinal				Interval		
1	*2*	*3*	*4*	*5*	*6*	*7*	*8*	*9*	*10*	*11*	*12*
1	1	2	0	1	6	3	0	56	1	17	2
1	3	5	1	8	8	5	2	55	9	21	2
2	2	1	0	2	16	5	2	48	0	2	6
1	3	1	0	8	20	5	4	55	5	19	8
3	1	4	2	8	8	4	3	58	7	25	11
2	2	2	0	3	7	6	1	57	7	24	9
1	1	5	0	9	25	7	3	90	7	20	5
3	2	2	0	0	7	10	4	55	4	20	2

Data (*continued*)

Nominal				Ordinal				Interval			
1	*2*	*3*	*4*	*5*	*6*	*7*	*8*	*9*	*10*	*11*	*12*
2	3	1	2	7	8	11	2	54	3	22	10
1	2	2	0	8	8	10	2	53	1	19	2
2	3	3	2	7	9	11	0	55	2	34	5
2	3	3	1	9	7	12	2	51	0	7	2
1	3	4	0	1	19	11	4	54	0	20	8
2	3	3	0	8	15	5	1	80	1	21	9
2	3	3	2	7	14	4	2	56	1	15	7
2	1	4	2	9	8	3	3	50	1	20	8
3	2	1	0	8	7	5	1	62	1	23	10
2	3	4	2	8	9	11	0	54	7	18	8
2	3	3	0	0	9	6	2	52	6	21	11
2	3	4	2	4	8	3	0	70	6	33	10
3	1	5	1	5	10	12	1	65	7	19	9
1	3	5	1	6	11	13	4	59	8	20	6
1	3	1	2	8	7	11	3	56	9	16	9
3	3	5	2	7	9	11	3	60	9	6	9
2	3	2	2	9	8	13	1	100	0	28	8

Task 2. Use the computer to analyze data provided by the instructor. Describe the variables:

 a. name of variables
 b. coding for each variable
 c. level of measurement of each variable
 d. bar graph or line graph for each variable
 e. appropriate measures of central tendency
 d. description of general shape of the distribution

REVIEW QUESTIONS

 1. For which of the following distributions would the variance be the greatest?

A	B	C
7	7	7
6	5	7
5	5	7
4	5	2
3	3	2

2. What is the level of measurement of each of the following measures?

   a. Degree of liberalism: 5 = strong liberal; 4 = liberal; 3 = moderate; 2 = conservative; 1 = strong conservative.
   b. Committee in the Senate: 1 = Armed Services; 2 = Appropriations; 3 = Foreign Relations; 4 = Finance; 5 = Government Operations.
   c. Support for farm price supports in the Senate: 1 = support on 0% to 20% of the bills; 2 = support on 21 to 40%; 3 = support on 41% to 60%; 4 = support on 61% to 80%; and 5 = support on 81% to 100%.
   d. Length of time served in prison: Code number of days in prison.

3. Construct a line graph showing a positively skewed distribution. Indicate the approximate values of the mean, median, and mode.

4. Find the mean, median, mode, range, and interquartile range of the following numbers: 4 6 5 2 2 7 9 0 1

5. Hypothetical data, United States cities:

City	Mean January Temperature*	Tax Burden per Capita[†]	In-migration Rate[‡]
Buffalo	1	7	1
Chicago	1	5	1
Dallas	3	3	1
Fresno	3	3	3
Frankfort	2	2	1
Galveston	3	5	3
Honolulu	3	4	3
Jackson	2	11	2
Juneau	1	10	3
Lubbock	3	2	2
Mobile	3	3	2
New York	1	8	1
Pittsburgh	1	4	2
Seattle	2	2	3
Syracuse	1	6	2
Toledo	1	9	2
Virginia	3	1	2

*Mean January temperature: 1 = below 30; 2 = 30–50; 3 = above 50.

[†]Tax burden per capita: in hundreds of dollars.

[‡]In-migration rate: 1 = losing population; 2 = slow increase; 3 = rapid increase.

Compute the percentage distribution for each variable, compute the mean, median, and/or mode (whenever they are appropriate), compute the interquartile range (if it is appropriate), and describe the general shape of each distribution.

CHAPTER NINE

REPORTING RELATIONSHIPS FOR CATEGORICAL INDEPENDENT VARIABLES

With this chapter we begin considering the analysis we use to determine whether the relationship between the variables is the one stated in the hypothesis. Every hypothesis asserts that variation in one property is dependent upon variation in another. The property that is considered to be dependent is measured by the dependent variable (sometimes called the effect variable); the property considered to cause the variation is measured by the *independent variable* (sometimes called the causal variable). The dependent variable is generally represented by the symbol Y; the independent variable, by the symbol X. This chapter considers ways of reporting the relationship between X and Y when the X variable is divided into a small number of categories.

Suppose the hypothesis is "College graduates are more likely to vote than nongraduates." Educational attainment is the independent (X) variable; voting is the dependent (Y) variable. The researcher must report how variation in educational attainment is related to variation in voting for the units in the sample.

The researcher reports a relationship by showing the distribution of the dependent variable (Y) for each category of the independent variable (X). Every hypothesis asserts that differences in X will generally cause differences in Y; consequently, the distribution of Y should be different for different categories of X. As we indicated earlier, the hypothesis must specify the manner in which these distributions of Y should differ.

Consider again the hypothesis that college graduates are more likely to vote than nongraduates. If the hypothesis is correct, the distribution of voters and nonvoters should be different for graduates and nongraduates. More specifically, there should be a higher percentage of voters among the graduates than among the nongraduates.

The researcher could demonstrate support for that hypothesis by showing that in the sample a higher percentage of graduates than nongraduates were voters. To make it easier for the audience to see the relationship between the properties, he or she might report the percentage comparisons as in Table 9–1.

TABLE 9-1   Percentage of Voters: College
Graduates and Nongraduates

	Graduates	Nongraduates
Voters	91%	67%
Nonvoters	9%	33%
Total	100%	100%
Sample Size (*N*)	(248)	(1156)

Source: Data from the *1980 Election Study;* access provided by the Inter-
University Consortium for Political and Social Research.

This chapter focuses on ways of reporting data so that the audience can
readily tell whether the hypothesized differences in distributions were actually
present in the sample. Such reporting might involve comparing percentage distributions, as in the example above. However, it might require comparing the
central tendencies of distributions, and it sometimes requires more complex statistical treatment. This chapter will deal with percentage comparisons and comparisons of central tendencies. More complex statistical techniques are often unnecessary when the relationships can be displayed in tables. Treatment of more
complex techniques is deferred until later chapters.

Where there are few (two or three) categories of the dependent variable, it
is always appropriate to report comparisons of percentage distributions. The tables comparing those distributions are called **percentage crosstables.** Where
there are few *Y* categories, the audience should have little trouble understanding
the percentage crosstables resulting from the analysis. Where there are more
than four or five categories of the dependent variable, it is usually clearer to report comparisons of central tendency. This can be done in a table showing the
mean or median value of *Y* for each category of *X*.

COMPARING PERCENTAGE DISTRIBUTIONS

The first step in creating a percentage crosstable is to divide the sample into
groups according to the *X* (independent) value of each unit. In the example
above, the researcher would separate the 248 graduates and the 1156 nongraduates.

The second step is to describe completely the frequency distribution of the
Y (dependent) values for each of the groups. In the example above the graduates
were distributed as follows:

Y value (Category)	Frequency Distribution (Number)
Voters	225
Nonvoters	23
Total	248

The nongraduates were distributed like this:

Y value	Frequency Distribution
Voters	776
Nonvoters	380
Total	1156

The third step in creating the percentage crosstable is to divide the number of each group in each Y category by the total number of units in that group. This changes the frequency distribution into a percentage distribution. For the graduates that would have been as follows:

Category	Frequency Distribution	Total in Group	Percentage
Voters	225	248	91%
Nonvoters	23	248	9%
Total	248		100%

For the nongraduates that would have been as follows:

Category	Frequency	Total in Group	Percentage Distribution
Voters	776	1156	67%
Nonvoters	380	1156	33%
Total	1156		100%

The final step in creating the percentage crosstable is simply to put the percentage distributions next to each other, giving each X group a separate column in the table and each Y category a separate row. The percentage distributions should then always add up to 100% for each column (except for occasional minor errors created by rounding off of the percentages).

In the example above, combining the two percentage distributions produced the first table of this chapter (repeated here for convenience):

TABLE 9–2 Percentage of Voters: College Graduates and Nongraduates

	Graduates	Nongraduates
Voters	91%	67%
Nonvoters	9%	33%
Total	100%	100%
Sample Size (N)	(248)	(1156)

Comparison across the rows shows that 91% of the graduates voted, as opposed to only 67% of the nongraduates. Also, 33% of the nongraduates did not vote, whereas only 9% of the graduates did not vote. This would support the hypothesis.

The crosstable should always show the number (N) of cases in each column (the number the percentages are based on). It may also show the N for each row. Because all of these Ns are generally shown in the margins of the table, they have come to be called **marginals.**

Each table should be accompanied by a discussion of what the researcher thinks the table shows. Tables cannot be assumed to be self-explanatory.

Percentages Rather Than Frequencies

The use of percentages rather than frequencies enables the audience to see the support for the hypothesis clearly despite the differences in the total number of graduates and nongraduates in the sample. As Table 9–3 shows, in this case, a frequency crosstable might have been confusing to some, because fewer graduates than nongraduates were voters.

To tell that the hypothesis is supported, the audience has to do just what you do in changing the frequencies into percentages: compare the number voting with the number in each group.

With very large samples, percentages have an added advantage over frequencies. Percentages never go beyond 100, and therefore they are easier to read and compare than numbers going into the thousands. To maintain that clarity, it is best not to go to more than one decimal place when presenting percentages, rounding off to the nearest percent is usually close enough.

Interpreting the Crosstable

To interpret the crosstable first determine if there are differences in the distribution of the dependent variable for different categories of the independent. In other words, determine if the percentages vary from one column of the table to another in any given row. If there are no differences, there is no support for the hypothesis.

TABLE 9–3 Number of Voters: College Graduates and Nongraduates

	Graduates	Nongraduates
Voters	225	776
Nonvoters	23	380
Sample Size (N)	(248)	(1156)

If differences in the distributions are observed, the second step is to determine if the differences observed are consistent with those hypothesized. If the hypothesis is that college graduates are more likely to vote than nongraduates, then the hypothesis would be supported only if a higher percentage of graduates than nongraduates vote.

If the percentage differences are in the hypothesized direction, then note the size of the differences. The larger the differences, the stronger the support for the hypothesis. For example, if 50% of the college graduates vote while only 49% of the nongraduates vote, the percentage differences would be in the hypothesized direction but the support would be very weak. If 90% of the college graduates vote while 10% of the nongraduates vote, the support would be much stronger.

Percentaging the Wrong Way

The most common mistake that students make in producing percentage crosstables is to base percentages on the total number in each category of the dependent (Y) variable, rather than on the total number in each category of the independent (X) variable. This may result from the student's mixing up the dependent and independent variables. More frequently it occurs when the student first creates a complete frequency crosstable (as we did just above), and then computes each cell frequency as a percentage of the row marginal rather than the column marginal. For this reason, this error is generally called *percentaging the wrong way*.

If the researcher had percentaged the wrong way in the example above, the crosstable would have been as follows:

TABLE 9-4 Percentage of College Graduates:
Voters and Nonvoters

	Graduates	Nongraduates	(N)
Voters	22%	78%	(1004)
Nonvoters	6%	94%	(203)

Since college graduates constituted a lower percentage of the voters than nongraduates, a careless viewer might assume that graduation reduces voting. Of course, the percentage of voters who were college graduates depended very much upon the percentage of all respondents who graduated from college. A comparison of the percentages of voters would tell nothing about the hypothesis unless you had a sample containing the same number of graduates as nongraduates. If the percentages are computed in the correct direction, the distributions can be compared regardless of the percentage of respondents in any particular row or column.

Misunderstanding the Crosstable

The most common mistake that students make in analyzing crosstables is to assume that the distributions must be radically different in order for the hypothesis to be supported. In the sample, the hypothesis was that college graduates are more likely to vote that nongraduates. This did not require that the majority of the college graduates be voters and the majority of the nongraduates be nonvoters. It simply required that a higher percentage of graduates than nongraduates vote.

Hypotheses can be so worded as to require that the majority of each X category be in a different Y category. Such a hypothesis would be "College graduates tend to vote, while nongraduates tend not to vote." Table 9–3 did not show support for that hypothesis.

Consider the hypothesis "The more intense the lobbying effort by an interest group, the more likely that group is perceived to be the major factor in determining a congressman's vote." The researcher could measure the dependent variable by asking congressmen what the major factors were in determining their votes. The independent variable could include three categories: (1) groups that made personal visits to the congressman, (2) groups that wrote letters but did not make personal visits, and (3) groups that made no effort to contact the congressman. If the hypothesis is correct, a higher percentage of groups in category 1 than in category 2 should be listed as major factors. Similarly, a higher percentage of those in group 2 than in group 3 should be listed.

Following the same procedure outlined earlier in this chapter, a researcher testing this hypothesis would begin constructing the percentage crosstable by separating the sample of interest groups by category. He or she would then determine the percentage in each category that were reported to be major factors in determining the votes of congressmen. We can present the results for each category as follows:[1]

	Importance of Group in Determining Vote
For groups that visited personally:	
Major Factor	75%
Not a Major Factor	25%
(*N*)	(48)
For groups that only sent letters:	
Major Factor	19%
Not a Major Factor	81%
(*N*)	(86)
For groups that made no contact:	
Major Factor	5%
Not a Major Factor	95%
(*N*)	(88)

TABLE 9-5 Intensity of Lobbying Effort and Importance of Interest
Group in Determining Vote of Congressmen

		Intensity of Lobbying Effort		
		Personal Contact	*Only Letter*	*No Contact*
Importance of Group	Major Factor	75%	19%	5%
	Not a Major Factor	25%	81%	95%
	(*N*)	(48)	(86)	(88)

The reseacher would then combine the percentage distributions to form a single
crosstable. As before, the crosstable would be set up so that each column shows
the percentage distribution of *Y* for a different category of *X*. Each row would
indicate a different *Y* category. If the *X* and *Y* variables are ordinal, the crosstable is traditionally set up so that the upper-left cell represents the highest value
for each variable; the lower-right cell would then represent the lowest value for
each variable.

For this sample, the finished product would look like Table 9–5.

This percentage crosstable shows support for the hypothesis because
groups that personally contacted congressmen were cited as being a major factor
in the congressmen's voting decision more often than other groups were, and
groups that contacted by letter were cited more often than groups that did not
contact the congressmen at all.

Several *X* Categories and Several *Y* Categories

This analysis is easily expanded to include cases in which both the *X* and *Y*
variables are divided into several categories. This type of analysis is done most
frequently when the hypothesis relates two ordinal variables.

There are two general types of relationships frequently hypothesized between ordinal variables:

1. As *X* increases, *Y* tends to increase (a **positive relationship**).
2. As *X* increases, *Y* tends to decrease (a **negative relationship**).

If the table is set up traditionally, and a positive relationship is substantiated, the
percentages will tend to increase from right to left across the top row, and from
left to right across the bottom row. The highest percentages for the middle rows
should tend to fall on the diagonal running from upper left to lower right. Table
9–6 shows a positive relationship.

A negative relationship would fall along the other diagonal, from upper
right to lower left. Table 9–7 is an example of a negative relationship.

The best general indicator of ordinal relationship is a consistent increase in
percentages in one direction across the top row and in the reverse direction

TABLE 9-6   Positive Relationship

		Independent Variable		
		High	*Medium*	*Low*
Dependent Variable	*High*	75%	50%	10%
	Medium	15%	40%	20%
	Low	10%	10%	70%

across the bottom row. Note that the two variables need not have the same range of values, but the upper-left cell should indicate the highest value for each variable.

TABLE 9-7   Negative Relationship Independent Variable

		6	5	4	3	2	1
	4	10%	15%	20%	30%	50%	70%
Dependent Variable	3	20%	40%	50%	40%	30%	20%
	2	20%	20%	10%	15%	10%	5%
	1	50%	25%	20%	15%	10%	5%

Eliminating Irrelevant Categories
From the Table

We have already considered that some categories of a measure may be usefully ignored in analysis. We noted that in presenting distributions, categories of missing data are often deleted. In most cases these data are not relevant to a description of the distribution. The same is true for bivariate tables. If a category is not relevant to the hypothesis being tested, eliminating it simplifies the table. For example, in testing the hypothesis relating college graduation to likelihood of voting, we eliminated from the analysis individuals who refused to disclose either their educational attainment or whether they had voted. Percentages were based on only those units for which we had meaningful values for both variables.

Missing values are not the only categories that are removed from a table. Often the hypothesis will make specific comparisons involving only some of the categories of the variables. Suppose we hypothesized that among identifiers with the major parties, Catholics are more likely to be Democrats than are Protestants. The measures of religion might also differentiate Jews, others, and those with no religion, but since they are not part of the theoretical population dealt with by the hypothesis, only Protestants and Catholics would be reported in the table. Also, only those identifying with the Republican and Democratic party would be included. In many cases, extraneous units in the table may be misleading. Extraneous rows and columns in Table 9-8 make it difficult to see that among people identifying with the major parties, Catholics are more likely than Protestants to be Democrats.

TABLE 9–8 Party Identification by
Religious Affiliation

		Religion		
		Protestants	*Catholics*	*Jews*
	Democrats	50%	56%	85%
Party	*Independents*	12%	14%	3%
	Republicans	38%	30%	13%
	(*N*)	(870)	(314)	(40)

Source: Data from the *1980 Election Study;* access provided by
Inter-University Consortium for Political and Social Research.

Excluding the irrelevant row and column makes the presentation clearer:

TABLE 9–9 Major Party Identification by
Religious Affiliation: Protestants and
Catholics

		Religion	
		Protestants	*Catholics*
	Democrats	57%	65%
Party	*Republicans*	43%	35%
	(*N*)	(770)	(271)

Advantages and Disadvantages of
Comparing Percentage Distributions

The main advantage of comparing percentage distributions is simplicity. Percentages will be familiar to the audience; this is rarely the case with more complicated statistical techniques. Percentage crosstables are also easy to construct, and they save time and reduce the probability of error in relation to other techniques.

The main disadvantage to using percentage crosstables is that the presentation is clear only if there is a small number of rows and columns. The strength of a relationship or the degree of support for a hypothesis shown in one table often cannot readily be compared with that in another table. A difference of 20% in one table may be less significant than a difference of 10% in another.

COMPARING CENTRAL TENDENCIES OF
DISTRIBUTIONS

Where the dependent (Y) variable has too many categories to permit simple comparison of the whole percentage distribution of Y for each category of X, it is preferable to compare just the central tendencies of the Y distributions. The measure of central tendency for the comparison should be the one that is most appropriate for the dependent variable. In practice, this means comparing either means or medians.

Comparing Medians

Where the dependent variable is ordinal, the researcher should compare the median values of Y for the different categories of X. The hypothesis may specifically call for such a comparison, as in "Females tend to have higher median grades than do males." Alternatively, the hypothesis may specify a comparison, but leave it up to you to determine that a comparison of medians is appropriate: "Females tend to have higher grades than do males."

The procedure for comparing medians is very similar to that for comparing percentages. Again, the first step is to divide the sample into groups according to each unit's value on the independent variable. The second step is also the same, the frequency distribution of Y must be computed for each group. Then, instead of translating the frequencies into percentages, compute the median Y value for each group. Then compare the medians to see if there is support for the hypothesis.

A hypothesis that might best be supported by a comparison of medians is "Nations with relatively homogeneous populations tend to allow their citizens greater civil liberties than nations that have heterogeneous populations." The extent of civil liberties allowed in each nation can be measured by the Gastil/Freedom House Index, an ordinal index ranging from 1 (most liberty) to 7 (least liberty). A crosstable comparing percentage distributions would have seven rows. Such a table would probably be too complicated to convey the findings clearly. A much simpler alternative would be to present the median civil-liberty rating for each type of population. For African nations in 1981 the results were as follows:

TABLE 9–10 Median Civil-Liberties Rating: Homogeneous and Heterogeneous Populations, Africa, 1981

	Type of Population	
	Homogeneous	*Heterogeneous*
Median Civil-Liberties Rating	5	6
(*N*)	(9)	(39)

Source: Raymond Gastil, *Freedom in the World: Political Rights and Civil Liberty, 1982* (Wesport, Conn.: Greenwood Press, 1982), Table 4.

This concisely conveys support for the hypothesis: The homogeneous nations allow more civil liberties than the heterogeneous nations.

When comparing measures of central tendency, always show the number of units on which the indicator of central tendency is based. In the African sample, the table indicates that there were only 9 nations with homogeneous populations and 39 nations with heterogeneous populations.

Comparing Means

Where there is an interval dependent variable, it is possible to compare the mean values of Y for each category of X. The form of the hypotheses and presentation of data is very similar to that for the comparison of medians.

The following hypothesis lends itself to a comparison of means: "In congressional races, the margin of victory for Democrats tends to be greater than the margin of victory for Republicans." If margin of victory is measured in percentage points separating the winner from his or her nearest competitor, the dependent variable has a range from 0 to 100, and it includes fractions as well as whole numbers. A comparison of the full distributions of margin of victory for Republicans and Democrats would require an extremely lengthy crosstable. Reporting only the mean margin of victory for Republicans and Democrats gives a much shorter and clearer presentation:

TABLE 9–11   Mean Margin of Victory by Party:
1980 U.S. House Races in California

	Democratic	Republican
Mean Margin of Victory	32.0%	35.7%
(*N*)	(23)	(20)

Source: Data from Michael Barone and Grant Ujifusa, *Almanac of American Politics: 1982* (Washington: Barone, 1982).

The above results would not support the hypothesis: The Republicans in California had the larger margin of victory in 1980. Note that, as with comparisons of medians, the number of cases that each indicator of central tendency is based on should be reported in the table.

SUMMARY

In this chapter we have discussed methods of presenting data that will clearly indicate whether the relationship observed is similar to the one hypothesized. These methods are appropriate when the independent variable is divided into a smaller number of categories. All of the methods involve comparing the distribution of Y values for the different categories of X. We discussed two principal approaches, comparison of percentage distributions and comparison of the central tendencies of the distributions. Where there are few categories of the dependent variable, the percentage comparison is preferred; where there are many categories, the comparison of central tendencies is necessary.

Endnote

[1]Data from John Kingdon, *Congressmen's Voting Decisions* (New York: Harper & Row, 1973) p. 143.

RESEARCH EXAMPLE

We have now progressed through enough material to consider a simple but fairly complete piece of research. The following is adapted from a published article by one of the authors of this book. (James Dyer, "Do Lawyers Vote Differently? A Study of Voting of No-Fault Insurance" *Journal of Politics,* 38 1976, 450–56.) Take note of the hypothesis, the properties, the measures, the sample, and the way the relationships are presented. Try to evaluate the work as you read it. What might be done to improve it?

DO LAWYERS VOTE DIFFERENTLY?

Explanation

Many lawyer-legislators at the state level are practicing attorneys. They can reasonably expect their business to be adversely affected by the passage of no-fault insurance legislation, for such legislation would reduce the demand for the services of attorneys. Nonlawyer legislators, however, would not have this economic incentive for opposing no-fault legislation. Though the professional literature indicates no differences have been found between lawyers and nonlawyers on other issues,[1] commentaries suggest otherwise on no-fault.[2]

Hypothesis

Therefore, we would expect that in state legislatures, lawyers are more likely to oppose no-fault insurance legislation than are nonlawyers.

Units of Analysis, Theoretical Population, and Sample

The hypothesis encompasses all legislators in all states for all time. Unfortunately, we cannot test all of those comparisons: Some legislators have not made their position clear on the issue because they have not voted on the issue. We also do not have access to information on all legislatures, particularly for all possible votes in the future.

However, if the hypothesis is correct, then in those states for which we do have data and for those legislators who did vote, the proportion of lawyers opposing no-fault should generally be higher than the proportion of nonlawyers opposing it. For purposes of illustration, this note analyzes the voting on two no-fault bills in the California Assembly, and one in the Florida House. [The original research note also includes data from New York and Minnesota—all of the states for which roll-call votes on no-fault were available.]

Properties

For California, brief biographies of the legislators were available. Thus, it was possible to determine which legislators had law degrees. Each of these was considered a lawyer; other legislators were defined as nonlawyers. Such biographies were not available for Florida. In that state, lawyers were identified as those listed in the *Martindale and Hubbell Law Directory* (Summit, N.J.: 1971). All other legislators were considered nonlawyers.

In both states, roll-call votes on no-fault legislation were used to define the percentage of those lawyers and nonlawyers opposed to the legislation. Abstentions were not counted—the percentage computed was the percentage of those taking a position on the issue. The roll call for the 1972 California vote was found in the *Assembly Journal,* May 25, 1972, p. 3974; the 1973 California vote was found in the *Los Angeles Times,* March 16, 1973, Section I, p. 24; and the Florida vote was in the *Journal of the House of Representatives,* June 4, 1971, p. 1177.

Relationship

Table A shows the relationship between the properties for each of the three votes.

In each of these three cases, the data strongly support the hypothesis. Lawyers were more likely to oppose no-fault legislation than were nonlawyers.[3]

TABLE A   Lawyer and Nonlawyer Opposition to No-Fault Legislation

	Percentage of Lawyers Opposed	Percentage of Nonlawyers Opposed
California, 1972	45	21
California, 1973	66	26
Florida, 1972	41	10

In the California House there were 29 lawyers and 38 nonlawyers in 1972. In 1973 that ratio was 29 to 42; in Florida it was 34 to 73.

Conclusion

This analysis indicates that in general, lawyers in state legislatures are less likely to support no-fault proposals that would adversely affect the business of the legal profession than are nonlawyers. It is also clear that the lawyers did not necessarily vote as a bloc against it. But even when the majority of lawyers voted in favor of it, they were less supportive than nonlawyers.

The question is, how important are these differences between lawyers and nonlawyers? Perhaps even more significant than the fact that a relationship was found between lawyers and no-fault voting was that it was not more dramatic. Seldom would there be an issue given more emphasis by the profession, and yet large numbers of lawyers voted contrary to that position.

Clearly, lawyers are a diverse group of people. But the outcomes of several votes would have been substantially different had lawyers not opposed no-fault insurance to the extent they did. Also, as Derge has indicated, lawyers are often in the key positions of leadership within legislative bodies, so the opportunities to influence decisions in a less public way than a record roll-call vote are great. It is suggested that the evidence presented here is only a reflection of other, more private arenas of legislative decision-making, in which lawyers may be expected to play an even more significant role in determining the outcome.

Notes for Dyer Article

[1]David W. Brady, John Schmidhauser, and Larry L. Berg, "House Lawyers and Support for the Supreme Court," *Journal of Politics,* 35 (1973), 724–29. David R. Derge, "The Laywer as Decision-Maker in the American State Legislature," *Journal of Politics,* 21 (1959), 408–33. David R. Derge, "The Lawyer in the Indiana General Assembly," *Midwest Journal of Political Science,* 6 (1962), 19–53. Justin Green, John Schmidhauser, and Larry Berg, "Lawyers in Congress: A New Look at Some Old Assumptions." *Western Political Quarterly,* 26 (1973), 440–52.

[2]For examples of such reports, see Helen Dewar, "Legislature Spins Wheels," *Washington Post,* March 11, 1973, Section D, pp. 1–2; and John Morris, "Inaction by States May Strengthen a New Drive for Federal No-Fault Insurance Law," *New York Times,* October 3, 1972, p. 23.

[3]In the original, tests of statistical significance are presented and a control for party is discussed. These are omitted here since controls and tests of significance will be discussed in the next two chapters. Data for New York are omitted here.

LABORATORY EXERCISES

The purpose of this laboratory is to give you experience in using crosstabulations and comparisons of medians to test bivariate relationships.

Task 1. You are to create the percentage crosstables that you will need in order to test the following hypotheses:

*H*1. Senators from large states tend to get more publicity than do senators from small states.

*H*2. Liberal senators tend to get more publicity than do conservative senators.

Use the data below to test the hypotheses. The data set includes nation-wide newspaper publicity score, size of state, and liberalism for a sample of United States senators for 1975–76. (Publicity scores computed by Eric Veblen: 1 = a positive Z-score, 0 = a negative Z-score; size: 1 = 10 or more electoral votes, 0 = 9 or less votes; liberalism: 1 = liberal (higher ADA scores than ACA scores), 0 = conservative.) Sample includes all senators with a high publicity score except the speaker, the majority leader, and the minority leader, and a systematic sample of 25 percent of all senators with a low publicity score.

Senator	Publicity	State Size	Liberalism
Young (N.D.)	0	0	0
Randolph	0	0	1
Leahy	0	0	1
Huddleston	0	0	1
McClure	0	0	0
Packwood	0	0	1
Scott (Va.)	0	1	0
Stevens	0	0	0
Biden	0	0	1
Beall	0	1	1
Chiles	0	1	0
Case	0	1	1
Byrd (Va.)	0	1	0
Griffin	0	1	0
Cannon	0	0	0
Hollings	0	0	0
Allen	0	0	0
Ribicoff	0	0	1
Mathias	0	1	1
Hart (Mich.)	0	1	1
Javits	1	1	1
Percy	1	1	1
Long	1	1	0
Stevenson	1	1	1
Baker	1	1	0
Buckley	1	1	0
Schweiker	1	1	1
Goldwater	1	0	0
Muskie	1	0	1
Bentsen	1	1	0
McGovern	1	0	1
Proxmire	1	1	1
Bayh	1	1	1
Dole	1	0	0
Mondale	1	1	1
Kennedy	1	1	1
Church	1	0	1
Humphrey	1	1	1
Jackson	1	0	1

a. What is the distribution of publicity scores among senators from large states?

	(*N*)	(%)
High		
Low		
(*N*)	( )	( )

b. What is the distribution of publicity scores among senators from small states?

	(*N*)	(%)
High		
Low		
(*N*)	( )	( )

c. Create the appropriate percentage crosstable:

		State Size	
		Large	*Small*
Publicity	High		
	Low		
	(*N*)	( )	( )

d. Following the same procedure, construct a percentage crosstable to test the second hypothesis.

e. Which of the two hypotheses is more strongly supported? Why?

Task 2. Using data from the House of Representatives, Ninety-fourth Congress, do a comparison of medians to determine if members from the West have higher conservative-coalition scores than members from the South or North.

West		South		North	
Name	*CC Score*	*Name*	*CC Score*	*Name*	*CC Score*
Anderson	28	Andrews	67	Abnor	90
Burgener	91	Boggs	42	Annunzio	29
Corman	8	Broyhill	88	Beard	17
Goldwater	82	Carter	75	Blanchard	15
Howe	36	Derrick	64	Broomfield	71
Lujan	73	Evins	35	Carr	17
McKay	57	Fountain	82	Cohen	50
Moorhead	89	Gude	19	Crane	89
Rousselot	86	Hefner	75	Devine	94
Stark	4	Jarman	83	Du Pont	50
Van Deerlin	23	Kelly	93	Esch	44
Wirth	21	Lott	92	Fithian	40
		Milford	79	Frenzel	61
		Neal	58	Green	3
		Roberts	80	Harkin	21
		Slack	59	Hillis	69
		Steelman	57	Hungate	39
		Thornton	66	Johnson	74
		Whitten	81	Kindness	87
				Madigan	70
				Metcalf	2
				Minish	25
				Mosher	38
				Myers	71
				O'Hara	18
				Pattison	16
				Randall	65
				Roe	26
				Russo	32
				Sharp	36
				Smith	28
				Stokes	4
				Thone	87
				Vigorito	29
				Yatron	40

a. Present the data as a comparison of medians.

b. Present the same data as a percentage comparison.

c. Do the two presentations lead to the same conslusion? If not, why not?

Task 3. Use the computer to analyze data provided by the instructor. Present the percentage crosstable that is appropriate for testing a hypothesis you write that can be tested with the data. Label the table completely and indicate whether or not it supports the hypothesis.

REVIEW QUESTIONS

1. Hypothesis: High school students from large cities tend to have lower SAT scores than students from small cities.

Data

Student	City Size*	SAT Score
A	1	1400
B	1	1400
C	1	1000
D	1	900
E	1	900
F	1	900
G	1	700
H	2	1200
I	2	900
J	2	700
K	2	700

*1 = large; 2 = small.

a. What is the dependent variable?

b. Is the data best reported as (1) a comparison of percentages, (2) a comparison of means, or (3) a comparison of medians?

c. Regardless of whether it is appropriate, construct a percentage crosstable. Label it completely.

d. Regardless of whether it is appropriate, show a comparison of medians. Again, label completely.

e. What do you conclude regarding support for the hypothesis?

2. Hypothesis: Democratic justices tend to favor judicial activism, whereas Republican justices tend to favor judicial self-restraint.

Hypothetical Data

Justice	Party*	Judicial Position[†]
A	9	1
B	1	1
C	1	1
D	1	2
E	2	1
F	2	1
G	2	1
H	2	2
I	2	2

*1 = Democrat; 2 = Republican; 9 = Unknown
[†]1 = favors judicial activism; 2 = favors judicial self-restraint

a. What is the dependent variable?
b. Is the data best reported as (1) a comparison of percentages, (2) a comparison of means, or (3) a comparison of medians?
c. Regardless of whether it is appropriate, construct a percentage crosstable. (Label it completely.)
d. Regardless of whether it is appropriate, show a comparison of medians. (Again, label completely.)
e. What do you conclude regarding support for the hypothesis?

3. Two researchers tested the hypothesis that the longer students study, the higher their grades tend to be. Their results:

		Researcher A Hours of Study				Researcher B Hours of Study		
		10+	5–9	0–4		10+	5–9	0–4
	A	80%	60%	50%	A	70%	33%	0%
Grades	B	10	10	10	B	30	33	50
	C	10	30	40	C	0	33	50
$N =$		10	10	10		10	9	10

a. Which relationship did researcher A find, positive or negative?
b. Which relationship did researcher B find, positive or negative?
c. The stronger relationship was found by which researcher?

CHAPTER TEN

CONTROLLING FOR OTHER VARIABLES

THE EFFECTS OF OTHER VARIABLES

In testing a hypothesis it is never enough to establish that a relationship exists between two variables while ignoring the possible effects of other variables. As we said in the beginning of this text, a hypothesis asserts a *causal* association between properties, and it is impossible to get any evidence on whether an association is causal without holding constant the effects of other variables.

Suppose that Republican senators are more likely than Democratic senators to support development of a weapons system. How do we know whether party pressures had any causal effect on the voting? Republicans may be conservative and ideologically inclined to vote for weapons systems whether or not those systems are supported by the party. Similarly, Democrats may be liberal and ideologically inclined to vote against weapons systems, also regardless of party pressure. How can we tell whether senators are voting their party's position or their own ideology?

To further complicate our analysis, party and ideology are not the properties that may be causing senators to vote for or against the weapons system. Senators may be influenced by the potential economic benefits to their states from passage of the legislation, by campaign contributors who would benefit from the system, by experiences they have had with the military, and so on.

We could be *certain* of whether party pressure was causing senators to vote for or against the weapons system only if senators were identical with respect to all other possible independent variables and differed only in their party affiliation. If all senators had the same ideology, came from states that would benefit equally from passage of the legislation, had the same experiences, and so on, but differed with respect to party, any variation in support for the weapons system would have to be the result of variation in party. But since we are unable to clone senators, giving them identical ideologies, districts, and life experiences, we cannot get a sample of senators who are identical with respect to all properties but the independent and dependent variables. Hence, we can never be certain of whether senators' votes are influenced by their party affiliation.

We can never be absolutely certain that any hypothesis is true. To be certain would require that we find a sample of units that are the same with respect to all properties other than the ones related in a hypothesis. In cases where we cannot manipulate the properties, the best we can do is find subsamples in which the units are similar with respect to at least one important property other than the two related in the hypothesis. If the hypothesis holds in all such subsamples, we can conclude that the association is likely to be causal and the hypothesis is likely to be true.

For example, if we were investigating the hypothesis that Republican senators are more likely to support development of a weapons system than are Democratic senators, we might look at one subsample of senators in which all were liberals, and at another subsample in which all were conservatives. Since all of the senators in each subsample would have the same ideology, any differences we observed in voting behavior within a subsample would have to be the result of variation in something other than ideology. If Republican senators appeared to favor the weapons system only because they tended to be conservatives—and that ideology was what caused them to support the weapons system—then we would not find Republican conservatives any more supportive of weapons systems than conservative Democrats. Similarly, we would find opposition among all liberals. If we found greater opposition among liberal Democrats than among liberal Republicans, then something more than ideology would have to be determining senators' votes.

Note that even if we found for both liberals and conservatives that Republicans were more supportive than Democrats, we still would not have conclusive proof that party was the causal variable. Other possible causal factors have not been ruled out. However, we would have eliminated one alternative explanation for why we found support for the hypothesis: The observed relationship between support for the weapons system and party could not solely be the reflection of ideological differences among senators.

Following the same procedure, we could eliminate other variables as alternative explanations for the hypothesis. We could look at subsamples of senators representing states that would benefit economically from passage of the legislation and subsamples representing states that would not benefit; at subsamples of older and younger senators; at subsamples of former lawyers, businessmen, and other occupational groups; at subsamples of Protestants, Catholics, and Jews. We could eliminate many plausible alternative explanations. Even though we could not eliminate every possible alternative explanation, if the hypothesis were supported in every subsample created from variables that could plausibly be causing the relationship between party and vote, we could be quite confident that senators were swayed by party pressures.

THE USE OF CONTROLS

When we test a hypothesis we observe the hypothesized relationship while holding constant other variables. This procedure is called **controlling** for the variable that we hold constant. In the example above, we would be controlling for ideology. Ideology would be held constant in each subsample because all senators in a subsample would have the same ideology. We could also control for state economic benefits, age, former occupation, religion, and so on. The variables held constant are called the **control variables.**

When we test the hypothesis that Republican senators are more likely to support weapons systems than are Democratic senators, and we control for ideology, then party would be the independent variable, support for the systems would be the dependent variable, and ideology would be the control variable. If we also test the hypothesis that conservative senators are more likely to support weapons systems than are liberal senators, and we control for party, the dependent variable would still be support for the weapons system, but ideology would now be the independent variable and party would be the control variable.

When considering several explanations for variation in a property, we need several hypotheses, each linking a different independent (X) variable to the same dependent (Y) variable. These may be diagramed as follows:

X_1, X_2, and X_3 represent three independent variables and Y the dependent variable. The arrows represent causal links between each of the independent variables and the dependent variable. When testing each hypothesis (for example, $X_1 \to Y$), you should control for each of the other possible independent variables (here, for X_2 and X_3).

Procedures for Controlling for Categorical Variables

This section discusses the general procedures to follow when controlling for variables that have relatively few categories. Other procedures are discussed in Chapter 14.

Controlling involves just two steps. First, divide the whole sample into subsamples so that all of the units in each subsample have the same value on the control variable or variables. Then, test the relationship between the independent and dependent variables for each subsample.

If we are testing the hypothesis that Republicans are more likely to vote for a weapons system than Democrats, and we are controlling for ideology, we first divide the sample of senators into groups according to their ideology. If the categories of ideology are liberal and conservative, we will have just those two subsamples. If there are three categories of ideology (for example, liberal, moderate, conservative), then we will have three subsamples.

After the subsamples are created, we test the relationship between party and support for the weapons system for each subsample. This relationship is best tested by percentage crosstables for each subsample. All crosstables would be la-

TABLE 10–1   Party Affiliation and Support for
the ABM (Whole Sample)

	Republicans	Democrats
For ABM	79%	56%
Against ABM	21%	44%
(N)	(43)	(54)

beled identically, with party as the independent variable and support for the
weapons system as the dependent variable.

The table used to present the relationship for the whole sample is called
the *bivariate table*. The tables presenting the relationship for each of the subsamples are called the *control tables*.

An example taken from actual research may clarify the procedure.[1] In
1970 there was a Senate vote on whether to develop an antiballistic-missile system (ABM). One hypothesis tested by researchers seeking to explain Senate voting on this system was that Republicans are more likely to support development
of a weapons system than are Democrats. The researchers constructed a bivariate table showing the association between party and support for the ABM for all
97 senators in the sample (see Table 10–1).

At this point in the analysis the hypothesis appeared to be supported, but
appearances can be deceiving. Controlling for ideology showed just how decep-
tive. The researchers looked separately at liberal and conservative senators.
There were 49 liberals in the sample; Table 10–2 shows the relationship between
party and support for the ABM for those liberals.

TABLE 10–2   Party Affiliation and Support for
the ABM (Liberals)

	Republicans	Democrats
For ABM	36%	37%
Against ABM	64%	63%
(N)	(11)	(38)

Table 10–3 shows the same relationship for the 48 conservatives.

TABLE 10–3   Party Affiliation and Support for
the ABM (Conservatives)

	Republicans	Democrats
For ABM	97%	100%
Against ABM	3%	0%
(N)	(32)	(16)

Note that in neither subsample were the Republicans more supportive than the
Democrats. Because there was no evidence that differences in party caused sena-

tors with similar ideologies to vote differently, the researchers found no support for the hypothesis.

When we are controlling, the cell frequencies in the control tables sum to equal the frequencies in the corresponding cells of the bivariate table. In the example above, Table 10–1 showed 34 senators in the upper-left cell (Republicans for the ABM); 4 of them appear in the upper-left cell of Table 10–2 (they were the liberals among the 34), and the remaining 30 (the conservatives) are in the upper-left cell of Table 10–3. This relationship holds because the control tables are constructed from subsamples of the original tables. Checking to be sure that the control tables sum to the bivariate table is a useful way of determining if an error has been made. If the sum of the like cells of the control tables does not equal the total in the corresponding cells of the bivariate table, there is an error. (This may not work if there are missing data on the control variable.)

Testing Two or More Hypotheses with the Same Dependent Variable

When testing two or more hypotheses having the same dependent variable, the researcher should test each hypothesis, controlling for all independent variables that are not in the hypothesis being tested. Suppose researchers are testing the following hypotheses:

1. Republican senators are more likely to support the ABM than are Democratic senators.
2. Conservative senators are more likely to support the ABM than are liberal senators.

To test the first hypothesis they would follow the procedures illustrated in Tables 10–1 through 10–3. Party would be the independent variable, support for the ABM would be the dependent variable, and ideology would be the control variable. To test the second hypothesis, they would follow a similar procedure. Support for the ABM would be the dependent variable, but the independent variable would be ideology and the control variable would be party. Table 10–4 shows the relationship between ideology and support for the ABM, controlling for party.

TABLE 10–4 Ideology and Support for the ABM, Controlling for Party

	Republicans		**Democrats**	
	Conservatives	*Liberals*	*Conservatives*	*Liberals*
For ABM	97%	36%	100%	37%
Against ABM	3%	64%	0%	63%
(*N*)	(32)	(11)	(16)	(38)

Regardless of party affiliation, conservatives are more supportive than liberals.

Controlling for Two or More Variables

It is possible to control for two variables at the same time by first dividing the sample into subsamples according to each unit's value on one of the control variables, and then dividing the subsamples into still smaller groups according to each unit's value on the second control variable. For each additional control variable, the sample is further subdivided in the same fashion. This can be continued as long as the subgroups created are large enough to provide meaningful comparisons. The relationship between X and Y must be reported for every subgroup created.

In the example above, the researchers wanted to control the relationship between party and support for the ABM for both ideology and potential economic benefits accruing to each state from adoption of the ABM program. They controlled for both variables simultaneously by dividing both conservative and liberal senators into groups depending upon whether they represented states that would benefit from the program or states that would not benefit. That created four subsamples: conservatives representing states that would benefit, conservatives representing states that would not benefit, liberals representing states that would benefit, and liberals representing states that would not benefit. Four control tables were created, each showing the relationship between party and support for the ABM for a different subsample (see Table 10–5).

Support was found for the hypothesis only among liberal senators representing states that would not benefit from passage of the ABM. But support is suspect even for that group because the difference is small and the Republican percentage is based on such a small sample.

Controls and Sample Size

In Chapter 3 we observed that the complexity of the analysis influences the size of the sample needed. This is quite clear in the case of controls. Requiring

TABLE 10–5   Party Affiliation and Support for the ABM, Controlling for Ideology and State Economic Benefits

| | CONSERVATIVES | | | |
| | State Would Benefit | | State Would Not Benefit | |
	Republican	Democrat	Republican	Democrat
For ABM	100%	100%	96%	100%
Against ABM	0%	0%	4%	0%
(N)	(9)	(5)	(23)	(11)

| | LIBERALS | | | |
| | State Would Benefit | | State Would Not Benefit | |
	Republican	Democrat	Republican	Democrat
For ABM	17%	45%	60%	33%
Against ABM	83%	55%	40%	67%
(N)	(6)	(11)	(5)	(27)

TABLE 10–6 Party Affiliation and Support for the ABM, Controlling for State Economic Benefits

	State Would Benefit		State Would Not Benefit	
	Republican	*Democrat*	*Republican*	*Democrat*
For ABM	67%	63%	89%	53%
Against ABM	33%	37%	11%	47%
(*N*)	(15)	(16)	(28)	(38)

that the sample be broken into subgroups on the basis of the categories of the control variable reduces the size of the groups evaluated.

To reduce the number of control tables, the researcher can reduce the number of categories for each of the control variables to as few as are needed to maintain the validity of those measures. For example, ordinal variables having several categories can often be recoded into just high and low categories.

If the sample size is still too small to allow us to draw meaningful conclusions after the number of control tables has been minimized, the researcher will have to control for each variable separately rather than controlling for all simultaneously. Because the sample size was small in the example above, the researchers might well have controlled for the two variables separately. They would have controlled for ideology as before (Tables 10–2 and 10–3). Then, instead of controlling simultaneously for both ideology and state benefits, they would have ignored the ideologies of the senators and controlled just for state economic benefits (Table 10–6).

These results show that the hypothesis is much more strongly supported by those senators representing states that would not receive economic benefits from passage. Note that controlling for each variable separately is not a completely satisfactory test of the effects of the control variables. Without controlling simultaneously for both ideology and state economic benefits, we cannot know whether the relationship observed among senators from states that would not benefit was due to ideology.

When the sample size permits, test each hypothesis by controlling simultaneously for all relevant independent variables not in the hypothesis. When the sample size is too small for simultaneous controlling, controlling separately for each of the other independent variables provides a limited test of the effects of the controls.

INTERPRETING THE RESULTS

After the bivariate and control tables have been produced, we can determine if the hypothesis is supported. Notice that the control tables, and not the bivariate table, determine the support for the hypothesis. Often, in fact, researchers present only the control tables in demonstrating support for the hypothesis. Control tables can demonstrate that a hypothesis is likely to be true under all conditions, unlikely to be true under any conditions, or likely to be true only under certain conditions.

Unconditional Support for the Hypothesis

Interpretation of the results of controlling is most straightforward when all control tables show support for the hypothesis. In that case, the researcher can claim that the hypothesis is supported for the sample studied.

In the study of voting on the ABM, the researchers found support in all subsamples for the hypothesis that conservatives are more likely than liberals to support a weapons system (see Table 10–7).

TABLE 10–7 Ideology and Support for the ABM, Controlling for Party and State Economic Benefits

| | REPUBLICANS | | | |
| | State Would Benefit | | State Would Not Benefit | |
	Conservative	*Liberal*	*Conservative*	*Liberal*
For ABM	100%	17%	96%	60%
Against ABM	0%	83%	4%	40%
(*N*)	(9)	(6)	(23)	(5)

| | DEMOCRATS | | | |
| | State Would Benefit | | State Would Not Benefit | |
	Conservative	*Liberal*	*Conservative*	*Liberal*
For ABM	100%	45%	100%	33%
Against ABM	0%	55%	0%	67%
(*N*)	(5)	(11)	(11)	(27)

The researchers may have failed to control for some other variable that would change the findings, but as far as they were able to determine, the hypothesis was supported for this 1970 vote on developing the ABM system. There probably was a causal association between ideology and support for the weapons system.

No Support in Bivariate Table. It is possible to find support for a hypothesis in all subsamples even when no support is evident for the sample as a whole. An example of this from actual research is presented at the end of this chapter. Even when the reverse of the hypothesis seems to hold for the bivariate table, controlling for other possible independent variables may indicate that the hypothesis is supported.

The hypothesized association can be found in the control tables and not in the bivariate table when the control variable has such a strong effect on both the independent and dependent variables that it obscures the hypothesized relationship. When that variable is controlled, its impact on the other two variables disappears and the hypothesized relationship becomes visible. If the variables are ordinal or interval, the relationships among the three variables can be diagramed thus:

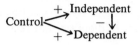

If this were the relationship, an increase in the value of the control variable would cause an increase in the value of both the independent and dependent variables, making it appear that those two variables were positively related. The negative relationship that actually exists might not be strong enough to be seen until the control variable is held constant.

No Support for the Hypothesis

When none of the control tables show support for the hypothesis, and especially if the researcher has controlled for several variables, it is unlikely that there is a causal association between the the independent and dependent variables. The bivariate table may show support for the hypothesis, but if that support is not evident in any control table, the association between the independent and dependent variables is probably not causal, but spurious.

Spurious Association. A **spurious association** is one in which two properties are associated because variation in a third property causes each of the first two properties to vary simultaneously. The association between party and support for the ABM, seen in the bivariate table (Table 10–1) may be spurious. If conservatives are more likely to support the development of weapons systems than are liberals, and if conservatives are also more likely to become Republicans than are liberals, then Republicans will appear to be more supportive of weapons systems than Democrats, even if party officials, members, or contributors have no influence at all on the way senators vote. We can diagram such a situation:

Ideology ⟶ Party Affiliation
⟶ Support for ABM

The dotted line indicates that an association between party and support will appear in the bivariate table but will disappear when ideology is controlled. In contrast, the arrows indicate that the associations between ideology and each of the other variables do not disappear when the third variable is controlled.

Indirect Association. Unfortunately, the disappearance of a bivariate association after a control is used does not always indicate that the bivariate association was spurious. The disappearance could instead indicate an *indirect association*—a causal association in which variation in the independent variable causes variation in an intervening variable, which in turn causes variation in the dependent variable. For example, if variation in party caused variation in ideology, which in turn caused variation in support for the ABM, then party would be an indirect cause of variation in support. This might be the case if senators who joined the Republican party tended to become more conservative than those who joined the Democratic party. We could diagram that relationship:

Party→Ideology→Support for ABM

If this were the case, the hypothesis would be correct but we would find no support for it in the control tables. Once ideology was controlled, any variation that party caused in support would disappear, and any association between party and support would disappear with it.

Distinguishing Spurious From Indirect Association. There is no way to distinguish spurious from indirect association just by looking at the tables. You must determine whether the control variable can reasonably be expected to be an intervening variable between the independent and dependent variables. If senators develop their ideologies before they join a party, for example, and those ideologies change little over time, then ideology cannot be an intervening variable between party and support for the ABM.

If an association evident in the bivariate table disappears when we control for what is clearly not an intervening variable, then the association is spurious and the hypothesis is not supported. If the association disappears when we control for a variable or variables that may be intervening, then the association may be indirect and the hypothesis may be correct.

Conditional Support for the Hypothesis

One Control Variable or Simultaneous Controls. When there is only one control variable, or when controls are used simultaneously, interpreting the results is fairly easy. If only some of the subsamples show support for the hypothesis, it is likely that a causal association exists only for that part of the theoretical population where the support is evident. For example, if you were controlling for age and support for the hypothesis was evident only among those over 65, you would conclude that the hypothesis was supported only for those over 65.

Occasionally support will be much more dramatic in one control table than in another. For example, Table 10–6 showed strong support for the hypothesis linking party and ABM support for senators from states that would not benefit from passage of the bill; there was virtually no support for the hypothesis among senators representing states that would benefit from passage. Where support varies dramatically from one control table to the next, it is proper to conclude that the independent variable seems to have the most impact on the dependent variable in that part of the theoretical population where support is the greatest. In our example, the control tables showed that party had more impact on support for the ABM in those states that would not benefit economically than in those states that would benefit.

Controls Used Separately. Interpretation is not as straightforward when several controls are used separately. Suppose one control shows no support for any subsample, another shows support for some subsamples, and still another shows support in all subsamples. What are you to conclude?

You should begin with the control variable where the least support for the hypothesis is shown. If after you control for one of the variables there is no support in any control table, any apparent association is probably spurious or indirect. If reason leads you to believe that the association is spurious, you should conclude that there is no support for the hypothesis, regardless of what the control tables show when you control for any other variable. If you decide that the association is indirect, go on and consider the control variable that shows the next lowest degree of support for the hypothesis. If that control variable shows support only for part of the theoretical population, then that is all the support you should claim.

In our example, when using the controls separately the researchers found no support for the hypothesis linking party and ABM support when controlling for ideology. They found some support when controlling for state economic benefits. Since they reasoned that the control for ideology disclosed a spurious relationship between party and ABM support, they were justified in concluding that the hypothesis was not supported.

When controls are applied separately, the general procedure should be to claim no more support for the hypothesis than is justified by the least supportive control variable. You may overlook some special conditions under which the hypothesis holds, but you will avoid the more serious error of claiming support for a hypothesis in instances where it does not hold.

Interpretation may be difficult when control variables are applied one at a time but because of sample size it is not possible to control for all variables simultaneously. In such cases check to see if you can apply two (but not all) controls simultaneously. The use of the two simultaneous controls may clarify the interpretation.

What Variables Should Be Used As Controls?

Select for controls variables that might plausibly cause variation in the dependent variable. It is particularly important to use as controls variables that might also cause variation in the independent variable. Variables that cause variation in both the independent and dependent variables may lead us to incorrect conclusions when we analyze bivariate tables. Observed relationships in the bivariate table may be spurious, or causal associations may be hidden by the effects of the control variables only when the control variables are associated with both the independent and dependent variables. Any control variable, whether or not associated with the independent or dependent variables, can indicate that there is conditional support for the hypothesis.

It should be noted that the dependent variable itself can never be used as a control. Obviously it makes no sense to observe a relationship, say, between gender and income and control for income. Income would always explain all of income.

COMPARISONS OF CENTRAL TENDENCY

The examples in this chapter have all used percentage crosstables to present relationships. However, the use of controls does not restrict the research to percentage comparisons. If comparisons of central tendency are appropriate in reporting the bivariate relationship between the independent and dependent variables, then they are also appropriate for reporting the relationship for each subsample when a control variable is used.

Suppose a researcher hypothesizes that among municipal bonds, general-obligation bonds tend to have higher ratings than do revenue bonds. If the dependent variable is measured by reference to *Standard and Poor's* ratings of municipal bonds (from D to AAA), then a comparison of medians would be the most appropriate way to present the bivariate relationship. A sample of bonds rated in October 1981 gives the following bivariate relationship:

TABLE 10-8 Median Bond Ratings by Type (Whole Sample)

	General Obligation	Revenue
Median Rating	A+	A
(*N*)	(38)	(77)

To control for the region of the country in which the bonds are issued, the sunbelt or the frostbelt, the researcher divides the sample of bonds into subsamples by region and then computes the median ratings for general obligation and revenue bonds within each subsample (Table 10-9).

TABLE 10-9 Median Bond Ratings by Type, Controlling for Region

	Sunbelt		Frostbelt	
	General Obligation	*Revenue*	*General Obligation*	*Revenue*
Median Rating	A+	A	A+	A
(*N*)	(15)	(36)	(23)	(41)

SUMMARY

Controlling for other variables may help substantiate your explanation by (1) eliminating alternative explanations in those cases where the subsamples show that the control variables do not affect an association found for the whole sample; and (2) disclosing associations in those cases where strong relationships between the X variable and the control variables have hidden or reversed the true $X-Y$ association for the whole sample. Control variables may also undermine support for an explanation by washing out an apparent relationship or by showing it to be spurious rather than causal. *You can never prove conclusively that variation in the independent property causes variation in the dependent property.* Only if you could control every other conceivable variable could you determine that variation in murder rate was caused solely by variation in the law on capital punishment. Of course, you can never control all of the other variables, so you can never be certain of causation. The best you can do is eliminate the most likely alternative explanations; this will make your explanation more convincing. Even if you cannot conclusively prove causation, you may be able to prove it beyond a reasonable doubt.

Controlling for other variables may uncover conditions under which your explanation is especially strongly or weakly corroborated. It may demonstrate that it does not hold at all for some of the population, even though it does for the rest. These conditioning effects may be true even if the control variable is not related to the other variables in any consistent manner.

Endnote

[1] Robert Bernstein and William Anthony, "The ABM Issue in the Senate, 1968–1970: The Importance of Ideology," *American Political Science Review,* 68, no. 3 (September 1974), 1198–1206.

RESEARCH EXAMPLE

This is a slightly modified version of a published article by one of the authors of this text (From *Western Political Quarterly,* 28, no. 4 [1975], 733–36. Reprinted with permission of the University of Utah.) It is a good example of the importance of controls because it shows how the uncontrolled relationship can be very misleading.

RACE, CLASS AND SUPPORT FOR FEMALE CANDIDATES

Robert A. Bernstein and Jayne D. Polly

Where will female candidates run well? Will their appeals meet readier acceptance in middle- and upper-class districts than in lower-class districts; in black districts than in white districts? What are the effects of race and class on support for female candidates? Bringing electoral data to bear on this question is particularly difficult because of the necessity for distinguishing support for female candidates from such other variables as support for incumbents, special issues, ethnic groups, and so on. A particularly favorable test case for examining empirical relationships did develop in the April 1, 1969 city council race in Dallas, Texas. In that contest it seemed possible to isolate support for female candidates in a relative way and to investigate the influence of race and class on that support.

The Election

Two males and two females competed for the at-large position on the city council. None had ever served as a council member previously. It was anticipated that any ethnic vote gained from sympathy with a minority group candidate would not be a determining factor in this election, because one male and one female candidate were Mexican-American.

Sex was raised as an issue in the campaign by Mrs. Anita Martinez. She said that ". . . a woman's sensitivity to 'people problems' will provide sound balance to the facts-and-figures abilities of our gentlemen representatives."[1]

None of the candidates appeared to make a special effort to gain the support of a particular class or race. The two women were sponsored by conflicting civic associations, and they primarily debated leadership, city planning, and zoning issues. The male independent argued for more council responsiveness and for upgrading the police force. The other male candidate was backed by the American Party and was therefore not particularly attractive to many blacks.[2]

Studying a single election, we cannot entirely control for personality, incumbency, ethnic group appeal, or for issues that might influence class or racial groups differently. It is our hope that in this city election, the circumstances were such that none of these factors significantly influenced any class or race to vote for candidates of either sex.

The Variables

At the time of this election, there were 195 voting precincts in the city. In order to ascertain support for female candidates, the number and percentage of persons voting for the female candidates in each precinct in the city were calculated.[3] Precinct boundaries were compared to census tracts (the percentage of blacks in each census tract first having been established) to determine which precincts were heavily populated by white persons and which were heavily populated by black persons. Any precinct in which at least 75% of the residents were black was designated a "black precinct," and any precinct in which at least 75% of the residents were white was designated a "white precinct." All precincts in which the population was racially mixed so that neither whites nor blacks constituted 75% of the residents were omitted from the anlaysis. Only 16 to 195 precincts were omitted by this measure.[4]

We also designated those precincts in which the average value of owner-occupied homes exceeded $15,000 as "middle- and upper-class precincts," and those in which the average value was less than $15,000 as "lower-class precincts." Eighteen white precincts, which included two or more census tracts, indicative of conflicting class designations, were also omitted from the analysis.[5] The omission of these precincts brought the total number of precincts eliminated to 34, or 17% of all precincts. The 161 precincts that were sufficiently homogeneous for us to analyze included 84% of all those who voted.

Results

Table A indicates the percentage supporting the female candidates for each of the groups we are concerned with.

TABLE A Race, Class and Support for Female Candidates[6]

Precinct Characteristics	Number of Votes Cast	Percent Voting for Two Female Candidates
Black Middle and Upper Class	792	73.5
White Middle and Upper Class	26,424	72.1
Black Lower Class	3,413	61.8
White Lower Class	5,347	56.7

Regardless of race, lower-class districts show significantly less support for female candidates than do middle- and upper-class districts. Black districts show somewhat greater support for female candidates than do white districts, but the difference is not significant in the middle- and upper-class districts. It is significant in the lower-class districts.

A Methodological Point

Because class is so strongly related to *both* support for female candidates and race, it was necessary to control for class before the casual relationship between race and support could be clearly observed. It is particularly instructive methodologically to note that if we had not controlled for class, the relationship between race and support would have been as follows:

TABLE B Race and Support for Female Candidates Without a Control for Class

Precinct Characteristic	Number of Votes Cast	Percent for Females
Black	4,205	64.0
White	31,771	69.5

Because the uncontrolled table would have confounded race and class, we might mistakenly have concluded that whites were more likely than blacks to support female candidates. Using a control variable kept us from an erroneous conclusion.

Class and Support

In their book *Class Differences and Sex Roles in American Kinship and Family Structure,* Schneider and Smith contend that sex-role distinctions are much more important norms for the lower class than for the middle and upper classes.[7] While there is a great deal of empirical evidence that ". . . it is common for the young child to acquire the assumption that 'politics is the man's business' . . . ,"[8] this is probably more common for lower-class children than middle- and upper-class children. This kind of early socialization may lead many lower-class voters to reject female candidates simply because they are female; among middle- and upper-class voters, the tendency may be to accept or reject candidates on other grounds.

Race and Support

Warren TenHouten, in a study of nearly 100 families in Los Angeles, found that among nuclear families, lower-class white families were more husband-dominated than lower-class black families; but he found very little difference in husband domination between middle- and upper-class black and middle- and upper-class white families.[9] It is probable that voters who are raised in a male-dominated household will expect male domination in politics, while those raised in more egalitarian households will be more willing to accept either male or female political leaders.

Additionally, there were a number of families in Dallas which had female heads of the household. It seems likely that these families would be especially receptive to female political leadership. Further, children raised in these relatively matriarchal families will likely look to females for political guidance, just as children raised in relatively patriarchal families tend to look to males for political leadership. While exact figures could not be obtained, in the middle- and upper-class districts, the percentage of black households with a female head was only slightly higher than that for white households (roughly 13% as compared to 9%). In the lower-class districts, the corresponding difference was about 36% to 40% as opposed to 13%.[10]

Conclusions and Suggestions

Unless we see marked changes in family structure and socialization, this analysis suggests that female candidates can expect a readier acceptance among middle- and upper-class voters than among lower-class voters; and especially within the lower class, a readier acceptance among black voters than among white voters.

In order to take advantage of special circumstances, the study was restricted to a specific election in Dallas. However, these conclusions tie in well with the limited conceptual and empirical work already done. And the special circumstances which increased the internal validity of this research design did nothing to lower its external validity. Hence, we expect this relationship to hold generally.

Further research is necessary to ascertain strength and general applicability of these relationships. However, controlling for possible alternative explanations such as issues, incumbency, ethnicity, and personality will continue to pose problems. It seems likely that large-scale comparative survey research will be necessary for a complete test of the hypotheses.

Notes for Bernstein and Polly Article

[1]Information for this and for the rest of this section was gathered from the *Dallas Morning News*, March 26–April 1, 1969.

[2]Yet the American Party candidate did receive 16.55% of the vote in the black districts, as opposed to just 16.70% of the vote in the white districts.

[3]While there would be some advantage to a survey rather than aggregate analysis, it is clearly impossible to do that now for a 1969 city council race. Yet circumstances present at that time, and unlikely to be duplicated elsewhere, make this a particularly desirable race to analyze. Therefore, we proceeded with the aggregate analysis, making every effort to use homogeneous precincts so problems relating to the "ecological fallacy" would be as limited as possible.

[4]In fact, this may understate the degree of homogeneity, for over 63% of the black precincts were more than 90% black.

[5]It was impossible to tell exactly how homogeneous each precinct was with regard to class, but, as noted, any precinct overlapping census tracts that were adjacent but not homogeneous enough to fall into the same class category was eliminated.

[6]Chi square analysis of the appropriate frequencies shows class differences in support to be significant at the .001 level. Racial differences in support among the lower class are also significant at the .001 level. Racial differences in support among the middle class are not significant.

[7]David M. Schneider and Raymond T. Smith, *Class Differences and Sex Roles in American Kinship and Family Structure* (Englewood Cliffs, N.J.: Prentice-Hall, 1973), p. 106.

[8]Fred I. Greenstein, *Children and Politics* (New Haven: Yale University Press, 1965), p. 119.

[9]Warren TenHouten, "The Black Family: Myth and Reality," *Psychiatry*, 33 (1970), 164.

[10]U.S. Bureau of the Census, *1970 Census of Population: General Population Characteristics, Texas* (Washington, D.C.: Government Printing Office, 1972), Table 25.

LABORATORY EXERCISES

The purpose of this laboratory is to provide you with experience in using data to test relationships while controlling for other variables.

Task 1. Use the hypothetical data below to test the following hypotheses:

*H*1. The more education individuals have, the less likely they are to favor increases in welfare spending.

*H*2. The more frequently individuals attend church, the more likely they are to favor increases in welfare spending.

Data

	Level of Education*	Welfare Spending†	Church Attendance‡
Smith	3	2	1
Jones	3	2	1
Davis	3	2	1
Kay	3	2	1
Hofman	3	2	2
Balicek	3	1	3
Coombs	3	1	2
Curtis	3	1	1
Richardson	3	1	1
Ford	3	1	2
Nye	2	2	1
Olsen	2	2	1
Mackland	2	2	1
Frey	2	2	1
McDonald	2	2	1
Bailey	2	2	2
Daniels	2	2	2
Wilson	2	2	3
Meyer	2	1	3
Albertson	2	1	3
Black	2	1	2
Duncan	2	1	2
Allison	2	1	1
Hobbs	2	1	3
Brown	2	1	3
Thompson	2	1	3
Reeves	1	2	2
McCoy	1	2	2
Douglas	1	2	1
Cleaver	1	2	3
James	1	2	3
Cannon	1	1	3
Gates	1	1	3
Michaels	1	1	3
Matthews	1	1	3
Johnson	1	1	2

*Education: 3 = completed college; 2 = completed high school but not college; 1 = did not complete high school.

†Welfare spending: 2 = favors increase in welfare spending; 1 = does not favor increase in welfare spending.

‡Church attendance: 3 = regularly; 2 = occasionally; 1 = very rarely.

a. Create a table showing the bivariate relationship appropriate for testing hypothesis H1.
b. Control for the frequency of church attendance. Create the appropriate control tables.
c. Is hypothesis H1 supported by the data? Why?
d. Create a table showing the bivariate relationship appropriate for testing hypothesis H2.
e. Control for education level. Create the appropriate control tables.
f. Is hypothesis H2 supported by the data? Why?
g. Create a table showing the bivariate relationship between education (treated as the independent variable) and church attendance.
h. Control for opinion on welfare spending. Create appropriate control tables.
i. Describe the relationship between education and church attendance.
j. Diagram the relationships among these variables as disclosed by the control tables.
k. Based on the analysis, explain why the first bivariate table showed no association between education and opinion on welfare spending.

Task 2. Use the computer to analyze data provided by your instructor. Create a bivariate table testing a hypothesis of your choice; then control for an appropriate third variable.

REVIEW QUESTIONS

1. Use the following information to respond to questions a–f.
   Hypothesis H1: The higher the tax rate in a state, the more likely businesses are to move out of the state.
   Hypothesis H2: The higher the crime rate in a state, the more likely businesses are to move out of the state.

Hypothetical Data

State	Tax Rate*	Crime Rate†	Percentage of Businesses Moving Out‡
Alabama	1	1	1
Arizona	1	1	1
South Carolina	1	1	2
South Dakota	1	1	2
Louisiana	1	2	1
Tennessee	1	2	1
Wyoming	1	2	1
Washington	1	2	1
Arkansas	1	2	2
Missouri	1	2	2

Hypothetical Data (*Continued*)

State	Tax Rate*	Crime Rate[†]	Percentage of Businesses Moving Out[‡]
Texas	1	3	1
Maine	2	1	1
New Hampshire	2	1	2
Vermont	2	1	2
Virginia	2	2	1
Indiana	2	2	2
California	2	3	1
Florida	2	3	1
Connecticut	2	3	1
Delaware	2	3	1
Rhode Island	2	3	1
Colorado	2	3	1
Georgia	2	3	1
New York	2	3	2

*Tax rate: 1 = low; 2 = high.
[†]Crime rate: 1 = low; 2 = medium; 3 = high.
[‡]Business movement out of state: 1 = low; 2 = high.

    a. Construct a bivariate table appropriate for testing hypothesis H1. Label it completely.
    b. Control for the crime rate. Present the appropriate tables below; label completely.
    c. Based on the analysis, is hypothesis H1 supported?
    d. What is the effect of the control variable on the hypothesized relationship?
    f. Construct a bivariate table appropriate for testing hypothesis H2. Label completely.
    g. Control for tax rate. Present the appropriate tables below; label completely.
    h. Based on the data, is hypothesis H2 supported?
    i. What is the effect of the control on the hypothesized relationship?

2. Use the following hypotheses and hypothetical data to respond to questions a–e.

Hypothesis H1: The more progressive the income-tax structure of a nation, the lower its savings rate is likely to be.

Hypothesis H2: The more unequal the distribution of wealth in a nation, the higher its savings rate is likely to be.

Hypothesis H3: The shorter the life expectancy in a nation, the lower its savings rate is likely to be.

(Savings rate is measured by percentage of disposable personal income not spent on consumption.)

Findings for Hypothesis H1

	Tax Structure	
	More Progressive	*Less Progressive*
Mean Savings Rate	5	15
(*N*)	(20)	(30)

Controlling for Distribution of Wealth

	WEALTH			
	More Unequal		More Equal	
	More Prog. Taxes	*Less Prog. Taxes*	*More Prog. Taxes*	*Less Prog. Taxes*
Mean Savings Rate (*N*)	12	12	8	8
	(15)	(10)	(5)	(20)

Controlling for Life Expectancy

	LIFE EXPECTANCY			
	Shorter		Longer	
	More Prog. Taxes	*Less Prog. Taxes*	*More Prog. Taxes*	*Less Prog. Taxes*
Mean Savings Rate (*N*)	5	5	5	17
	(5)	(25)	(20)	(5)

    a. Do these findings show support for hypothesis H1?
    b. What was the effect of controlling for distribution of wealth?
    c. What was the effect of controlling for life expectancy?
    d. Is the distribution of wealth strongly and consistently related to the savings rate, regardless of the type of tax structure?
    e. Is life expectancy strongly and consistently related to the savings rate, regardless of the type of tax structure?

3. Assume that (a) there is no causal relationship between X and Y; (b) there is a positive association between Z and X; (c) there is a negative association between Z and Y. When X increases, Y will appear to _____.

CHAPTER ELEVEN

CHANCE AND TESTS OF SIGNIFICANCE

Even after appropriate controls have been used we sometimes find apparent associations that may be the result of chance (luck). Since all units do not appear in the sample, it is possible for units with properties indicating association to appear in the sample even though the units in the theoretical population would not show such an association. By chance the researcher may have selected a sample that shows the hypothesized association.

In this chapter we will show how to avoid taking chance relationships seriously. We do this by applying a test to the association discovered that enables us to say something like "In only 5 cases out of 100 would two variables unrelated in the theoretical population show an association as strong as the one found in the sample." Notice that we cannot be absolutely certain that the variables are not related by chance. We can only say that the odds are very small—for example, less than 5%—that we are taking a chance relationship seriously.

THE EFFECT OF CHANCE

Let us look at an example to see how chance can cause a researcher to draw the wrong conclusions. Suppose we have a class of six male students and six female students. A researcher selects a sample of half of the males and half of the females to test the hypothesis that females have a higher median grade than males. Let us suppose that in fact the medians of the males and females are the same. The data on the population are as follows:

Males		Females	
Identification #	*Grade*	*Identification #*	*Grade*
1	A	1	A
2	B	2	B
3	C	3	C
4	C	4	C
5	D	5	D
6	F	6	F

Given (1) that the two groups have identical grades, each with a median of C, and (2) that the researcher's sample includes half of each group, you might expect the sample medians for males and females to be equal. In fact, there is less than a 50% chance that they will be equal, and there is a 28% chance that the researcher will be able to substantiate his hypothesis. Let's see why that is so.

The Possible Samples

Using the identification numbers in the data above, let us identify all the possible samples of three males that could have been drawn. There are 20 possible combinations:

1,2,3	1,3,4	1,5,6	2,4,6
1,2,4	1,3,5	2,3,4	2,5,6
1,2,5	1,3,6	2,3,5	3,4,5
1,2,6	1,4,5	2,3,6	3,4,6
	1,4,6	2,4,5	3,5,6
			4,5,6

Since the samples were to be selected by chance, each of these combinations was equally likely to be chosen.[1] This is like saying that heads and tails have an equal chance of coming up when you throw a coin.

The researcher was to select the three females in the same way, and thus the possible combinations for the females and the probability of each combination being selected is exactly the same as for the males.

Sampling Distribution for the Median

We can now establish a **sampling distribution** for the median for each group. A sampling distribution is a probability distribution of all possible values of a descriptive statistic that occur in all the unique samples of a specific size from a specified population. In the example, it indicates what the likelihood is of drawing a sample of males (or females) with a median of A, B, C, D, and F. To find the sampling distribution we simply take all the possible combinations we could get in a sample and find the median grade for each combination. The number of times each median grade occurs tells us how likely it is that a sample with that median will be drawn. The possible combinations and the medians are as follows:

Combination	Values	Median
a. 1, 2, 3	A, B, C	B
b. 1, 2, 4	A, B, C	B
c. 1, 2, 5	A, B, D	B
d. 1, 2, 6	A, B, F	B
e. 1, 3, 4	A, C, C	C
f. 1, 3, 5	A, C, D	C

Combination	Values	Median
g. 1, 3, 6	A, C, F	C
h. 1, 4, 5	A, C, D	C
i. 1, 4, 6	A, C, F	C
j. 1, 5, 6	A, D, F	D
k. 2, 3, 4	B, C, C	C
l. 2, 3, 5	B, C, D	C
m. 2, 3, 6	B, C, F	C
n. 2, 4, 5	B, C, D	C
o. 2, 4, 6	B, C, F	C
p. 2, 5, 6	B, D, F	D
q. 3, 4, 5	C, C, D	C
r. 3, 4, 6	C, C, F	C
s. 3, 5, 6	C, D, F	D
t. 4, 5, 6	C, D, F	D

We find that there are no medians of A or F, 4 medians of B, 4 of D, and 12 of C. When stating probabilities, we usually use a decimal fraction to represent the likelihood of an occurrence. There were 20 possible combinations, and 4 of them resulted in a median of B. Thus, the probability of getting a median of B is .2 (4 out of 20, or 4 divided by 20). The entire sampling distribution for our example would be as follows:

Median	Probability
B	.2 (4 out of 20)
C	.6 (12 out of 20)
D	.2 (4 out of 20)

What this means is that if we were to draw 10 random samples of three from our six male (or female) students, we would expect two of the sample to have a median of B, six to have a median of C, and two to have a median of D. Thus, estimating the median for either sex, based on a sample of three, would be correct only 60% of the time.

Sampling Distribution for the Difference Between Medians

Our problem was to determine the likelihood that we would reach the correct conclusion about the hypothesis. In other words, we wanted to be able to say that the hypothesis that women have a higher median grade than men is false. Using the probability for finding particular medians for each group, males and females, we can determine what the probability of finding a difference between the medians is.

We can see that if among the 20 possible combinations for our example the researcher happened to pick combination *g* for the males, which happens to have a median of C, and combination *m* for the females, which also happens to have a median of C, the difference would happen to be correct. We would draw the correct conclusion that there was no difference between the medians. But you can see that many of the combinations would lead to an incorrect conclusion about the difference between medians. Suppose the researcher had picked combination *t* for the males and the combination *a* for the females. He would have found a median of B for the females and D for the males and concluded, quite incorrectly, that the hypothesis was supported.

What we want to do is judge the total likelihood that the sample of three males and three females from a population of six of each will mislead the researcher. There were 12 chances in 20 (a 60%, or .6, probability) that he would select a female combination with a median grade of C. If this had happened, there was a 20%, or .2, probability that the females would have had a higher median than the males (4 out of 20 male combinations had a median of D). The combined probability of those two things happening together was $(.6) \times (.2) =$ .12. That is, 12% of the time the researcher was likely to select three females with a median grade of C and three males with a median grade of D.

In a similar fashion we can compute the rest of the sampling distribution for the difference between medians. The whole distribution is as follows:

Females Higher	Probability
Females, B; Males, C	$.2 \times .6 = .12$
Females, B; Males, D	$.2 \times .2 = .04$
Females, C; Males, D	$.6 \times .2 = \underline{.12}$
Total	.28

Sexes Equal	Probability
Females, B; Males, B	$.2 \times .2 = .04$
Females, C; Males, C	$.6 \times .6 = .36$
Females, D; Males, D	$.2 \times .2 = \underline{.04}$
Total	.44

Males Higher	Probability
Females, C; Males, B	$.6 \times .2 = .12$
Females, D; Males, B	$.2 \times .2 = .04$
Females, D; Males, C	$.2 \times .6 = \underline{.12}$
Total	.28

There is thus a 28% chance that by pure luck the researcher would have selected a sample substantiating his erroneous hypothesis that females had a higher median grade than males. The researcher also had a 28% chance of selecting a sample in which the males had the higher median than the females, and a 44% chance of selecting groups with the same median.

LEVELS OF STATISTICAL SIGNIFICANCE

In the previous example, suppose the researcher had simply presented evidence showing that in his sample the females had the higher median grade. If we had not known that the population medians for the two sexes were equal, how convincing would his evidence have been? Most of the time, when researchers find supportive evidence for their hypothesis, that hypothesis is true for the general population from which their sample was drawn. Even in the example above there was only a 28% chance that the researcher could support his hypothesis when it was wrong. But for most political scientists a 28% chance is too large for them to accept the hypothesis. Before most scientific jurors would be willing to convict sex rather than chance as the cause of difference in grades, they would want to be convinced beyond a reasonable doubt. Just what that level of reasonable doubt should be is a matter of some debate. But most of us would want to be sure that the sample results would occur by chance no more than 5% or 1% of the time if the hypothesis were untrue.

The level of chance we are willing to accept is referred to as the **level of statistical significance.** We might report finding an association that was significant at the .05 level. That would mean that the chance that we would find such an association when no association actually existed in the theoretical population would be only 5 out of 100. The level of statistical significance in this case is .05. But just because an association attains a statistically significant level does not prove the relationship to be significant in any other way. The size of the relationship may indicate that it is very weak, and it can still be spurious. Statistical significance means only that the probability that the finding was attributable to chance is at or below a specified acceptable level.

The scientific community fears the acceptance of an untrue hypothesis much more than the failure to accept a true hypothesis. This may stem from the perception of the researcher as an advocate, for an advocate may fudge her findings ever so slightly in order to favor her hypothesis. But it probably stems primarily from the fact that if the hypothesized relationship is true for the population, it is usually fairly easy to demonstrate significance at the .05 or .01 level.

There are three ways in which researchers can decrease the probability of accepting a chance relationship. First, they can increase the size of the sample. In the example above, increasing the number of students would have decreased the chance of getting incorrect medians. Second, they can take another sample. In the example above, the probability is small that two independent samples of students would both have substantiated the hypothesis. Third, they can require deviations from chance to be large before rejecting chance as the cause of the relationship. In the example above, if the researcher had decided that he would accept his hypothesis only if the females got a median grade two grades or more above that of the males, then his odds of drawing a sample leading to the incorrect conclusion would have been .04 instead of .28.

If two variables are not associated in the theoretical population, then the distribution of the dependent variable (Y) will be the same for every category of the independent variable (X). If we take a sample of that theoretical population, however, we are likely just by chance to find some differences in the distribution of Y across the X categories. Those differences may be of the type that the hypothesis predicted we would find.

To avoid confusing chance findings with empirical verification of hypotheses, we must estimate the probability that any observed differences result from a chance sample of a population in which X and Y are not associated, rather than from a sample of a population in which X and Y are associated as predicted by the hypothesis.

If X and Y are not related in the whole population, differences in the distribution of Y across categories of X are likely to be small. The greater the differences in the Y distributions, the lower the probability that those differences are just the result of chance, and consequently the more likely they are to reflect the hypothesized association between X and Y.

The magnitude of the differences in the Y distributions is the key to estimating statistical significance.

TESTS OF STATISTICAL SIGNIFICANCE

Tests of statistical significance are statistical operations that allow us to estimate what the probability is that the association we find between variables in the sample occurred by chance. These tests involve calculating a statistic that reflects the magnitude of the differences in the Y distributions across categories of X. The greater the magnitude of the Y differences, the greater the value of the statistic.

Statistics used for tests of significance have known sampling distributions. Once we calculate the statistic, we know the probability that the statistic, and the differences in Y on which the statistic was based, occurred by chance.

There are dozens of tests of statistical significance. For almost every way that has been developed to determine the degree of association between two variables, a corresponding statistic has been developed that can be used to test the significance of the association. The next several chapters discuss measures of association and their associated tests of significance. When using one of those measures, you should calculate the appropriate statistic for testing the significance of that measure.

The rest of this chapter is devoted to tests of significance for differences between percentage distributions and differences between medians. The tests are based on calculation of the chi-square statistic and are most appropriately used as tests of significance for a specific hypothesis when the percentage distributions are presented in tables with just two columns and two rows (2 × 2 tables), or when two medians are being compared.[2]

THE CHI-SQUARE STATISTIC

The chi-square statistic (χ^2) is designed so that it will equal zero when the percentage distributions of Y are the same for every X category. That is, $\chi^2 = 0$ when there is no association between the independent and dependent variables.

If the Y distributions are not the same for each category of X, chi-square will have a value other than zero. The greater the differences in the Y distributions, the greater the value of the chi-square. With the same differences in the Y distributions, the greater the sample size, the greater the chi-square.

If X and Y are not associated in the theoretical population, the researcher would be the unlikely to find a sample, especially a large sample, in which the Y distributions were much different for different categories of X. Hence, if X and Y are not associated in the theoretical population, the researcher would be unlikely to get a very large value for χ^2. The greater the value of chi-square, the more confidence we can have that the X and Y variables are associated in the theoretical population.

When to Calculate χ^2

The researcher calculates a chi-square value *only if the sample shows support for the hypothesis.* Remember, the purpose behind a test of significance is to estimate how likely it is that the support found in a sample is the result of chance. If no support is found, there is no reason to check whether the nonsupport occurred by chance.

Consider a researcher investigating the hypothesis "Candidates who face divisive primaries are more likely to lose Senate races than are candidates who do not face such primaries." It would be appropriate to calculate χ^2 if his results were these:

TABLE 11–1   Effect of Divisive
Primaries on Winning

	Type of Primary	
	Divisive	*Nondivisive*
Won	50% (8)	79% (22)
Lost	50% (8)	21% (6)

Source: Robert Bernstein, "Divisive Primaries Do Hurt: U.S. Senate Races, 1956–1972," *American Political Science Review,* 71 (June 1977) 540–45. Results are for candidates of the stronger party in open-seat races in unbalanced competitive states.

Calculating χ^2

Since the χ^2 value must reflect both differences in the Y distributions and the sample size, it must be calculated from the *frequency crosstable* and not from the percentage crosstable. The chi-square statistic is based on the deviation of *observed frequencies* (F_o) in a crosstable from the frequencies that would have been most *expected by chance* (F_c) had there been no association between the two variables. The general formula for calculating χ^2 is to apply the following equation to each cell in the table and then sum the results:

$$\frac{(\text{frequency expected by chance} - \text{frequency observed})^2}{\text{frequency expected by chance}}$$

or

$$\sum \frac{(F_c - F_o)^2}{F_c}$$

(The Σ means to sum the results of the individual cells.)

Frequencies Expected By Chance (F_c)

The frequency most expected by chance can be determined for any cell of a crosstable from the distribution of Y for the sample as a whole. If X and Y are not associated and a given percentage of the whole sample is in category 1 of Y, then that percentage of the units in every X category would be expected to be in category 1. For example, Table 11 displays the results of 44 primaries. Candidates won 68% of all of the primaries (30 of 44). Therefore, by chance, 68% of those with divisive primaries would be expected to win, as well as 68% of those with nondivisive primaries. In this case there were 16 divisive primaries; 68% of 16 is 10.9, and so 10.9 is the number of winners to be most expected by chance if divisiveness of the primary has no effect on winning.

There is a shortcut to calculating the expected frequencies. The expected frequency for any cell in a crosstable is the product of the row (R) and column (C) marginals for that cell, divided by the number of units in the whole crosstable (N):

$$F_e = \frac{R \times C}{N}$$

In the example above, the marginals were as follows:

	Divisive	Nondivisive	(N)
Won			(30)
Lost			(14)
	(16)	(28)	44

The frequency expected for winning after a divisive primary would be (30) (16)/44 = 10.9. The frequencies expected for the whole table would be these:

	Divisive	Nondivisive
Won	10.9	19.1
Lost	5.1	8.9

Frequencies Observed

The frequencies observed are taken from the table (in this case, Table 11–1, repeated here for convenience):

TABLE 11–1   Effect of Divisive
Primaries on Winning

	Type of Primary	
	Divisive	*Nondivisive*
Won	8	22
Lost	8	6

The F_0 for each cell is simply the frequency in that cell.

Final Computation of χ^2.

To calculate the value of chi-square, substitute the values of F_e and F_0 for each cell into the formula given earlier:

$$\frac{(F_e - F_0)^2}{F_e}$$

For each cell of the table, we square the difference between the expected and observed frequencies and divide by the expected frequency. We then sum the results from each cell to obtain the chi-square. For the example above, the computation would be as follows:

$$\chi^2 = \frac{(10.9 - 8)^2}{10.9} + \frac{(19.1 - 22)^2}{19.1} + \frac{(5.1 - 8)^2}{5.1} + \frac{(8.9 - 6)^2}{8.9}$$

$$\chi^2 = .77 + .44 + 1.65 + .94 = 3.80.$$

Note that in a 2×2 table the numerator is the same for all four cells.

Sampling Distribution of χ^2

What we need to know now is how likely it is that a deviation from what is expected by chance will occur. Specifically, we want to know how likely an χ^2 of the size we have is likely to occur by chance. To discover this we need to look at a sampling distribution for χ^2. Sampling distributions for χ^2 are determined mathematically and are reproduced in a wide number of sources. They indicate the level of significance for a given χ^2 at a specified degrees of freedom (df). The degrees of freedom is a reflection of the number of cells in the table, computed as follows:

$$df = (\text{number of rows} - 1) \times (\text{number of columns} - 1)$$

In our example,

$$df = (2 - 1) \times (2 - 1) = 1$$

The χ^2 distribution is reproduced in the appendix of this book. Here is a small part of it:

df	Level of Significance	
	.05	*.01*
1	2.71	5.41
2	4.61	7.82

Each column of the table indicates a particular level of significance. Each row indicates the degrees of freedom. To find the level of significance for the df and χ^2 you have computed, you must find the row for the df and proceed across the columns until you find the place where the χ^2 in one column is smaller (or equal) to yours, and the χ^2 in the next column is bigger than yours. You look at the heading of the column in which the χ^2 is smaller than or equal to your χ^2, and this indicates the level of significance of this χ^2. For example, we found an χ^2 of 3.8 with 1 degree of freedom. Looking at the row for a df of 1, we find that 3.8 is bigger than the χ^2 in the first column but smaller in the second. Thus, we look at the heading of column 1 and find that the level of significance is .05.[3] This means that the relationship in the table is significant at the .05 level.

The apparent association in our example between divisiveness and losing is probably not the result of chance. If divisiveness were not associated with losing in the theoretical population, we would get sample results that strongly support the hypothesis purely by chance less than 5% of the time.

Testing Significance of a Difference in Medians

Researchers also use the chi-square statistic to test the significance of a difference in medians. For this test, the researcher must first summarize the relationship in a frequency crosstable set up like Table 11–2, and then compute a chi-square value for the crosstable.

TABLE 11–2 Form of Crosstable for Testing the Significance of a Difference in Medians

		Independent Variable	
		Category A	*Category B*
Dependent Variable	*Above the Median for the Sample*		
	Below the Median for the Sample		

TABLE 11–3 Ratings of Individual Freedom: Former British and French Colonies, 1976–1980

Former British Colonies	Freedom Rating*	Former French Colonies	Freedom Rating*
Mauritius	68	Morocco	44
Nigeria	53	Upper Volta	44
Ghana	42	Ivory Coast	25
Zimbabwe	42	Madagascar	25
Lesotho	39	Tunisia	25
Kenya	36	Algeria	17
South Africa	30	Chad	14
Zambia	30	Mauritania	14
Sierra Leone	28	Congo	11
Sudan	28	Niger	8
Tanzania	17	Togo	8
Uganda	11	Central African Rep.	3
Malawi	11	Mali	3
		Guinea	0
Median	30		14

*Freedom ratings are from Raymond Gastil, *Freedom in the World: Political Rights and Civil Liberties, 1982* (Westport, Conn.: Greenwood Press), Table 20.

The researcher finds the number of units in each category of X that have above and below median values for Y. The chi-square value is computed for the resulting crosstable just as for any other frequency crosstable. Only if the difference in medians shows support for the hypothesis, *and* the χ^2 is statistically significant, is it proper to conclude that the observed relationship supports the hypothesis.

For example, a researcher might use the data in Table 11–3 to test the hypothesis that former British colonies in Africa allow their citizens more freedom than do former French colonies. A comparison of medians would tend to support the hypothesis, so we would have to compute a chi-square value to determine the probability that the difference in medians occurred because of a fortunate sample selection.

Since the median for the whole sample of 27 nations is 25, we may summarize the data in Table 11–3 as follows in order to calculate a χ^2 value:

	Former British Colonies	Former French Colonies
Above the Median Freedom Rating	10	2
Below the Median Freedom Rating	3	9

The chi-square value for this summary table is 8.22. With 1 df, that value is significant at the .005 level. The probabilities are very high that there is an association between a nation's former colonial experience and the amount of freedom it allows its citizens. If colonial experience were unrelated to freedom allowed, we would observe this degree of support for the hypothesis less than five times in a thousand.

CONSIDERATIONS ON THE USE OF TESTS OF STATISTICAL SIGNIFICANCE

Now that we have seen how tests of significance are used, and have been introduced to a common test, let us look at some considerations that affect how we can apply these tests. Tests of statistical significance measure the probability that the relationship holds true for the theoretical population only if the sample has been randomly drawn from the population. Additionally, virtually all of the tests assume that the researcher hypothesized the relationships before making the analysis. Finally, the various tests of significance assume that a variety of specified conditions are true before the tests can be considered valid. We will briefly consider these points.

Random Samples

In Chapter 3 we talked about the selection of the sample. You may recall that we said for true random samples it was possible to test the extent to which the findings of the sample were likely to reflect the population. It is through the tests of significance that we can do this. Note that all of these tests assume that a random sample has been drawn.

We stated in Chapter 3 that there are very few random samples. Samples may approximate a random sample, and the closer the sample is to a random sample, the more confidence we can have in inferences from it.

This brings us to an interesting question: Should tests of statistical significance be run on samples that are not random? The answer is yes. If the apparent association is not strong enough to be statistically significant for a random sample, that is reason enough to ignore the association. If the association is found to be statistically significant, we cannot be as confident as with a random sample that it would hold for the theoretical population. Thus, the test serves as a veto in the case of nonrandom samples, but is less powerful as a reason to accept the conclusion than in the case of random samples.

Tests of significance should also be applied when the sample includes all units that exist at a single time or in a single place and when at the same time the theoretical population is assumed to include units from other times or places. Samples limited to a time or place are nonrandom, but they should not be mistaken for populations. Consequently, tests of significance are necessary for those samples.

Hypothesizing Before the Test of Significance

Almost all tests of statistical significance assume that researchers determine before they look at the data the associations they expect to find. If they do not, and simply look through a set of variables to find any that happen to associate, the probability that the finding is a chance occurrence is very much higher than is indicated by the usual test of significance.

Consider an extreme example. Suppose people were interviewed and gave random responses to each of 100 questions. If a researcher created all of the possible tables (2450 of them), she would find that about 122 of them had a relationship significant at the .05 level. If she then reported these findings, along with their acceptable level of significance, we would obviously be misled. If these relationships had been hypothesized in advance, only then would the .05 level be useful. Otherwise, it can be an exaggeration, and in some cases a gross exaggeration.[4]

This does not mean that we cannot look at unhypothesized relationships. It does mean that we must be more cautious when accepting conclusions based on this kind of research.

There are tests of statistical significance that do not require the relationship to be hypothesized in advance, but they require much stronger relationships for the same size samples in order to be considered statistically significant. The best practice is to work out carefully in advance the explanations to be tested, and then analyze the data and apply the usual tests of significance.

Other Limits

Because we do not know what the population actually looks like, tests of significance must assume certain things about the variables. Different tests make different assumptions, and the tests are most useful when those assumptions can be met. For example, the χ^2 can only be used when the distribution of the variables is such that the expected frequency in any cell is greater than 1 and the expected frequency in at least 80% of the cells in the table is greater than 2. Most tests of significance on interval variables assume that the variables are normally distributed in the population. That is, if their distributions were to be plotted, they would look like the bell-shaped line graph in Figure 8–4. Tests of statistical significance on variables that do not approximate such a distribution may not be useful. When such limits have been placed on the test of significance, the researcher must be careful not to violate the rules for the particular test she is using.

SUMMARY

We know that if we randomly assign values of variables to objects, some of the time the variables will appear to be related, even though they are not. As the apparent association becomes stronger, however, the likelihood of a larger deviation from what would be expected by chance becomes very small. Tests of statistical significance measure the probability that the association could have occurred by chance.

In the chapters ahead we will refer to different tests of statistical significance and show you how they are used in specific circumstances being considered. Remember that they are all based on principles of probability. The logic of all tests of statistical significance is fundamentally the same.

Providing evidence that the relationship you claim is not likely to have occurred by chance is the last step in the data analysis. The extent to which your work will be accepted must be a function of the probability that it is not explainable by chance. Thus, this is a necessary part of the verification process.

Endnotes

[1] By chance samples we mean random, independent samples.

[2] We can compute chi-square values for larger tables to determine whether the frequencies are distributed as would be expected on the basis of chance. However, a significant χ^2 for such a table would not necessarily indicate that the hypothesis was supported. For larger tables, the best test of significance is one that tests the significance of an appropriate correlation coefficient (see Chapter 12).

Chi-square can be computed for all 2×2 tables in which all expected cell frequencies are greater than 1 and $N > 9$. If the expected frequencies are smaller than that, use the Fisher-Yates Exact Test.

Technically, the computed chi-square value, when computed as shown in the text, should be reduced slightly for 2×2 tables. The adjustment is very slight and is unlikely to affect your conclusions unless the chi-square value is just marginally significant or N is very small. The chi-square value should be reduced by a percentage equal to 100 divided by the difference between the products of the two cells along each diagonal. This is the Pirie-Hamden correction factor recommended by N. M. Downie and R. W. Heath, *Basic Statistical Methods*, 4th ed. (New York: Harper & Row, 1974), pp. 197–98.

[3] We are assuming that χ^2 is being computed as a test of the significance of results supporting a specific, directed hypothesis. Therefore, the chi-square distributions are for one-tail tests. For more on that decision, see Downie and Heath, p. 200.

[4] See James Payne and James Dyer, "Betting After the Race is Over: The Perils of Post Hoc Hypothesizing," *American Journal of Political Science* 19, (August 1975), 559–64, for a critique of a piece of research that suffers seriously from this problem.

LABORATORY EXERCISES

The purpose of this laboratory is to give you experience in computing and interpreting a commonly used test for statistical significance. We use the χ^2 statistic to test the statistical significance of a crosstable and a comparison of medians.

Task 1. In this task we compute and evaluate χ^2 for a crosstable. Table 10–5 in the text relates party and support for the ABM, controlling for ideology and state economic benefits. Using those control tables, test the hypothesis that Republicans are more likely to support the development of a weapons system than are Democrats.

  a. Compute χ^2 statistics where appropriate.
  b. Are any of the χ^2 values significant at the .05 level?
  c. On the basis of these results, is the hypothesis supported?

Table 10–7 presents similar evidence regarding the hypothesis that conservatives are more likely to support the development of a weapons system than are liberals.

  d. Compute χ^2 statistics where appropriate for those control tables.
  e. Are any of the χ^2 values significant at the .05 level?
  f. On the basis of these results, is the hypothesis supported?

Task 2. Compute and interpret the χ^2 for a difference of medians. The data below give the ages of male and female candidates who faced candidates of the opposite sex in primary races for open-seat nominations to the House of Representatives, 1978. The hypothesis is that males tend to be younger than females in these races.

Candidate	Sex	Age
Mikulski	F	40
Daker	F	36
Cooper	F	51
Caray	F	50
Maurer	F	53
Marting	F	42
Davis	F	46
Henderson	F	58
Garrot	F	59
Wilson	F	34
Fabula	F	43
Albertson	F	51
Gallucci	F	46
Flippo	M	38
Familian	M	34
Bradham	M	47
Barnard	M	34
Bell	M	41
Davis	M	30
Markey	M	30
Pierce	M	46
Stockman	M	29

Candidate	Sex	Age
Bonoir	M	31
Skelton	M	44
Maxfield	M	35
Volkmer	M	45
Lederer	M	38
Gore	M	28
Hogan	M	52
Curran	M	44
Avara	M	43
Byrnes	M	36
Celebrezze	M	34
Celebrezze	M	37

a. Compute and compare the median age of males and females. If appropriate, compute the χ^2 test to see if the difference is significant.

b. On the basis of your analysis, is the hypothesis supported?

Task 3. Use the computer to analyze data provided by your instructor. Test a hypothesis and control for the effects of a third variable. If support for the hypothesis is found, test its significance.

REVIEW QUESTIONS

1. Hypothesis: Families receiving food stamps are less likely to shop at the store with the lowest prices in town than families that do not get food stamps. Bivariate Relationship:

		Receive Food Stamps	
		Yes	No
Shop	Yes	20%	80%
Lowest Prices	No	80%	20%
	(N)	(100)	(200)

Controlling for whether the store with lowest prices is within two miles of the family residence:

		WITHIN 2 MILES Food Stamps	
		Yes	No
Shop	Yes	80%	85.6%
Lowest	No	20%	14.4%
	(N)	(20)	(180)

		OUTSIDE OF 2 MILES	
		Food Stamps	
		Yes	*No*
Shop	*Yes*	5%	30%
Lowest	*No*	95%	70%
	(N)	(80)	(20)

a. Compute χ^2 values for each control table.
b. For each level of significance below, indicate whether each value is significant. Use S for significant, N for nonsignificant.

	.1	.05	.01	.005
Within 2 Miles	————	————	————	————
Outside of 2 Miles	————	————	————	————

c. On the basis of the computations above and standard levels of significance, is the hypothesis supported?
d. What is the effect of the control variable (if any)?
e. If the percentage crosstables had remained the same but the Ns for each had been doubled, would the probability that the results had shown support just by chance be greater, lesser, or unchanged?

2. Use the following hypothesis and hypothetical data to respond to questions A through G.
   Hypothesis: High school graduates tend to earn more than high school dropouts.

	Hourly Earnings ($)	
	High School	*Dropouts*
	30	20
	20	13
Males	20	3
	10	7
	15	8
	40	11
	12	6
	10	5
Females	7	3
	5	
	3	

a. Use a comparison of medians to test the hypothesis. Control for gender; show both the bivariate and control comparisons.
b. Calculate χ^2 values to determine whether the differences in medians show statistically significant support for the hypothesis. Show all work.

d. How many degrees of freedom are there for each table?
e. Which tables show statistically significant support for the hypothesis at the .05 level? At the .01 level?
f. What do you conclude regarding the hypothesis?
g. What do you conclude was the effect of the control variable?

CHAPTER TWELVE

CORRELATION COEFFICIENTS AND TESTS OF SIGNIFICANCE: NOMINAL AND ORDINAL LEVELS

Up to this point we have used crosstables and comparisons of means or medians to report relationships between variables. This chapter and the two that follow will deal with an alternative method for reporting relationships, the **correlation coefficient**—a single number indicating the extent to which two variables are related.[1]

Correlation coefficients have two principal advantages over tables in reporting relationships. First, coefficients give reliable estimates of the extent of association. Different researchers looking at two tables might differ in their estimates of which association was stronger; different researchers using the same correlation coefficient would come to the same conclusion. Second, coefficients make possible more concise presentation of several relationships. A number of coefficients can be reported in the space that would be required for a single table.

A single measure cannot communicate all that a researcher might observe about a relationship by studying a table, and he or she must be careful to present tables when summary measures prove inadequate. When correlation coefficients are used without tables, the reader has to trust the researcher's evaluation of the usefulness of the measure, for there is no way to reconstruct the table from the measure. More information can almost always be reported when both the cross-tabulations and the appropriate correlation coefficients are presented. Thus, *if space permits,* both tables and correlation coefficients should be presented.

EXTENT OF ASSOCIATION

The extent of association between two variables may vary greatly. If the values of the independent *(X)* and dependent *(Y)* variables are paired in such a way that one can perfectly predict the absolute or relative value of Y for each unit by knowing either the absolute or relative value of X, then we say there is **perfect association** between the variables. If, however, the X and Y values are paired in such a way that knowing the X value of a unit is of no help in predicting its Y value, we say there is **zero association** between the variables. Zero association occurs when X and Y are statistically independent—that is, when each Y value is equally likely to be paired with each X value.

If sex were the X variable and ideology the Y variable and you could always predict a person's ideology by knowing his or her sex, then sex and ideology would be perfectly associated. This could happen if all males were conservatives and all females liberals. However, if 40% of the males and 40% of the females were conservatives, then knowing the sex of a person would not help you guess his or her ideology. In that case, sex and ideology would be statistically independent; there would be no association between the two variables.

Perfect association can also occur when the hypothesis relates one or more relative properties. For example, if social-class background were the X variable and degree of conservatism were the Y variable, and if for every pair of people the person with the higher social-class background was the more conservative, then social class and degree of conservatism would be perfectly associated. We could predict perfectly the *relative* Y value of each unit by knowing the *relative* X value of each unit. All upper-middle-class individuals would not have to have a specific Y value—for example, being slightly conservative. Perfect association would exist as long as they had the same relative Y value—for example, as long as they were all more conservative than all those in the middle class and less conservative than all those in the upper class. There would be zero association between social class and degree of conservatism if knowing the relative social class of two individuals was of no help in predicting which was the more conservative.

Strength of Association

The closer an observed relationship is to perfect association, the *stronger* we find the association to be. The magnitude of the correlation coefficient, ignoring the $+$ or $-$ sign, indicates its strength of association. For most correlation coefficients the magnitude will be between 1 and 0. The nearer it is to 1, the stronger the relationship; the nearer to zero, the weaker the relationship. A correlation of 1 between sex and party would indicate a perfect association between those two variables; a correlation of 0 would indicate no association between them.

Direction of Association

A perfect association between sex and ideology could result from all males being conservative and all females being conservative, but it could, of course, also result from all females being liberal and all males being liberal. In addition to the strength of the association, a researcher needs to report its *direction*—that is, how the Y values tend to be paired with X values. The direction of association is reported by the sign ($+$ or $-$) of the correlation coefficient. When the data are nominal, the sign usually indicates direction with respect to the hypothesis: A $+$ indicates that the hypothesis tends to be supported; A $-$ indicates that it tends not to be supported. Some coefficients for ordinal and interval variables also use the sign to indicate whether the relationship supports or contradicts the hypothesis. It is more common, however, when the data are ordinal or interval to let the sign indicate whether high values of one variable tend to be paired with high values of the other (indicated by a positive sign and called a *positive correlation*), or whether high values of one tend to be paired with low values of the other (indicated by a negative sign and called a *negative correlation*).

If the direction is as hypothesized and as indicated by the sign, then the larger the coefficient is, the more support there will be for the hypothesis. Thus, a coefficient of .8 would indicate that the pattern of the relationship was closer to the one hypothesized than would a coefficient of .6. Since we can seldom expect perfect association, a correlation of .8 or .9 would show extremely strong support for the hypothesis. A correlation of .1 or .2 would be at best weak support, and 0 would be no support at all.

Tests of Significance

Just as very small differences in percentage tables may be due to chance, so may very small correlation coefficients. For this reason, tests of significance are available for most correlation coefficients. These tests, such as the χ^2 test introduced earlier, indicate the likelihood that a coefficient of the magnitude observed could have occurred by chance when in fact there was no association between the variables in the theoretical population.

KINDS OF CORRELATION COEFFICIENTS

There are many correlation coefficients commonly used for measuring the degree of association between nominal and/or ordinal measures. Some are appropriate only if the hypothesis relates specific (not relative) X values to specific (not relative) Y values. An example of that type of hypothesis is the one relating sex and ideology that we used above. The next section of this chapter treats a coefficient of that type, del_k (Δ_k).[2]

Other correlation coefficients are appropriate if the hypothesis involves relative values of either X or Y. An example of that type of hypothesis is the one linking social class and degree of conservatism, which we discussed at the start of this chapter. The last section of the chapter treats two coefficients of that type: del_l (Δ_l), and gamma (γ).

HYPOTHESES RELATING SPECIFIC X AND Y VALUES

Hypotheses relating specific X and Y values assert that some pairings of X and Y values are more likely to occur than others. For example, the hypothesis "Women are more likely to be token candidates of the major parties than are men" asserts that token female candidates and nontoken male candidates are more probable than token males and nontoken females. If the sample shows that there are only token female candidates and only nontoken male candidates, then sex and token nomination are perfectly associated in the hypothesized direction for that sample. Del_k, the correlation coefficient summarizing the association between those variables, will be 1.0. If the proportion of token candidates among females is greater than the proportion of token candidates among males, the association may not be perfect, but it will be in the hypothesized direction and Δ_k will be positive. If the proportion of token females exactly equals that of token males, there will be zero association and the correction coefficient will be 0. If there is a lower proportion of token candidates among females than among males, the association will not be in the predicted direction and the correlation coefficient will be negative.

Del_k (Δ_k)

Theoretical Foundation. Del_k is based on the extent of deviation from what a set of data would look like if the two variables were in perfect association. To compute it, the researcher first asks how far the observed pairs of X–Y values deviate from what would be expected if X and Y were perfectly associated as predicted by the hypothesis. The researcher then determines how far the pairs of X–Y values would have deviated from perfect association if the X and Y values had been statistically independent (paired by chance). Let us call the first type of deviation *error observed* (E_o) and the second type *error expected by chance* (E_c). Del_k coefficient is simply the proportion by which E_o is smaller than E_c:

$$\Delta_k = \frac{E_c - E_o}{E_c}$$

Del_k tells us how much closer the observed relationship is to perfect association than would be expected by chance. If the association predicted by the hypothesis is perfect, than $E_o = 0$ and thus $del_k = 1.0$. If the association is zero, then $E_o = E_c$; thus, $del_k = 0$. If the observed relationship deviates less from perfect association than would be expected by chance, then $E_o < E_c$ and del_k is positive. If the observed relationship deviates further from perfect association than would be expected by chance, then $E_o > E_c$ and del_k is negative. The stronger the association, the higher the magnitude of del_k.

Computation. The first step in computing del_k is to set up an empty crosstable, one correctly labeled for the variables but without numbers in the cells. For example, if the hypothesis is that women are more likely than men to be token candidates of the major parties, the crosstable would be as follows:

		Sex	
		Women	*Men*
Candidate	*Token*		
	Nontoken		

The second step is to determine which cells, according to the hypothesis, would be empty if the association were perfect in the direction predicted by the hypothesis. In this example, if the association were perfect (if type of candidacy could be predicted correctly for each person on the basis of his or her sex), then all women would be token candidates and all men would be nontoken candidates. If the association were perfect, all units would fall in the token-women and nontoken-men cells, and the nontoken-women and token-men cells would be empty. The cells that would be empty if the association were perfect are called *error cells* and all of the units falling in those cells are considered *errors* (actually they are deviations from perfection). The crosstable below shows the error cells for this hypothesis:

		Sex	
		Women	*Men*
Candidate	*Token*		error
	Nontoken	error	

The third step in computing del_k is to calculate from the actual marginals the frequency expected by chance in each error cell—that is, the frequency to be expected in each error cell if the variables were statistically independent. That frequency is calculated the same way as expected frequencies are calculated in the computation of χ^2. The expected frequency for each cell equals the row marginal times the column marginal for the cell, divided by the N for the table.

To continue our example, the following crosstable shows the frequencies expected by chance in each error cell, based on nonincumbent nominations for the House of Representatives, 1964–1968:

		Sex		
		Women	*Men*	*(N)*
Candidate	*Token*		564.1	(577)
	Nontoken	14.1		(629)
	(N)	(27)	(1179)	

The sum of the expected frequencies for all error cells is E_c, the error expected by chance. In this case $E_c = 578.2$.

The fourth step in computing del_k is to add the frequencies actually observed in the error cells. The following crosstable shows the observed results:

TABLE 12–1   Sex and Type of Candidacy: House Races, 1964–1968

		Sex	
		Women	*Men*
Candidate	*Token*	17	560
	Nontoken	10	619

The sum of the observed frequencies for all error cells is E_0, the error observed. In this case, $E_0 = 570$.

The final step in computing del_k is to substitute E_c and E_0 into the general formula for del. Del is simply the proportion by which the error observed is smaller than the error expected by chance:

$$\Delta = \frac{E_c - E_0}{E_c}$$

In this case,

$$\Delta_k = \frac{578.2 - 570}{578.2} = .01$$

Note that Δ_k is positive because the percentage crosstable supports the hypothesis. Here is that crosstable:

		Sex	
		Women	*Men*
Candidate	*Token*	63%	47%
	Nontoken	37%	53%

Interpretation. There were 1% fewer errors observed than would have been expected by chance. Put another way, the observed pairing of values is 1% closer to perfect association than would have been expected by chance. The correlation can be interpreted as showing a very weak association in the direction that was hypothesized.

Whenever the percentage crosstable supports the hypothesis, the total of the errors observed is less than that expected by chance, and del is positive. Del_k can only reach $+1.0$ when there are no errors observed: That would be perfect association.[3] Whenever the percentage crosstable does not support the hypothesis, the total of the errors observed will be more than that expected by chance, and del_k is negative. Whenever the percentage crosstable shows zero association (the same percentage in each cell of any given row), the totals for the observed and expected errors are identical, and del_k is zero.

Del_k for Tables Larger Than 2 × 2. The procedure used in calculating del_k for tables larger than 2 × 2 (tables having more than two columns or rows) is the same as for 2 × 2 tables. Suppose we have the hypothesis that former British and French colonies are less likely to have compulsory military service than are former colonies of other nations. If the hypothesis perfectly predicted association between former colonial status and type of military service, then former British and French colonies would all have voluntary service, while former colonies of other powers would all have compulsory service. Hence the error cells

TABLE 12–2 Former Colonial Status and Type of Military Service

		Former Colonial Status		
		British	*French*	*Other*
Military Service	*Voluntary*	29	12	15
	Compulsory	5	10	24

Source: Michael Kodron and Ronald Segal, *The State of the World Atlas* (New York: Simon & Schuster, 1981), Map 30.

are British-compulsory, French-compulsory, and other-voluntary. The actual relationship for 1972 is portrayed in Table 12–2.

Following the same procedure as for the 2×2 tables, we find that $E_c = 46$ and $E_0 = 30$. Del_k, therefore, is .35. This is a stronger association than the one found in the previous example. It shows the association to be 35% closer to perfect association than would be expected by chance.

Testing the Significance of Del_k. Whether any del_k is statistically significant depends largely upon both the sample size and the amount of the sample expected to be in the error cells. The magnitude of del_k will not automatically tell you whether it is statistically significant; for that information you must compute a χ^2 value for del_k, and then use a table of χ^2 distributions to determine the probability of getting, just by chance, a χ^2 as high as the one you did get. The test of significance is computed only when the hypothesis is supported (only when Δ_k is positive).

To compute the χ^2 value for del_k, substitute the values already computed for E_c and E_0 into the following formula:

$$\chi^2 = \frac{(E_c - E_0)^2}{E_c} + \frac{(E_c - E_0)^2}{N - E_c}$$

In our token-candidate example, $E_c = 578.2$, $E_0 = 570$, and $N = 1206$. Therefore,

$$\chi^2 = \frac{8.2^2}{578.2} + \frac{8.2^2}{627.8} = .23$$

Chi-square values for del_k have only one degree of freedom, regardless of the size of the crosstable. But even with one degree of freedom, .23 is not a high enough chi-square value to be significant at the .05 level. We cannot conclude that the hypothesis is supported, based on this sample. The weak support we found may have been the result of a fortunate choice of years to examine; sex and token candidacy may not be associated for the whole theoretical population.

Testing the significance of the .35 del_k coefficient that we computed for our second example, we get a chi-square value of 10.78. With one degree of freedom, that value is significant at the .005 level.

HYPOTHESES INVOLVING RELATIVE VALUES
OF EITHER *X* OR *Y*

To verify hypotheses involving relative values of either X or Y, the researcher must compare the X and Y values of *pairs* of units rather than the X and Y values of individual units. Consider the hypothesis "The higher the social-class background of children, the higher their grades tend to be." That hypothesis does not assert that all upper-class children get A's or that all lower-class children get F's. All it asserts is that if you compare the grades of pairs of students having different social-class backgrounds, the students from the higher class will tend to have the higher grades. To test that hypothesis the researcher cannot compare grade and background for each individual. To know that Bill is middle-class and received a C does not help determine how nearly perfect the association is. If the upper-class children received D's, then Bill's grade would indicate a deviation from perfect association. If they received A's or B's, then Bill's grade would not indicate such a deviation. The only way the researcher can tell whether the association is perfect is to compare Bill's C with the grades received by other children. All pairs in which upper-class children did better than C or lower-class children did worse than C would be in accord with perfect association.

Del$_I$ (Δ_I) and gamma (γ) measure association when the hypothesis involves relative values of either X or Y. The magnitude of either coefficient reaches 1.0 when the paired comparisons show perfect association; it reaches 0 when the comparisons show zero association. A positive correlation indicates that the units with the higher-coded values of X tend also to be the ones with the higher-coded values of Y; a negative correlation indicates that units with the higher-coded values of X tend to be those with the lower-coded values of Y.

Del$_I$

Theoretical Foundation. Hypotheses involving relative values of either X or Y are typically of this form: the higher the code value of the X variable, the higher the code value of the Y variable tends to be. If the hypothesis is not stated in that form, one variable can be recoded so that it will fit the form. Once the hypothesis is in that form, perfect association exists when *in all comparisons of pairs of units that differ with respect to* X *the unit with the higher* X *value also has the higher* Y *value.*

To compute del$_I$, the researcher must examine all pairs of units that differ with respect to X to see if the units with the higher X values have the higher Y values. If all pairs meet that condition, the association is perfect.

Any pair in which the unit with the higher X value does not have the higher Y value is a deviation from perfect association (an error). From the marginals, it is possible for the researcher to compute the number of errors that would have been expected by chance if there were zero association between X and Y. Del$_I$

measures the proportion by which the observed error (E_O) is smaller than the error expected by chance (E_c):

$$\Delta_I = \frac{E_c - E_0}{E_c}$$

Del$_I$ tells us how much closer the observed relationship is to perfect association than would be expected by chance. If the association predicted by the hypothesis is perfect, $E_0 = 0$ and thus del$_I = 1.0$. If the association is zero, $E_0 = E_c$ and thus del$_I = 0$. If the observed relationship deviates less from perfect association than would be expected by chance, $E_0 < E_c$ and del$_I$ is positive. If the observed relationship deviates further from perfect association than would be expected by chance, $E_0 > E_c$ and del$_I$ is negative. The stronger the association, the higher the magnitude of del$_I$.

Computation. Before computing Δ_I, check to see whether the hypothesis asserts that the units with the higher-coded values of X also tend to be the ones with the higher-coded values of Y. If that is the case, no recoding is necessary. If the hypothesis asserts an association between the higher-coded values of X and the lower-coded values of Y, reverse the coding for one of the two variables. Then construct the frequency crosstable with the rows and columns ordered so that the lowest X and Y values are in the upper-left corner and the highest values are in the lower-right corner of the table.

Suppose the hypothesis is "The larger the city, the lower the turnout is likely to be for municipal elections." If the researcher used ordinal measures for both properties and coded so that the largest cities and the highest turnouts were given the highest code numbers, then before computation of del$_I$, the code numbers for one of the two variables would have to be reversed. If turnouts of over 50% had been coded 3, those from 40 to 50%, 2, and those under 40%, 1, then the 1 and 3 codes would be switched before computing Δ_I. The frequency crosstable would be constructed with the columns from left to right indicating increasing city size, and the rows from top to bottom indicating decreasing turnout. Table 12–3 is set up in that fashion.

TABLE 12–3 City Size and Turnout in Municipal Elections: San Francisco Bay Area

		City Size	
		Small	*Large*
	High	26	3
Turnout	*Medium*	23	6
	Low	19	10

Source: Gordon Black, "Conflict in the Community: A Theory of the Effects of Community Size," *American Political Science Review,* 68, no. 3 (September 1974), 1251.

Note the 3 large cities with high turnout: They are larger than all of the 68 small cities. If the variables were perfectly associated in the hypothesized fashion, those 3 cities would have lower turnout rates than all of the small cities. Since none of the 3 has a lower rate than any of the smaller cities, any comparison between any one of the 3 cities and any of the 68 smaller cities would show a deviation from perfect association (3 × 68 = 204 errors).

Next, consider the 6 large cities with medium turnout. If there were perfect association, all of the smaller cities would have a higher turnout rate than any of those 6. However, 42 of the smaller cities do not have a higher turnout than any of the 6. Any comparison between any of the 6 and any of the 42 would be a deviation from perfect association (6 × 42 = 252 more errors).

Finally, consider the 10 larger cities with low turnout. There are 19 smaller cities that do not have higher turnouts. Therefore, there are 190 more errors (10 × 19).

Adding all of those errors together (204 + 252 + 190) gives us 646 errors observed, (E_o = 646).

The general procedure for computing E_o, regardless of the number of rows or columns in the crosstable, is as follows: *Sum, for all cells, the product of each cell frequency and the total frequency of those cells that are to the left of, but not above, that cell.* In the preceding example, 6 was multiplied by 42 because 42 was the total frequency of units in the cells to the left of, but not above, the cell with the 6 in it.

Note that this researcher did not distinguish medium-sized cities. Had there been a column for medium-sized cities, as in Table 12–4, the same procedure would have been followed. Cell frequencies in the rightmost column would be multiplied by the total frequency in the two columns to the left but not above. Cell frequencies in the middle column would be multiplied by the total frequency in the leftmost column but not above. In Table 12–4, 4 would be multiplied by 23 and 7 by 12. E_o for this example is 509 (3 × 40 + 4 × 23 + 3 × 7 + 9 × 20 + 7 × 12 + 4 × 3).

To compute Δ_p, we must also compute the number of errors expected by chance—that is, the number expected if there were no association between the X and Y variables. That we do by computing the cell frequencies that would be most likely to occur by chance based on the row and column marginals. We determine the expected cell frequencies just as we did when computing χ^2, by dividing the product of the row frequency and column frequency for each cell by

TABLE 12–4 City Size and Turnout in Municipal Elections: Hypothetical Data

		City Size		
		Small	*Medium*	*Large*
	High	8	9	3
Turnout	*Medium*	9	7	4
	Low	3	4	3

the number in the whole table ($R \times C/N$). For the cities in the San Francisco Bay area, the frequencies most expected by chance are shown in Table 12–5:

TABLE 12–5 City Size and Turnout: Frequencies Expected by Chance

		City Size		
		Small	*Large*	*(N)*
	High	22.7	6.3	(29)
Turnout	*Medium*	22.7	6.3	(29)
	Low	22.7	6.3	(29)
	(N)	(68)	(19)	

Following the same error-counting procedure that we used with the observed data, we can compute the number of errors that would most likely have occurred had there been no association between city size and turnout. For Table 12–5, E_c, the total number of errors expected by chance, is 858.1 (6.3 × 68.1 + 6.3 × 45.4 + 6.3 × 22.7).

We compute Del$_l$ by substituting the values for E_o and E_c into the general equation for del$_l$:

$$\Delta_l = \frac{E_c - E_o}{E_c} = \frac{858.1 - 646}{858.1} = .25$$

Interpretation. There are 25% fewer errors than would be expected if there were zero association between the two variables. Put another way, there are 25% fewer errors than would be expected by chance. This sample shows weak to moderate support for the hypothesis that the larger the city, the lower the turnout tends to be.

Testing the Significance of del$_l$. When del$_l$ supports your hypothesis, you can determine if that support is statistically significant at a specified level by referring to the graphs in the appendix. These show the minimum del$_l$ value needed for significance for different sample sizes. There are curves for the .05 level and the .01 level: Find the appropriate graph and locate on the grid (X axis shows sample size; Y shows del) the del$_l$ and sample size for your research. If the point representing your del and sample size is above the curve for the specified level of significance, then the del is significant. Following this procedure for the del computed in the previous example will show that it is significant at the .05 level.

Gamma (γ)

Theoretical Foundation. Gamma measures how useful it is to know the relative value of X for each unit in predicting the relative value of Y for those units. To find the predictive value of X, the researcher first determines the amount of error he would have made in predicting the Y values of the units without knowledge of each unit's X value. He then determines the amount of error he would have made in predicting the Y values of the units if he had based his estimates of Y on the X values of the units. If X has any predictive value, there will be less error when the predictions are based on X. If the minimum error made with *knowledge of X* is called E_k, and the amount of error made *without knowledge of X* is called E_w, then the predictive value of X is measured by the extent to which E_k is smaller than E_w. Specifically, the magnitude of the correlation coefficient is defined as $\frac{E_w - E_k}{E_w}$. This is often called the proportional-reduction-in-error (P–R–E) made possible by knowledge of X.

If the X values perfectly predict Y values (if there is perfect association), then E_k is zero and the magnitude of the correlation coefficient is $\frac{E_w - 0}{E_w}$, or 1.00. The P–R–E is 100%. If the X and Y values are paired in such a way that knowing X is of no help in predicting Y (that is, if there is zero association), then E_k equals E_w and the magnitude of the correlation coefficient is $\frac{E_w - E_w}{E_w}$, or 0. In this case, there is no P–R–E. If the X values are of some help in predicting Y but do not allow perfect prediction, then E_k is smaller than E_w and the magnitude of the correlation coefficient is between 0 and 1; the greater the magnitude, the greater the association. In this case, the magnitude indicates the P–R–E.

Computation. In evaluating the predictive value of X, gamma compares all pairs of units that differ with respect to both X and Y. For example, if the researcher were using gamma to determine the strength of association between city size and turnout in municipal elections (both measured as ordinal variables), he would compare all pairs of cities in which the cities are of different sizes and have different turnout rates. No paired comparisons are evaluated in which both cities are either the same size or have the same turnout rate.

For each paired comparison, the researcher predicts that the Y value of one unit will be higher than the Y value of the other unit. Without knowledge of the relative X values of the units, the researcher will probably be in error (guess the wrong unit has the higher value) half of the time. Hence, E_w equals half of the number of paired comparisons.

Knowing the relative X values of units, the researcher can generally improve her prediction of the relative Y values by either (1) predicting that the unit with the higher X value will have the higher Y value (a positive association) or (2) predicting that the unit with the higher X value will have the lower Y value (a negative association).

Suppose the researcher was measuring the association between city size and turnout for Table 12–6.

TABLE 12–6 City Size and Turnout in Municipal Elections

		City Size	
		Small	*Large*
Turnout	*Low*	City A	City B
	Medium	City C	City D
	High	City E	

The paired comparisons between A and D, B and C, B and E, and D and E would be the only ones to be evaluated. Other possible pairs, such as A and B, are not evaluated because they do not differ with respect to one variable or the other.

Without knowing the relative size of the cities, the researcher would be expected to correctly predict which city of each pair had the lowest turnout rate half of the time. In the four paired comparisons noted above, two errors in prediction would be expected without knowledge of X ($E_w = 2$).

The researcher could reduce the number of errors in prediction by predicting that the larger city in each pair would have the lower turnout. With respect to the A–D pair, she would predict that D had the lower turnout. For B–C, the prediction would be that B was lower; for B–E, that B was lower; and for D–E, that D was lower. Using that prediction rule and knowing the relative sizes of the cities, the researcher could reduce the errors in prediction to just one (A is incorrectly predicted to have a lower turnout than D). Therefore, $E_k = 1$.

Substituting for E_w and E_k in the formula for gamma yields

$$\gamma = \frac{E_w - E_k}{E_w} = \frac{2 - 1}{2} = .50$$

Knowledge of X cuts the errors in predicting the relative values of Y from 2 to 1. The proportional reduction in error is .50, the magnitude of gamma. In this case gamma would be $-.50$, the negative sign indicating that the larger cities had the lower turnout rates.

This example involved just five cities, no two of which had the same $X–Y$ values. Even listing the paired comparisons becomes difficult when there is a substantially larger sample with many units having the same $X–Y$ values. Fortunately, it is possible to determine E_w and E_k without listing all of the paired comparisons and determining which are in error.

To calculate E_w and E_k, first set up the frequency crosstable so that the lowest-coded values of X are in the left column and the lowest-coded values of Y are in the top row. Code values for X must increase from left to right across the columns; code values for Y must increase from top to bottom down the rows.

Once the table is set up in that fashion, the general procedure for finding the total number of paired comparisons, counting each pair only once, is as follows:

1. Sum for all cells the product of each cell frequency and the total frequency of those cells that are below and to the right of that cell.

2. Add to that the sum for all cells the product of each cell frequency and the total frequency of those cells that are below and to the left of that cell.

(The reason for computing the two sums separately and then adding them together will become apparent shortly.)

Consider Table 12–7.

TABLE 12–7 City Size and
Turnout in Municipal Elections:
San Francisco Bay Area

		City Size	
		Small	*Large*
	Low	19	10
Turnout	*Medium*	23	6
	High	26	3

Source: Gordon Black, "Conflict in the Community: A Theory of the Effects of Community Size," *American Political Science Review*,
68, no. 3 (September 1974), 1251.

Each of the 19 small cities with low turnout can be compared with the 9 cities
that are larger and have either medium or high turnout. That would be a total of
171 (19 × 9) paired comparisons. Each of the 23 small cities with medium turnout can be compared with the 3 large cities with high turnout and the 10 large
cities with low turnout. That would be another 299 paired comparisons (23 × 3
+ 23 × 10). Each of the 26 small cities with high turnout can be compared with
each of the 16 larger cities with medium or low turnout, another 416 paired
comparisons (26 × 16). Without counting any pair twice, we come up with 886
possible paired comparisons between cities differing in both size and turnout.

We could have obtained this total by following the two general procedures
listed above:

Procedure 1 (cell frequency times below and to right)	Procedure 2 (cell frequency times below and to left)
19 × 9 = 171	10 × 49 = 490
23 × 3 = 69	6 × 26 = 156
240	646

Summing the two numbers gives us the total number of paired comparisons,
886.

Since E_w is equal to half of the paired comparisons, $E_w = 443$. That is,
without knowledge of the relative sizes of cities, the researcher would expect to
make 443 incorrect predictions regarding which of the cities in each of the 886
paired comparisons had the higher turnout rate.

E_k can also be determined from the procedures above. It is equal to the
smaller of the sums for the two procedures. Procedure 1 yields the number of
paired comparisons that would be incorrectly predicted by the researcher if he
had hypothesized that the larger city in each pair had the lower turnout. Procedure 2 yields the number of paired comparisons that would be incorrectly predicted by the researcher if he had hypothesized that the smaller city in each pair

had the lower turnout. In this case the larger cities tended to have the lower turnout. Thus, the researcher would have made the fewest errors in prediction by hypothesizing a negative relationship between size and turnout. By making use of the relative value of X (relative size of city), the researcher could have reduced errors in prediction to 240. Therefore, $E_k = 240$.

Substituting E_w and E_k into the formula for the magnitude of gamma gives the following results for this case:

$$\gamma = \frac{E_w - E_k}{E_w} = \frac{443 - 240}{443} = .46$$

Since we would make fewer errors by predicting a negative rather than a positive association, the sign of the coefficient is negative: $\gamma = -.46$.

The steps in computing γ may be summarized as follows:

1. Sum for all cells the product of each cell and the total frequency of those cells that are below and to the right of that cell. This is the number of paired comparisons showing positive association.
2. Sum for all cells the product of each cell and the total frequency of those cells that are below and to the left of that cell. This is the number of paired comparisons showing negative association.
3. Add the sums found in steps 1 and 2 and divide by 2. This is E_w, the amount of errors expected without knowledge of X.
4. Take the smaller of the sums found in steps 1 and 2. This is E_k, the amount of errors made with knowledge of X.
5. $\gamma = \dfrac{E_w - E_k}{E_w}$
6. If the sum for step 1 is bigger than the sum for step 2, γ is positive; if it is smaller, γ is negative.

Interpretation. Gamma indicates perfect association (1.0 or -1.0) when the relative value of Y can always be correctly predicted from the relative value of X (that is, when $E_k = 0$). Gamma indicates zero association (0) when knowing the relative value of X is of no help in predicting the relative value of Y (that is, when $E_k = E_w$). When X is of some help in predicting Y but the association is not perfect, the magnitude of gamma indicates the P–R–E made possible by knowledge of X. In the previous example the magnitude of gamma was .46, which indicates that knowing relative city size reduced errors in predicting relative turnout by 46%.

The sign of the coefficient indicates the direction of association. In the previous example the negative sign for gamma indicates that the larger cities tended to have the lower turnout rates.

Testing the Significance of Gamma. We determine the statistical significance of gamma by computing a t value and then referring to the t table in the appendix to find whether the t value for the gamma is great enough to be significant at a specified level. The t value for gamma is

$$t = \gamma \sqrt{\frac{2\,E_w}{N(1 - \gamma^2)}}$$

The degrees of freedom equal 2 E_w–2, and the t table assumes that t will be computated only when gamma supports the hypothesis.

For Table 12–7, $\gamma = -.46$, $E_w = 443$, $E_k = 240$, and $N = 87$. Hence,

$$t = -.46 \sqrt{\frac{886}{87\,(1 - .21)}} = 1.65$$

With 884 degrees of freedom, the t value, and hence the gamma value, is significant at the .05 level. This analysis supports the hypothesis "The larger the city size, the lower the turnout rate tends to be for municipal elections."

Choosing Between Del$_I$ and Gamma

When at least one of the variables is quantitative, you will want to choose either del$_I$ or gamma to summarize the relationship. Gamma is the more widely used of the two, and is more likely to be familiar to your audience.[4] This is of some importance because your findings are more likely to be accepted if they are based on statistical analysis with which the readers are familiar.

Gamma, however, has the drawback of being based on only those paired comparisons in which the units differ on both the X and Y variables. In extreme cases gamma could reflect the strength of association for only a small minority of all possible paired comparisons. Because it is based on only the most clear-cut cases, the magnitude of gamma is usually higher than that of del$_I$ (almost twice as high in the previous example). Again treating the extreme case, gamma always has a magnitude of 1.0 for 2 × 2 tables if any one cell of the table is empty. Some of your audience may be hesitant to accept findings based on what they perceive to be inflated correlation coefficients.

Technically, these two correlation coefficients are appropriate for testing slightly different hypotheses. Del$_I$ is more appropriate when the researcher hypothesizes that higher levels of X are necessary and sufficient to cause higher levels of Y. Gamma is more appropriate when higher levels of X are seen as necessary but not sufficient to cause higher levels of Y. However, the technical distinctions between the two correlations are so fine, and the wording of our hypotheses usually so vague, that you can generally select whichever you prefer.

SUMMARY

This chapter has introduced correlation coefficients appropriate for reporting relationships in which the dependent variables are treated as nominal or ordinal.

Because correlation coefficients summarize the magnitude and character of association in a single number, they are easier to present and to comprehend than an entire table. They are especially valuable when several variables are each being related to each other. We may easily compare coefficients of the same type to see which relationship is stronger.

Although there are many different correlation coefficients, they all indicate the strength of association between variables. Some also indicate the direction of association. At this point you should be able to generally interpret correlation coefficients used by others, and to calculate at least one appropriate coefficient whenever you have a nominal or ordinal dependent variable. If you find a supportive correlation coefficient, you should test it for statistical significance.

Endnotes

[1]Social scientists typically refer to any measure of association as a correlation coefficient. Statisticians typically restrict that term to measures of linear association.

[2]For a more detailed treatment of del, see David Hildebrand, James Laing, and Howard Rosenthal, *Prediction Analysis of Cross Classifications* (New York: John Wiley, 1977). See also their article "Prediction Analysis in Political Research," *American Political Science Review,* 70 (June 1976), 509–35. We have expanded their analysis to include additional measures at the ordinal and interval level.

[3]Del_k cannot equal 1 when the marginals of the tables are distributed in such a way that there must be errors in prediction. For example, suppose Democrats were hypothesized to vote yes and Republicans no on a roll call. If the party split was 50%/50%, and the roll-call vote was split 70% yes to 30% no, at least 20% of the Democrats would have to be in error. Thus, del_k could not equal 1. Some measures of association define perfect association as when the relationship is as strong as it can be given the distribution of the variable. Del_k does not.

[4]For a recent article showing multiple uses for del_l, see Lee Sigelman and Yung-mei Tsai, "Personal Finances and Voting Behavior," *American Politics Quarterly,* 9, no. 4 (October 1981), 371–400.

LABORATORY EXERCISES

This laboratory is designed to give you experience with measures of association as they are applied to crosstables. You will determine which measures are the most appropriate, calculate the measures, and evaluate the meaning of them in different situations.

Task 1. In this task you will determine which correlation coefficient to use. After each of the following hypotheses indicate the correlation coefficient you would use to summarize the relationship between the independent and dependent variables.

Hypothesis H1: Upper- and lower-class voters are more likely to support conservative candidates than are middle-class voters.

Hypothesis H2: The higher the socioeconomic class of voters, the more likely they are to vote for conservative candidates.

Hypothesis H3: The greater the degree of central control exercised over a nation, the less likely it is to trade with other nations.

Hypothesis H4: Senatorial candidates who win divisive primaries are less likely to win the general election than are senatorial candidates who do not have to compete in divisive primaries.

Hypothesis H5: Urban residents tend to complete a higher level of education than do rural residents.

Task 2. In this task you will compute and interpret a correlation coefficient while working with quantitative independent and dependent variables. The following table shows hypothetical data appropriate for testing hypothesis H1 in Task 1. Compute a correlation coefficient to summarize the table.

		Class		
		Upper	*Middle*	*Lower*
Vote	*Conservative*	18	19	13
	Other	12	31	7

a. Does the correlation show support for the hypothesis? How strong is the support, if any?

b. Test the significance of the correlation to determine if it is significant at the .05 level. Is it significant?
   Assume this relationship was controlled for level of education with the following results:

Education	Correlation	Significance
College	.62	.05
High School	.41	.01
Grade School	.33	.05

c. For which education level is the hypothesized association between class and vote the strongest?

d. For which education level is the probability the lowest that the observed support for the hypothesis is a result of sample selection?

Task 3. In this task you will compute and interpret a correlation coefficient for relative variables. The following table is a crosstable testing hypothesis H3 in Task 1. The variables are measured by Guttman scales, with 6 being the highest score and 1 the lowest. The data are from a sample of 35 nations in the late 1950s.

		Centralized Control					
		1	*2*	*3*	*4*	*5*	*6*
	1		1		1	2	
	2		1	6			1
Trade	3		2	1		2	
	4					2	1
	5	2	3		2	1	1
	6	3	2	1			

a. Compute the correlation coefficient.
b. Does the correlation show support for the hypothesis? How strong is the support, if any?
c. Determine whether the correlation is statistically significant at the .05 level.
d. Does the analysis show support for the hypothesis?

Task 4. Use the computer to analyze data provided by your instructor. Develop a hypothesis relating two categorical variables, select an appropriate control variable, and, using appropriate measures of association, complete the analysis. Indicate what you found.

REVIEW QUESTIONS

1. Use the following hypothesis and hypothetical data to respond to questions a–d.
   Hypothesis: Delegates to national party conventions are more likely to support candidates from their own state than candidates from other states.

		Delegate's State			
		TX	*NY*	*OH*	*IL*
	NY	5	25	10	10
Candidate's State	*IL*	0	0	10	20
	TX	15	5	0	0
	OH	0	10	10	0

   a. Compute an appropriate correlation coefficient for the above table. Show all work. Reorder columns or rows if necessary.

    b. Determine the significance level of that correlation. Show all work.

    c. Does the bivariate table show support for the hypothesis?

    d. If you had tested this same hypothesis, controlling for the ideology of the delegates, and the correlations were as follows, what would you conclude regarding the hypothesis?

       1) for liberals: $-.25$

       2) for conservatives: .15, not significant at the .05 level

    What conclusions would you draw from this?

2. Use the following hypothesis and hypothetical data to respond to questions a–d.

    Hypothesis: As a president's popularity increases, his success with Congress tends to increase.

		Presidential Popularity		
		High	*Medium*	*Low*
	High	10	5	5
Success With Congress	*Medium*	5	5	0
	Low	5	10	5

    a. Compute an appropriate correlation coefficient for the above table. Show all work. Reorder columns or rows if necessary.

    b. Determine the significance of that correlation. Show all work.

    c. Does the bivariate table show support for the hypothesis?

    d. If you tested this same hypothesis, controlling for whether Congress was in the hands of the same party as that of the president, and the correlations were as follows, what would you conclude regarding the hypothesis?

       1) Congress controlled by party of president: .40, sig. at .05 level

       2) Congress controlled by other party or split: .13, not sig.

CHAPTER THIRTEEN

REPORTING RELATIONSHIPS AND SIGNIFICANCE: INTERVAL DEPENDENT VARIABLE

In this chapter we will consider ways of reporting and determining the significance of relationships in which the dependent variable is treated as interval. We
first look at those cases in which the independent variable is nominal or ordinal,
and then treat the cases in which both variables are interval.

NOMINAL OR ORDINAL INDEPENDENT VARIABLE

As we suggested in Chapter 8, when the independent variable is nominal or ordinal and the dependent variable is interval, the most appropriate presentation of
the relationship is often a comparison of the means of the dependent variable for
each of the categories of the independent variable. For example, the comparison
of means shown in Table 13–1 would be an appropriate test of the hypothesis
that metropolitan areas in the sunbelt have higher projected rates of growth in
employment than do metropolitan areas in the snowbelt.

TABLE 13–1 Projected Growth Rates in
Employment, 1979–1990: Metropolitan Areas in
the Sunbelt and the Snowbelt

	Sunbelt	Snowbelt
Mean Projected Growth Rate	2.7%	1.4%
(*N*)	(10)	(13)

Source: Chase Econometrics Regional Forecasting Service; reported in *The
World Almanac and Book of Facts, 1983* (New York: Newspaper Enterprise Association), p. 82.

A comparison of means is generally a clear and concise enough presentation of
the relationship between two variables that it is not necessary to use a correlation coefficient to summarize the presentation. However, when several compari-

sons of means are presented and the researcher wishes to reliably compare the strengths of association, a correlation coefficient is useful. The correlation coefficient most commonly used to summarize comparisons of means is eta^2.

Eta^2

Theoretical Foundation. Eta^2 is based on the assumption that perfect association between a categorical variable and an interval variable exists when we can exactly predict the value of the interval variable for each unit by knowing the category that unit falls into on the categorical variable. In the example above, region and growth in employment would be perfectly associated if all sunbelt metropolitan areas had one projected rate and all snowbelt metropolitan areas had another. The researcher could then always predict the growth rate by knowing the region of the metropolitan area. Put another way, if the association were perfect, there would be no variation in growth rates *within* the sunbelt or *within* the snowbelt, but there would be variation in the rates *between* the two areas. All of the variation observed in the Y values would be accounted for by differences between X categories; none would be accounted for by differences within X categories.

To calculate eta^2, the researcher apportions the total variation in Y into that part which can be accounted for by variation between X categories and that part which can be accounted for by variation within X categories. Eta^2 is equal to the proportion of the total variation in Y that can be accounted for by the variation between categories of X. In the example above, eta^2 would be equal to the proportion of the total variation in growth rates that could be accounted for by differences between the sunbelt and the snowbelt.

Computation. We can measure variation in Y values by summing the squares of the difference between each Y value and the mean Y value. This is the same procedure that we follow when we compute the variance in Y. The sum of the squared deviations about the mean is called the *total sum of squares (SS$_T$)*. SS_T can be broken down into two components, the within sum of squares (SS_W) and the between sum of squares (SS_B). ($SS_T = SS_W + SS_B$.)

The within sum of squares measures the variation in Y values within X categories. It is the sum of the squared deviations about the mean Y value for each category of X. To see how SS_W is calculated, consider the growth rates for the metropolitan areas summarized in Table 13–2.

Anaheim deviates 0.7 from the mean projected growth rate in employment for sunbelt metropolitan areas. Squaring that deviation gives .49, the first of the squared deviations that we must sum to get SS_W. Squaring the 0.6 for Atlanta contributes .36 more. We continue the process for each area, concluding with the .01 contribution from the squared deviation for Washington. For this sample, $SS_W = 14.36$.

The between sum of squares measures the variation in Y values between X categories. To compute SS_B, we multiply the number of units in each category

TABLE 13-2 Projected Growth Rate in Employment by Region: Data for Each Metropolitan Area

Sunbelt	Growth	Deviation From Mean	Snowbelt	Growth	Deviation From Mean
Anaheim	3.4	0.7	Bridgeport	1.3	0.1
Atlanta	2.1	0.6	Buffalo	0.2	1.2
Honolulu	2.0	0.7	Cincinnati	1.4	0.0
Memphis	1.4	1.3	Columbus	1.3	0.1
Miami	2.6	0.1	Denver	3.0	1.6
Phoenix	3.7	1.0	Hartford	1.4	0.0
Riverside	2.6	0.1	Kansas City	1.3	0.1
San Antonio	2.8	0.1	Milwaukee	1.5	0.1
San Jose	3.2	0.5	New York	0.1	1.3
Tampa	3.2	0.5	Pittsburgh	0.8	0.6
			Rochester	1.1	0.3
			Salt Lake	3.3	1.9
			Washington	1.5	0.1
Mean	2.7			1.4	
(N)	(10)			(13)	

by the squared difference between the category mean and the mean of the entire sample. After computing those products we add them together.

The mean projected rate of growth in employment for all 23 metropolitan areas in Table 13-2 is 1.97. The sunbelt areas, which have a mean growth rate of 2.7, deviate from the sample mean by .73. That deviation must be squared and, since there are 10 sunbelt areas, multiplied by 10 for us to find the sunbelt contribution to SS_B. That contribution would be 5.3. The same procedure applied to the snowbelt areas shows their contribution to be $(.57)^2$ (13) = 4.16. If we add those two values together, then $SS_B = 9.46$.

We measure the total variation in Y (SS_T) by summing SS_W and SS_B. (To check your results, make sure SS_T equals N times the variance in Y.) In this case, $SS_T = 23.82$.

Eta^2 is equal to the proportion of the total variation in Y that can be attributed to the variation between categories. In this case

$$\text{Eta}^2 = SS_B \div SS_T = 9.46 \div 23.82 = .40$$

For this sample, differences between the sunbelt and the snowbelt account for 40% of the variance in projected growth rates in employment. The other 60% of the variance is attributable to other factors that cause variation in growth rates among cities within each of the regions.

Interpretation. As with other correlation coefficients we have studied, eta^2 varies between 0.0 and 1.0. It is 0.0 when there is no difference in the mean value of Y for the different categories of X (in this case, $SS_B = 0$). Eta^2 is 1.0 when there is no difference in Y values within each category of X (in this case, $SS_W = 0$ and $SS_B = SS_T$). The greater the association between X and Y—that is, the more useful differences in X are in predicting Y values—the closer eta^2 will be to 1.0. The magnitude of eta^2 equals the proportion of the variation in Y that can be attributed to differences in X.

As with gamma, eta^2 measures how useful knowledge of X is in predicting Y. To find the predictive value of X, the researcher first determines the amount of error she would have made in predicting the Y values of the units without knowing each unit's X value. She then determines the amount of error she would have made in predicting the Y values of the units if she had based her estimates of Y on the X values of the units. If X has any predictive value, there will be less error when the predictions are based on X. If the amount of error made *with knowledge* of X is called E_k, and the amount of error made *without knowledge* of X is called E_w, then the predictive value of X is measured by the extent to which E_k is smaller than E_w. That is, eta^2 is equal to $(E_w - E_k)/E_w$. Put another way, eta^2 is equal to the proportional-reduction-in-error (P–R–E) made possible by knowledge of X.

Where Y is an interval variable E_w is equal to SS_T. By basing his predictions on X, the researcher can reduce errors to just those attributable to variation within X categories; that is, $E_k = SS_W$. Therefore,

$$\text{eta}^2 = \frac{E_w - E_k}{E_w} = \frac{SS_T - SS_W}{SS_T} = \frac{SS_B}{SS_T}$$

If the X values perfectly predict Y values (if there is perfect association), then E_k is zero and the magnitude of the correlation coefficient is $\frac{E_w - 0}{E_w}$, or 1.00. The P–R–E is 100%. If the X and Y values are paired in such a way that knowing X is of no help in predicting Y (if there is zero association), then E_k equals E_w and the magnitude of the correlation is $\frac{E_w - E_w}{E_w}$, or 0. In this case, there is no P–R–E. If the X values are of some help in predicting Y but do not allow perfect prediction, then E_k is smaller than E_w and the magnitude of the correlation coefficient is between 0 and 1; the greater the magnitude, the greater the association. The magnitude indicates the P–R–E.

Testing the Significance of Differences in Means

When a comparison of means indicates support for the hypothesis (regardless of whether eta^2 is computed), it is necessary to calculate a test of significance in order to determine the probability that the observed difference in means occurred by chance. The appropriate test of significance is called the F-test because it involves computing a value for F, a statistic with a known sampling distribution.[1] The distribution of F for different levels of significance is presented in the appendix.

The formula for computing F is

$$F = \frac{SS_B(N-C)}{SS_W(C-1)}$$

Where SS_B and SS_W are computed as shown earlier in this chapter, $N =$ the number in the sample, and $C =$ the number of categories of X.
For the data in Table 13–2,

$$F = \frac{9.46(23-2)}{14.36(2-1)} = 13.83.$$

Each F has two different values for degrees of freedom—one for the numerator, which is equal to $C - 1$, and one for the denominator equal to $N - C$. In the example, the degrees of freedom would be 1 and 21.

There is a separate F table for each level of significance. Each table shows the F value required for significance at the level given the number of degrees of freedom for the numerator and denominator. The F tables for the .05 and .01 levels are in the appendix. Here is a portion of the F table for the .05 level:

		Degrees of Freedom (df) for Numerator		
		1	2	3
Degrees of	10	3.28	2.92	2.73
Freedom (df)				
for Denominator	20	2.97	2.59	2.38

To determine whether the F calculated in the above example is significant at the 0.5 level, you would look for the column showing 1 df for a numerator and find the row showing 21 df, or as near to but less than 21 df, for the denominator. The value of F shown there is 2.97. Since the calculated value of 13.83 is larger than 2.97, the observed differences in means are significant at the .05 level.

INTERVAL INDEPENDENT VARIABLE

Visual Presentation

Scatterplots. Let us start by considering two ordinal measures that we have cross-tabulated with each other in order to find the extent of relationship between the two. Suppose that the independent variable is years of education and

TABLE 13–3 Hypothetical Relationship Between Education and Income (Ordinal Level Measures)

		Education		
		High	*Medium*	*Low*
Income	*High*	80%	10%	10%
	Medium	10	80	10
	Low	10	10	80
		(10)	(10)	(10)

the dependent variable is income. These two variables are each divided into three categories—high, medium, and low. Table 13-3, using hypothetical data, presents an example of a fairly high level of relationship between the two variables.

This is the visual presentation of this relationship by means of a cross-tabulation. We can quickly observe that there is a high positive relationship between these two variables. We find most of the cases along the main diagonal of the table, starting in the upper left and going to the lower right.

It is obvious that each of these ordinal-level variables could be measured with interval-level measures. Instead of categorizing the individuals into high, medium, and low on each variable, the actual number of years of education and the actual number of dollars of income could be considered.

If the two variables had been treated as interval, we could not have used a crosstable to present the data, for it would have required too many rows and columns. Instead we would use a scatterplot, a graphic presentation in which a dot represents the *X* and *Y* value of each unit. Figure 13–1 is a scatterplot representing a hypothetical relationship between income and education.

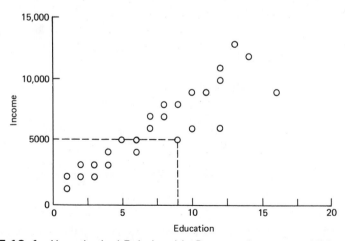

FIGURE 13–1 Hypothetical Relationship Between Income and Education

As with the cross-tabulation, the two dimensions of the scatterplot represent the two variables. The horizontal dimension represents the independent variable; the vertical dimension represents the dependent variable. Using the two dimensions together, we can represent each unit in terms of its position on the two measures. Suppose we had a respondent who earned $5000 per year and had eight years of school. To place him we would move to the $5000 position on the income dimension and run an imaginary line from that point parallel to the bottom of the plot. From the point indicating eight years of education on the education dimension, we would run an imaginary line parallel to the side of the plot. These lines are indicated in Figure 13–1 by the dotted lines. The two lines intersect, and at that point a dot is placed to represent the person who earns $5,000 and went to school for eight years. Note that this is similar to what we do with a table, except that instead of a limited number of categories we now have an infinite number of possible categories. Each unit may have its own category.

Interval relationships are similar to ordinal relationships. If an association

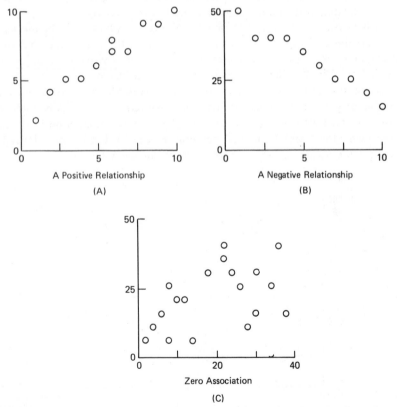

FIGURE 13–2 (A) A Positive Relationship; (B) A Negative Relationship; (C) Zero Association

TABLE 13–4 Women in the Work Force and Disapproval of Intermarriage: Western Europe, 1970

Nation	Women in Work Force	Disapproving of Intermarriage
West Germany	33%	25%
Italy	21	25
France	26	19
Netherlands	18	22
Belgium	27	22
Luxembourg	11	30
Great Britain	40	19
Portugal	27	25
Austria	40	34
Switzerland	33	26
Sweden	49	10
Denmark	38	13
Norway	23	30
Finland	41	16
Spain	15	33
Ireland	25	34

Source: *Survey of Europe Today* (London: Reader's Digest Association, 1970). The dependent variable is the mean percentage of adults disapproving of each of four types of intermarriage: across racial, religious, national, and social-class lines.

exists, then as one variable grows larger the other variable grows commensurately larger or smaller. If both grow larger at the same time, the association is positive. If one grows larger while the other grows smaller, the association is negative.

Figure 13–2 consists of simple scatterplots that reflect these kinds of relationships. The names of the variables do not matter. Figure 13–2A is a fairly strong positive relationship: One variable tends to grow larger as the other does. Figure 13–2B is a negative relationship: One variable grows smaller as the other grows larger. Figure 13–2C indicates zero association: The points are distributed randomly, and no association exists between the variables.

Now let us consider an example that uses actual data. Table 13–4 shows the relationship, for Western European nations, between the percentage of females in the work force and the percentage of adults who disapprove of intermarriage. Figure 13–3 shows the scatterplot for these data. Note that there is a tendency for disapproval of intermarriage to drop as the percentage of females in the work force rises. That is a negative association.

Pearson's r and r^2

When several relationships have to be presented and the strengths of each compared, it is especially cumbersome and unreliable to present scatterplots for

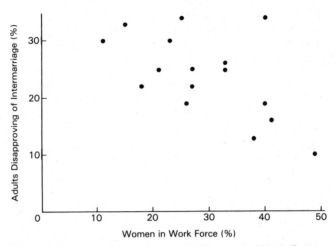

FIGURE 13–3 Scatterplot: Percentage of Women in Work Force and Disapproval of Intermarriage

each. Instead, we use correlation coefficients called Pearson's r and r^2 to summarize the relationships. As is the case with other correlation coefficients, Pearson's r and r^2 allow us to present relationships concisely and to make reliable comparisons of their direction and relative strength.

As was the case with the correlation coefficients introduced in the last chapter, r and r^2 vary in magnitude from 0.0 to 1.0. A correlation of 0.0 indicates no association between the two variables; a correlation of 1.0 indicates perfect association between the variables. Magnitudes between 0.0 and 1.0 indicate an association that is not perfect.

TABLE 13–5 Hypothetical Data Showing Perfect Linear Association

Unit	X	Y
A	10	21
B	9	19
C	8	17
D	6	13
E	6	13
F	6	13
G	5	11
H	4	9
I	3	7
J	2	5
K	1	3
L	0	1

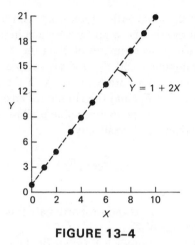

FIGURE 13–4

Pearson's r and r^2 measure the extent to which the Y values of units can be predicted from the X values of those units by using the equation $Y' = a + bX$ (where a and b are specific numbers). Because of this, r and r^2 are said to measure the extent of *linear association* between X and Y.

If X and Y are perfectly associated, a scatterplot of the X–Y values will show all of the data points to fall on a straight line, and r and r^2 will have a magnitude of 1.0. There will be some equation of the type $Y' = a + bX$ that will perfectly predict every observed Y value from every observed X value. Table 13–5 and Figure 13–4 illustrate a perfect association. Note that the equation $Y' = 1 + 2X$ correctly predicts all Y values from the X values.

If there is zero association between X and Y, no linear equation will predict the Y values any better than one could do by simply estimating that the Y value of each unit is equal to the mean Y value of all units. If there is no linear equation that will be of any help in predicting Y values, then r and r^2 will be 0.0.

Strength of Association. The closer the observed relationship is to perfect association, the more nearly the data points on the scatterplot will fall on a straight line, and the higher will be the magnitude of r and r^2. A correlation of .90 would indicate a very strong linear association between X and Y; a correlation of .10 would indicate a very weak association.

Direction of Association. When r is reported, a negative sign indicates a negative association, and a positive sign a positive association. When r^2 is reported, direction is not indicated because r^2 is always positive (squaring a negative r gives a positive r^2).

Theoretical Foundation for r^2. As with gamma and eta^2, Pearson's r^2 measures how useful knowledge of X is in predicting Y. To find the predictive value of X, the researcher first determines the amount of error he would have made in predicting the Y values of the units without knowing each unit's X value. He then determines the amount of error he would have made in predicting the Y values of the units if he had based his estimates of Y on the X values of the units (by using a linear equation linking X and Y). If X has any predictive value, there will be less error when the predictions are based on X. If the amount of error made *with knowledge* of X is called E_k, and the amount of error made *without knowledge* of X is called E_w, then the predictive value of X is measured by the extent to which E_k is smaller than E_w. Specifically,

$$r^2 = \frac{E_w - E_k}{E_w}$$

Pearson's r^2 is therefore equal to the proportional-reduction-in error (P–R–E) made possible by knowledge of X.

   If the X values perfectly predict Y values (if there is perfect association), then E_k is zero and the magnitude of the correlation coefficient is $\frac{E_w - 0}{E_w}$, or 1.00. The P–R–E is 100%. If the X and Y values are paired in such a way that knowing X is of no help in predicting Y (if there is zero association), then E_k equals E_w and the magnitude of the correlation coefficient is $\frac{E_w - E_w}{E_w}$, or 0. In this case, there is no P–R–E. If the X values are of some help in predicting Y but do not allow perfect prediction, then E_k is smaller than E_w and the magnitude of the correlation coefficient is between 0 and 1; the greater the magnitude, the greater the association. The magnitude indicates the P–R–E.

Theoretical Foundation for **r.** Pearson's r is based on the extent of deviation from what a set of data would look like if the two variables were in perfect association. The researcher first determines how far the observed pairs of X–Y values deviate from what would be expected if there were a perfect positive association between X and Y. She then determines how far the pairs of X–Y values would have deviated from perfect association if the X and Y values had been statistically independent (paired by chance). If the first type of deviation is called the error observed, E_o, and the second type of deviation is called the error expected by chance, E_c, then r is the proportion by which E_o is smaller than E_c:

$$r = \frac{E_c - E_o}{E_c}$$

   Pearson's r tells us how much closer the observed relationship is to perfect positive association than could be expected by chance. If the association is perfect, then $E_o = 0$, and therefore $r = 1.0$. If the association is zero, then $E_o = E_c$ and hence $r = 0.0$. If the observed relationship deviates less from a perfect positive association than would be expected by chance, then $E_o < E_c$ and r will be a positive number between 0.0 and 1.0. If the observed relationship deviates more from a perfect positive association than would be expected by chance, $E_o > E_c$ and r will be a negative number between 0.0 and -1.0. The stronger the association, the higher the magnitude of r.

Computation. Computation of Pearson's r is quite complicated and is generally done by machine. We will briefly discuss one of the simplest ways of computing r.

Computation of r is greatly simplified if both the X and Y variables are first z-scored. You may remember that z-scores were introduced earlier as a method for weighting variables equally. We compute the z-score of each value by subtracting the mean of the variable from the value and then dividing the difference by the standard deviation of the variable. Thus, a z-score of 2 would mean that a value was 2 standard deviations above the mean value for that variable. We will use Z_x to stand for the z-score of an X value and Z_y to stand for the z-score of a Y variable. Table 13–6 shows the z-scores for each of the Western European nations on the X and Y variables that we have been using as an example: percentage of women in the work force and percentage of adults disapproving of intermarriage.

TABLE 13–6 Z-Scores for Percentage of Women in the Work Force (Z_x) and Percentage Disapproving of Intermarriage(Z_y)

Nation	X	Z_x	Y	Z_y
West Germany	33	.37	25	.15
Italy	21	− .80	25	.15
France	26	− .31	19	− .70
Netherlands	18	−1.09	22	− .27
Belgium	27	− .21	22	− .27
Luxembourg	11	−1.78	30	.85
Great Britain	40	1.06	19	− .70
Portugal	27	− .21	25	.15
Austria	40	1.06	34	1.42
Switzerland	33	.37	26	.29
Sweden	49	1.94	10	−1.97
Denmark	38	.86	13	−1.55
Norway	23	− .61	30	.86
Finland	41	1.16	16	−1.12
Spain	15	−1.39	33	1.28
Ireland	25	− .41	34	1.42
Mean	29.2		23.9	
Standard Deviation	10.3		7.1	

Z_x for West Germany is .37 because the X value for West Germany, 33, is .37 of a standard deviation above the X mean of 29.2. Roughly put, Germany's z-score indicates that it has slightly more women in the work force than is average for these nations. Similarly, Sweden's Z_y of -1.97 indicates that disapproval of intermarriage is much lower in that nation than is average for this sample.

We compute Pearson's r by multiplying the Z_x value for each unit by the Z_y value for that unit. This is called finding the crossproducts for the units ($Z_x Z_y$). Pearson's r is the mean of those crossproducts for the whole sample:

$$r = \frac{(Z_x Z_y)}{N}$$

In this case the researcher multiplies .37 by .15 for West Germany, $-.80$ by .15 for Italy, and so on. The mean of those crossproducts is $-.60$. Thus, Pearson's r is $-.60$ and r^2 is .36.

Interpretation. The negative sign for r shows that as the percentage of women in the work force increases across this sample, disapproval of intermarriage tends to decrease.

The magnitude of r indicates that the association is not perfect. A perfect linear association requires that the absolute value of Z_x equal the absolute value of Z_y for each unit. In this sample those values are not equal, but they are much closer to being equal than would be expected by chance.

If the percentage of women in the work force and the percentage of the adult populace disapproving of intermarriage had been perfectly associated, then the mean of the $Z_x Z_y$ crossproducts would have been ± 1. If there had been no association between the two variables, the mean of the crossproducts would have been 0. As it was, the mean was $-.60$, or 60% closer to perfect association than would have been expected by chance if there had been no association.

The r^2 indicates that knowing the percentage of women in the work force will reduce errors in predicting the percentage of adults disapproving of intermarriage. Without knowing the percentage of women in the work force, the best estimate of disapproval of intermarriage in each country would be the mean disapproval rate for all countries in the sample, 23.9%. Although 23.9% would have been the best prediction for Y for each nation, those predictions would not have been accurate. The error in those predictions would have been equal to the variance in Y. The r^2 tells us that there is a linear equation relating X and Y that will give us estimates of disapproval that are closer to the actual disapproval rates than we can get by always estimating Y to be 23.9%. The estimated Y values given by the linear equation will not be equal to the actual Y values, but the error in predicting Y will be 36% less than the error we would have made by always estimating Y to be 23.9. The error in predicting Y will be 36% less than the variance in Y (P–R–E = .36).

Put another way, there is a linear equation relating women in the work force to disapproval of intermarriage that can account for 36% of the variation observed in the disapproval rates. (This interpretation of r^2 is very similar to the interpretation of eta^2 discussed earlier in this chapter.) In the next chapter we discuss how to determine the specific linear equation that best predicts Y from X.

SUMMARY

This chapter has focused on the test of significance for comparisons of means, scatterplots for visually displaying relationships between interval variables, and correlation coefficients that are appropriate for measuring association between interval variables. Of particular importance is Pearson's r correlation coefficient. Not only is it widely used, but the presentation of r in this chapter lays the foundation for all the work in the next chapter.

Endnotes

[1]Where there are only two categories of X, a t-test may be substituted for the F-test. The t distribution is simply the square root of the F distribution with one degree of freedom in the numerator.

LABORATORY EXERCISES

The purpose of this laboratory is to give you experience with measures of association and significance tests when interval-level variables are involved.

Task 1. In this task you will test the significance of difference in means and compute the measure of association between a categorical variable and an interval variable. Using the data tabulated below, you will test the following hypothesis.

Hypothesis: Republican candidates tend to spend more money on campaigns for the House of Representatives than do Democratic candidates.

Data: Candidate, party, and expenditure data from the 1980 *Almanac of American Politics.* We used a systematic sample of alternate districts, excluding races in which a candidate was nominated by both the Democrats and the Republicans or where candidates were unopposed.

Candidate	Party	1978 Expenditures (x \$10,000)
Randolph	D	8
Ambro	D	8
Carman	R	31
Wydler	R	8
Matthews	D	6
Ferraro	D	38
Dellibovi	R	11
Scheuer	D	2

Candidate	Party	1978 Expenditures (× $10,000)
Huhu	R	0
Solarz	D	2
Carasso	R	0
Murphy	D	19
Peters	R	5
Peyser	D	11
Martinelli	R	14
Fish	R	8
Ozols	D	0
McHugh	D	20
Wallace	R	14
Solomon	R	17
Pattison	D	16
Lee	R	16
Bernardi	D	7
Conable	R	6
Repicci	D	3
Nowak	D	4
Poth	R	0
Lundine	D	9
Maguire	R	7

a. Compute the comparison of means that you need in order to test the hypothesis.

b. What do you conclude about the hypothesis?

c. Since the hypothesis is not supported, you should not compute a test of significance. Assume for the sake of practice, however, that you had correctly hypothesized that Democrats spent more. Compute an F-test in order to see if the differences in means would show statistically significant support for that hypothesis.

d. Does the F value show support at the .05 level? The .025 level?

e. What would you conclude regarding that hypothesis?

Task 2. In this task you will test the bivariate relationships between interval variables.

Hypothesis: The greater the public support for a bill, the greater the support it is likely to have among groups having registered lobbyists.

Data: The bill, degree of public support, and measure of lobby-group support are presented. The sample includes all bills considered by the Iowa legislature, 1969–77, for which there are data on both public opinion and support by lobby groups. The data are adapted from data provided by Norman Luttbeg.

Bill	Public Support (as measured by statewide polls)	Lobby Support (weighted by group size)
Optional City Tax, 1969	40%	0%
Optional City Tax, 1973	40	40
City Aid From the State	80	100
Private School Aid*	80	100
Voting Age to 19	60	80
Voting Age to 18	50	80
Legalize Abortion*	80	100
Legalize Bingo*	80	0
Legalize Longer Trucks	50	100
Legalize Marijuana	30	40
Legalize Parimutuel Bets* 1971	60	0
Legalize Parimutuel Bets* 1977	60	80
Raise Public Drinking Age*	80	10
Restrict Public Smoking	70	90

Data are rounded off to nearest 10.

a. Construct a scatterplot which properly displays the relationship between public and group support as hypothesized.

b. Does the scatterplot tend to show support for the hypothesis?

c. Compute an appropriate correlation coefficient with which to test this hypothesis.

d. Does that correlation show statistically significant support for the hypothesis at the .05 level? At the .01 level?

e. What do you conclude regarding the hypothesis?

f. Control for whether the bill was one on which Iowa churches had generally taken a position (indicated by *). Below, construct scatterplots, for church-related and non-church-related bills.

g. Does either scatterplot tend to show support for the hypothesis?

h. Compute an appropriate correlation coefficient for both categories of the control variable.

i. Does either correlation show statistically significant support for the hypothesis at the .05 level?

j. What do you conclude regarding the hypothesis?

k. What do you conclude regarding the effect of the control variable?

Task 3. Use the computer to analyze data provided by your instructor.

a. Develop a hypothesis relating two interval variables.

b. Plot the relationship between the two variables; compute Pearson's *r*.

c. Is the correlation coefficient at the .05 level?

d. Do the data support the hypothesis?

REVIEW QUESTIONS

1. Use the following hypotheses and hypothetical data to respond to questions a and b.

   Hypothesis H1: The greater the margin of victory of a congressman, the more money he is likely to raise for his next campaign.

   Hypothesis H2: Congressional candidates who have won divisive primaries are likely to raise less money for their campaign than are congressional candidates who did not have to face divisive primaries.

   Measures:

       Margin of Victory: percentage of vote for congressman minus the percentage of the vote for his nearest opponent

       Divisive Primary: a primary in which the winner has a margin of 10% or less over his nearest opponent

       Money Raised: in dollars, as reported to the Federal Election Commission

   If you were testing these two hypotheses, which of the techniques might you properly use to present relationships and to test them for statistical significance?

2. For which of the following would the F value be the largest (assuming same sample size and same number of columns)? Compute the largest F for $N = 50$, $C = 2$.

       a. $SS_B = 98$; $SS_W = 200$

       b. $SS_B = 200$; $SS_W = 98$

       c. $SS_B = 98$; $SS_W = 98$

       d. $SS_B = 200$; $SS_W = 200$

3. Use the following hypothesis and hypothetical data to respond to questions a–d.

   Hypothesis: The higher the percentage of GNP spent on the military, the higher the rate of inflation tends to be.

Countries	Inflation Rate (%)	Military Spending as % of GNP
Israel	200	40
Argentina	100	25
Vietnam	50	40
Italy	40	5
Yugoslavia	40	4
Poland	20	10
U.S.S.R.	20	10
U.S.	10	5
South Africa	5	20
Switzerland	5	1

a. Present a scatterplot, labeled completely, showing the bivariate relationship.

b. Compute an appropriate correlation coefficient for the relationship, showing all work.

c. Does the bivariate relationship show support to be significant at the .05 level?

d. Suppose, for a larger sample, that we had computed the r correlations for the bivariate relationship, and for the relationship controlling for form of government, and the results were as follows:

whole sample: $r = .55; N = 34$
Communist nations: $r = .78; N = 12$
Western nations: $r = .61; N = 22$

Is the hypothesis supported at the .05 level of significance?

CHAPTER FOURTEEN

REGRESSION, EXPLANATION, AND CONTROLS: INTERVAL-LEVEL VARIABLES

The researcher attempts to explain variations in the dependent variable. Explanation of the variation may be done more or less precisely; sometimes all that is possible is an observation that as X increases Y increases. When the independent and dependent variables are interval, the researcher can usually estimate *how much* Y tends to increase for each increase of 1 in the value of X. Furthermore, it is usually possible to estimate a base value for Y—that is, the value of Y when X is zero. Having a base value for Y and an estimate of how much Y increases for each increase of 1 in X, the researcher can estimate the precise Y value for any unit, as long as its X value is known.

REGRESSION

The estimation of Y from X is done by **regression equation.** This equation is of the form $Y' = a + bX$, where Y' is the estimated Y value, b (the **slope**) is the amount that Y is estimated to increase for every increase of 1 in X, and a (the **intercept**) is the base value of Y.

In a study of attitudes toward intermarriage, for example, the regression equation was $Y' = 10.9 + 0.26 X$.[1] The dependent variable (Y) was the percentage of the population opposing intermarriage, and the independent variable (X) was the percentage attending church regularly. Since the intercept was 10.9, a nation with no one attending church regularly would be expected to have 10.9% of the population opposed to intermarriage. Since the slope was 0.26, each additional 1% of the population attending church would be expected to raise the opposition to intermarriage by 0.26%. The equation predicted a precise Y value for each X value. For example, for $X = 20$, Y was predicted to be $10.9 + (0.26)(20)$, or 16.1. A country with 20% of the population attending church regularly was estimated to have 16.1% of the population opposed to intermarriage.

If there is a perfect linear association between X and Y, the regression equation will correctly estimate Y for every unit in the sample. If, however, there is no perfect linear association, the estimated Y values will differ from the observed Y values for at least some of the units. The differences between the estimated and observed values $(Y' - Y)$ for the units are called **residuals.**

Determining the Regression Equation

The regression equation is the linear equation that produces the smallest squared sum of residuals. This equation will have a slope of $\frac{r\sigma Y}{\sigma X}$ and an intercept of $\overline{Y} - \frac{r\sigma Y\overline{X}}{\sigma X}$, where r is the Pearson's coefficient discussed in the last chapter, σX and σY are the standard deviations of X and Y, and $\overline{X}$ and $\overline{Y}$ are the means of X and Y. The regression equation, therefore, is,

$$Y' = \overline{Y} - \frac{r\sigma Y\overline{X}}{\sigma X} + \frac{r\sigma Y}{\sigma X}X$$

Let us return to the example in which opposition to intermarriage is explained as a result of increased numbers of people attending church regularly. Suppose the sample had shown the relationship appearing in Table 14-1.

TABLE 14-1 Hypothetical Relationship Between Church Attendance and Opposition to Intermarriage

Percentage Opposing Intermarriage		Percentage Attending Church Regularly
26		20
34		30
42		40
50		50
58		60
66		70
74		80
50	Mean	50
16	Standard Deviation	20

Pearson's r for that relationship would have been 1.0 (perfect association). The regression equation would have been

$$Y' = 50 - \frac{(1)\,16\,(50)}{20} + \frac{(1)\,(16)}{20}X, \text{ or}$$

$$Y = 10 + .8X$$

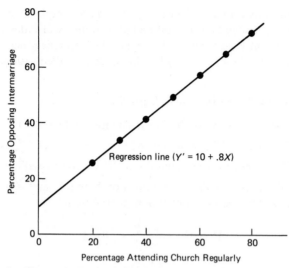

FIGURE 14–1 Scatterplot and Regression Line Showing Perfect Association

TABLE 14–2 Church Attendance and Opposition to Intermarriage: Western European Nations, 1970

Nation	Percentage Opposing Intermarriage	Percentage Attending Church Regularly
West Germany	25	53
Italy	25	71
France	19	38
Netherlands	22	48
Belgium	22	37
Luxembourg	30	71
Great Britain	19	27
Portugal	25	66
Austria	34	60
Switzerland	26	49
Sweden	10	32
Denmark	13	25
Norway	30	32
Finland	16	26
Spain	33	81
Ireland	34	98
Mean	23.9	50.9
Standard Deviation	7.1	21.2

Source: *A Survey of Europe Today* (London: Reader's Digest, 1970), Tables 8 and 66.

This equation defines a straight line (called a regression line) that we can super-impose over a scatterplot to show how far the predicted Y values differ from the observed Y values. The regression line and scatterplot are shown in Figure 14–1.

Since the hypothetical data show a perfect association between X and Y, all of the points in the scatterplot fall on the regression line. The percentage oppos-ing intermarriage is estimated correctly in every case, and each *residual* $(Y' - Y)$ is zero.

The actual sample, however, did not show a perfect association. Instead, the relationship was that shown in Table 14–2.

Pearson's r for this relationship is .77. The regression equation is

$$Y' = 23.9 - \frac{(.77)(7.1)(50.9)}{21.1} + \frac{(.77)(7.1)}{21.1} X, \text{ or}$$

$$Y' = 10.9 + 0.26X$$

Again, the regression equation defines a straight line, but in this case the regres-sion line does not go through all of the points on the scatterplot, as shown in Figure 14–2.

The residuals and squared residuals for this example are shown in Table 14–3. The sum of the squared residuals is the minimum possible for any linear equation given those X–Y values.

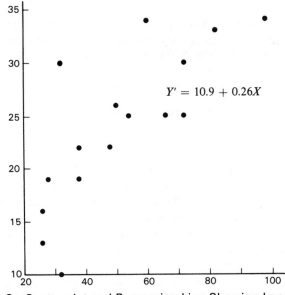

FIGURE 14–2 Scatterplot and Regression Line Showing Imperfect Associa-tion

TABLE 14–3   Residuals

Percentage Attending (X)	Percentage Opposing (Y)	Estimated Y ($Y = 10.9 + .26X$)	Residual ($Y' - Y$)	Squared Residual
53	25	24.5	0.5	0.3
71	25	29.1	−4.1	16.8
38	19	20.6	−1.6	2.6
48	22	23.2	−1.2	1.4
37	22	20.4	1.6	2.6
71	30	29.1	0.9	0.8
27	19	17.8	1.2	1.4
66	25	27.8	−2.8	7.8
60	34	26.3	7.7	59.3
49	26	23.5	2.5	6.3
32	10	19.1	−9.1	82.8
25	13	17.3	−4.3	18.5
32	30	19.1	10.9	118.8
26	16	17.6	−1.6	2.6
81	33	31.6	1.4	2.0
98	34	36.0	−2.0	4.0
		Sum of the squared residuals		328.0
		Mean of the squared residuals		20.5

EXPLANATION

You may recall from Chapter 8 that one measure of the variation in a property is the variance. Explanation can be viewed as an attempt to account for the variance in the dependent variable, Y. The total variance in Y is the mean of the squared difference between each Y value and the mean of Y:

$$\text{total variance} = \frac{\Sigma(Y - \overline{Y})^2}{N}$$

Some of the total variance in Y may be accounted for by the regression equation. If the regression equation estimates every Y value correctly, it is said to account for all of the variance in Y; then the mean of the squared differences between the estimated and observed values of Y would be reduced to zero.

If the regression equation estimates the mean Y value to be the value of Y for each unit, the variance in Y would still remain unexplained. Thus, the mean of the squared differences between the estimated and observed Y values would still be the total variance in Y.

If the regression equation does not estimate every Y value correctly, but comes closer to estimating those values than the mean of Y would, some of the variance would be explained and some unexplained. The unexplained variance would be equal to the mean of the squared differences between the estimated and observed Y values:

$$\text{unexplained variance} = \frac{\Sigma(Y' - Y)^2}{N}$$

Since $\frac{\Sigma(Y' - Y)^2}{N}$ is the mean of the squared residuals, the variance that cannot be explained is measured by the mean of the squared residuals. Because the regression equation holds the mean of the squared residuals to a minimum, it also holds unexplained variance to a minimum. The researcher has accounted for as much variation in Y as is possible on the basis of a linear association with X.

Researchers should report the proportion of the variance in Y that can be explained. They do so as follows:

$$\text{proportion of variance explained} = \frac{\text{total variance} - \text{mean of the squared residuals}}{\text{total variance}}$$

Returning to our example of imperfect association, the variance in Y is 49.9 and the mean of the squared residuals is 20.5. Hence, the proportion of the variance that can be explained is $\frac{49.9 - 20.5}{49.9} = .59$. In other words, 59% of the variation in Y is accounted for by the variation in X.

While the mathematics of the proof are too involved to present here, the proportion of the variance that can be explained by a linear association between X and Y is always equal to the square of the Pearson's r correlation coefficient for the association. In our example, Pearson's r was .77; r^2 would then be .59.

Had there been a perfect association, r and r^2 would have been 1, and 100% of the variance would have been explained. Had there been zero association, r and r^2 would have been 0, and none of the variance would have been explained.

REGRESSION AND EXPLANATION: MULTIPLE INDEPENDENT VARIABLES

Regression equations can be determined that estimate Y from more than one independent variable. The form of the multiple-regression equation is analogous to that of the simple-regression equation we saw at the beginning of the chapter: $Y' = b_1 X_1 + b_2 X_2 + b_3 X_3 \ldots + a$, where Y' is the estimated Y value of each unit; $X_1, X_2, X_3 \ldots$ are the values of the independent variables for each unit; $b_1, b_2, b_3 \ldots$ are **regression coefficients;** and a is the intercept. Like the slope for a simple regression, b_1, b_2, b_3, . . . each show how much Y is estimated to increase for each increase of 1 in the values of X_1, X_2, X_3 . . . , respectively, and as in simple regression a shows the estimated Y value when all X values are zero.

As with simple regression, the differences between the estimated and observed Y values ($Y' - Y$) are called the residuals. The multiple regression equation is the linear combination of the independent variables that minimizes the mean of the squared residuals.

A Pearson's r coefficient can be computed for the multiple regression; it is usually written as a capital R to indicate that it is based on a multiple regression euqation.[2] The proportion of the variance that can be explained by a multiple regression equation is R^2. As with the simple regresssion analysis, the proportion of the variance explained is equal to the

$$\frac{\text{total variance} - \text{mean of the squared residuals}}{\text{total variance}}$$

The combined effect of two or more variables in explaining Y is usually *not* the sum of their individual effects. To find the proportion of the variance accounted for by two or more variables, we cannot simply add together the variances accounted for by each. The only way to determine the combined explanatory effect of two or more variables is to compute the regression equation, determine the residuals and the total variance in Y, and then plug the results into the equation given in the previous paragraph.

Because the same variance in Y might have been explained by either one variable or another, the combined explanatory effect of two or more variables is usually less the sum of their separate effects. (That is, R^2 is usually less than the sum of the r^2 between Y and each independent variable.) Occasionally, the combined explanatory effects will be equal to or greater than the sum of their separate effects.[3]

Previously we studied a relationship in which church attendance accounted for 59% of the variance in opposition to intermarriage. We will now examine the combined explanatory effect of church attendance and reading books on opposition to intermarriage. The additional independent variable is the percentage of the population that regularly reads books. First, we look at the relationship between reading books and opposition to intermarriage (Table 14–4).

This relationship accounts for 32% of the variance in Y. However, reading books and church attendance are not statistically independent. Some of the 32% of the variance explained by reading was already explained by attendance. Thus, although attendance accounts for 59% of the variance in opposition to intermarriage, and reading accounts for 32%, together they do not account for 91% of the variance. Taken together, in fact, church attendance and reading books account for only 61% of the variance in opposition to intermarriage ($R^2 = .61$).

TABLE 14-4   Reading Books and Opposition to
Intermarriage: Western European Nations, 1970

Nation	Percentage Opposing Intermarriage	Percentage Reading Books Regularly
West Germany	25	17
Italy	25	9
France	19	33
Netherlands	22	35
Belgium	22	21
Luxembourg	30	33
Great Britain	19	39
Portugal	25	15
Austria	34	14
Switzerland	26	23
Sweden	10	27
Denmark	13	39
Norway	30	24
Finland	16	27
Spain	33	15
Ireland	34	27

Pearson's $r = -.56$ Regression Equation: $Y' = 35.0 - 0.45X$

Source: *A Survey of Europe Today* (London: Reader's Digest, 1970), Tables 34
and 66.

The computation of the mulitple-regression equation for estimating Y from
more than one X is beyond the scope of this text. It is generally done by computer. For our Western European sample, the multiple-regression equation is

$$Y' = 16.5 + 0.22\,X_1 - 0.15X_2$$

where X_1 is percentage attending church regularly and X_2 is percentage reading
books regularly. This equation indicates that a nation having no regular church
attenders or book readers would be estimated to have 16.5% opposition to intermarriage. For every increase of 1% in the percentage attending church, opposition would be expected to increase 0.22%; for every increase of 1% in the percentage reading books, opposition would be expected to decrease 0.15%.

Table 14–5 shows how well the multiple-regression equation estimates
each Y value. The estimates are closer to the observed Y values than was possible if we used simple regression, yet they are still not correct. The mean of the
squared residuals is reduced from 20.5 for the strongest of the simple regressions
(the one relating church attendance and opposition) to 19.3 for the multiple regression. This leaves 39% of the variance unexplained.

TABLE 14–5   Residuals for the Multiple-Regression Equation

X_1	Estimated Y X_2	Y	$(Y' = .22X_1 = .15X_2 + 16.5)$	Residual	Squared Residual
53	17	25	25.5	− .5	.3
71	9	25	30.7	−5.7	32.5
38	33	19	19.8	− .8	.6
48	35	22	21.7	.3	.1
37	21	22	21.4	.6	.4
71	33	30	28.6	1.4	2.0
27	39	19	16.4	2.6	6.7
66	15	25	28.7	−3.7	13.6
60	14	34	27.5	6.5	42.0
49	23	26	23.7	2.3	5.2
32	27	10	19.4	−9.4	87.6
25	39	13	16.0	−3.0	8.9
32	24	30	19.8	10.2	103.4
26	27	16	18.0	−2.0	4.2
81	15	33	32.0	1.0	1.0
98	27	34	33.9	.1	0.0

Sum of the squared residuals   308.5
Mean of the squared residuals   19.3

Summary

The combined variance accounted for by the independent variables is dependent upon both the variance accounted for by each independent variable and the extent to which the independent variables are correlated with each other.

CONTROLLING FOR INTERVAL VARIABLES

We can combine what we know from simple and multiple regression to determine how strongly each independent variable is associated with Y, *controlling for the other independent variables.* This is measured by a Pearson's r correlation coefficient called a **partial** r.

Up to this point, when we have discussed controls we have always used categorical control variables, divided the sample into groups of units with the same X value, and then done our analysis (tables, correlations, and so on) within those groups. This procedure is not possible, however, when the X variable is not categorical, as is generally the case with interval control variables. There might be only one unit in each control category, and no analysis would be possible.

The alternative procedure involves first determining how much of the variance in *Y cannot* be accounted for by the control variables, and then determining the proportion of this unexplained variance that *can* be accounted for by the independent variable. That proportion is equal to the partial r^2 between X and Y. The square root of that is the partial r. A partial r between X and Y controlling for Z is written $r_{xy.z}$.

Suppose, in the example above, that we had wanted to find the association between the percentage attending church and the percentage opposing intermarriage, controlling for the percentage reading books. Since reading accounted for 32% of the variance in opposition, only 68% of the variance could additionally be explained by church attendance. Church attendance did add to the total variance explained. It added 29%, bringing to 61 the percentage of the variance accounted for by the combination of church attendance and reading ($R^2 = .61$). Thus, church attendance was able to account for 29% of the 68% that had been unexplained by reading. The partial r^2 between church attendance and opposition is, therefore, 29/68 = .43. The partial r is .65.

The partial r between reading and opposition, controlling for attendance, could be calculated in the same way. Since attendance, by itself, explains 59% of the variance in opposition, and attendance plus reading explains 61%, reading adds only 2% to the overall explanation. That is 2% out of the 41% that was unexplained by attendance. Therefore, the partial r^2 between reading and opposition, controlling for attendance, is 2/41 = .05. The partial r is $-.22$. (The partial r is negative because the regression coefficient of reading is negative in the multiple-regression equation. It indicates that after controlling for the effects of church attendance, opposition tends to be lower when a higher percentage are reading regularly.)

General Formula for the Partial r^2

The general formula for the partial r^2 is

$$r^2 = \frac{R^2_{\text{all}} - R^2_{\text{controls}}}{1 - R^2_{\text{controls}}}$$

where R^2_{all} is the R^2 between Y and all of the independent and control variables, and R^2_{controls} is the R^2 (or r^2, if only one control) between Y and all of the control variables.

Tests of Significance

The statistical significance of the partial r may be determined from the table in the appendix for the significance of Pearson's r. The table shows the magnitude of the correlation needed for significance at the .05 and .01 levels. The degrees of freedom for the partial r are equal to the number of observations (N) minus the total number of variables (independent, dependent, and control).

In our example, the partial r between attendance and opposition was significant at the .01 level; the partial r between reading and opposition was not significant at the .05 level. (In both cases, there were $16 - 3$, or 13, degrees of freedom.)

A researcher investigating the hypothesis "The higher the percentage of the population regularly attending church, the greater the opposition in the nation to intermarriage" would have found support from the data in this sample. He or she would have failed to find support for the hypothesis "The greater the percentage of the population regularly reading books, the lower the opposition to intermarriage."

SUMMARY

When we are dealing with interval variables, we can determine regression equations that estimate Y values from the X values of one or more independent variables. The squared correlation coefficient tells us how close the regression equation comes to accounting for all of the variance in Y.

Based on the multiple-regression equation, we can determine the proportion of the total variance in Y accounted for by each independent variable. Based on both the multiple and the simple correlation coefficients, we can determine the partial correlation between two variables. The partial correlation measures the association between two variables, controlling for the effects of other variables.

Endnotes

[1]There is a test of significance for R. It requires the computation of an F value: $F = \dfrac{R^2}{1 - R^2} \cdot \dfrac{N - I - 1}{I}$, where I is the number of independent variables. The numerator has I degrees of freedom and the denominator has $N - I - 1$ degrees of freedom.

[2]Based on study by Robert Bernstein, "Determinants of National Social Tolerance," presented at the meeting of the International Studies Association, Mexico City, April 7, 1983.

[3]R^2 can be greater than the sum of the r^2 when there is a strong correlation between the second independent variable and the residuals from the regression equation between Y and the first independent variable.

LABORATORY EXERCISES

The purpose of this laboratory is to give you experience in using simple multivariate techniques for analyzing interval-level data.

Task 1. Use the computer to analyze data provided by your instructor.

a. Develop a hypothesis relating two interval variables.

b. Select and justify the selection of a control variable (hereafter designated as Z).

c. Find the Pearson's r correlation between each pair of variables:
   $r_{xy} =$ $r_{zy} =$ $r_{xz} =$

d. Find the partial correlation coefficients:
   $r_{xy.z} =$ $r_{zy.x} =$ $r_{xz.y} =$

e. Which (if any) of the correlation coefficients are significant at the .05 level?

f. Based on the correlations above, diagram the probable causal links among the variables.

g. What do you conclude regarding the hypothesis?

h. What do you conclude regarding the effect of the control variable?

i. Compute R^2 to find the total proportion of the variance in Y that can be accounted for by the variance in X and Z together.

j. Which is more important, X or Z, in explaining the variation in Y?

k. How much of the variance in Y can be accounted for by variance in X?

l. How much of the variance in Y can be accounted for by variance in Z?

m. How much of the variance in Y can be accounted for by X and Z together?

n. Why is the answer to question m not equal to the sum of the answers to questions l and k?

o. Find the multiple-regression equation.

p. Find the largest residual. Show the X, Z, Y, and Y' values for that residual.

REVIEW QUESTIONS

Use the following hypotheses and hypothetical analysis to answer questions 1–6.

Hypothesis: As A increases, C tends to increase.
Hypothesis: As B decreases, C tends to increase.
$N = 50$ Regression equation $C' = 4A + 3B - 14$.
$r_{AC} = .4$ $r_{BC} = .8$ $r_{AC.B} = .22$
$r_{BC.A} = .77$ $R^2 = .66$

1. Is the first hypothesis supported? Why?
2. Is the second hypothesis supported? Why?

3. Does a change of 1 in the value of A have more or less of an impact on C than does a change of 1 in the value of B? Why?

4. Variation in B alone accounts for what percentage of the variance in C? Why?

5. How much additional variance in C can be accounted for by the variance in A (after B has accounted for all it can)? Why?

6. Diagram the probable causal links among A, B, and C, using $+$ or $-$ to indicate the direction of association for each link.

CHAPTER FIFTEEN

PUTTING THINGS TOGETHER: THE RESEARCH DESIGN AND REPORT

We have now considered all of the basic steps of the research process that we outlined in the introduction. You have learned enough to design and carry out a complete research project. In this chapter we will consider putting everything together into the design of a research project, and then modifying the design into the final research report. Very little new material will be introduced, but the larger perspective should help you increase your understanding of what we have covered in the previous chapters.

In the introduction to this book we presented a diagram that outlined the basic steps in the research process. That diagram is reproduced in Figure 15–1. We will use the steps of the research process as the outline for the research design and research report.

The first step of the research process is to develop tentative explanations of what we have previously observed about behavior. This step involves library research in the professional literature, as well as consideration of popular commentaries and observations from exploratory research. The result of this step is the positing of one or more hypotheses, along with reasons for offering them. Those hypotheses are to be tested in the research.

The second step is to define and measure the properties. The words designating the properties must be given precise definition in the context of the research. The methods of measuring the properties must be given in sufficient detail to allow another researcher to follow the procedures as outlined and, as a result, to classify the units in exactly the same way as did the original researcher.

The third step is to collect the data. A sample of the theoretical population must be drawn. Using the measurement procedures, the researcher must classify each unit of the sample on each of the properties. The data must be recorded in such a way that the researcher can retrieve them easily in his or her analysis.

The next step is the analysis. The data that have been collected are used to test the explanations. Alternative explanations and conditioning influences of other properties are evaluated by the use of controls. The role of chance is evaluated through tests of statistical significance.

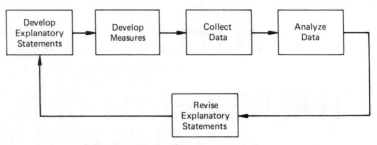

FIGURE 15-1   The Research Process

Finally, the research is concluded through a reevaluation of what has been presented as an explanation. Hypotheses may be altered to account for what the research appears to indicate. New hypotheses may be suggested. These can be the starting point for another cycle through the research process by the same or another researcher.

THE RESEARCH DESIGN AND REPORT

The research design is a statement of precisely what the researcher is going to do and how he or she is going to do it. All too often the research design exists in outline form in the researcher's head while the research is being done. This practice tends to be inefficient, because it leads to waste of resources as unanticipated problems arise that could have been avoided by more complete preparation. As students, you will generally be required to write formal research designs and thus be spared the problems of proceeding without one.

The research report repeats the information contained in the research design and presents the empirical data and the analysis of these data. The research design and the research report are virtually identical. If the research design is complete, the research report will involve little more than filling in blanks in the design. Thus, the organization of the research design and report are identical. We can discuss them simultaneously.

There are many reasonable ways to organize a research design or report. We are going to follow the steps of the research process as we have outlined them. Most important is that all of the relevant information be included.

Develop Explanatory Statements

Developing the hypotheses that the research is testing is a critical part of the research. The professional literature and informed commentary should be searched for all information relevant to the explanation of the behavior under observation. Exploratory research, either casual observations or formal data gathering, is combined with the information from the literature review. Using this information, the researcher can then offer the best possible explanation given the present state of knowledge. This search for explanation not only helps provide the best explanation, but it allows the researcher to avoid duplication of research that has already been done by another researcher. It also allows the results of the research to be easily placed in the existing literature.

The literature search needs to be more or less exhaustive, depending on the complexity of the research problem, the subject matter, and the demands of the audience of the researcher. From a practical point of view, an undergraduate term paper will require a less exhaustive literature search than a paper by a professional, even if on the same topic.

The hypotheses must be in good form, following the rules stated in Chapter 1. They must relate two properties in a precise manner. The units of analysis and theoretical population must be either specified or obvious. Value statements cannot be part of the hypotheses.

Often the researcher will test several interrelated hypotheses. The explanation that variation in property A causes variation in property B, which in turn causes variation in property C, is an explanation that involves two hypotheses. One hypothesis relates A to B, the other B to C. The discussion in this section of the design must make clear how multiple hypotheses are interrelated.

Generally the researcher will suggest several explanations that the research will test. For example, in Chapter 10 we examined two hypotheses, each explaining voting on the ABM. One hypothesis used party as the explanatory factor, the other ideology. When proposing multiple explanations the researcher must state all of the hypotheses and should discuss the merits of each.

It is also necessary to discuss properties other than the ones hypothesized that might account for the behavior. The researcher must use these properties as controls to demonstrate that the hypothesized relationship is not spurious. Though no researcher can take all factors into account, the explanation should suggest why the alternative explanations considered are the most plausible ones.

The researcher also uses controls to observe conditioning effects. Some relationships may hold true under some circumstances and not under others. The discussion should include the researcher's expectations about conditioning effects and why these expectations have arisen.

Develop Measures

There are two tasks to accomplish in this step: definition of the properties and development of measures for them. In order to give preceise meaning to the hypotheses, we have to be certain that the audience is using the words in the same way that we are. This is particularly important in scientific analysis, in which exact communication is required. Almost all words have many meanings. For this reason, it is generally necessary to define every property essential to the explanation. Only those few properties enjoying universal agreement as to their definition are exempt. Notice that the control properties must be defined, as well as those used in the hypothesis.

The measurement must be described in sufficient detail that anyone in the audience could replicate the study, if the units are still available, by using the description of the measurement. If the researcher asks a question in order to obtain data on a property, the question itself should be reported. How the question is asked—by phone, personal interview, questionnaire, and so on—should also be reported. When the data are to be retrieved from secondary sources, the citations to these sources should be given in full. Often such data may come from sources not readily available. It is a good idea to indicate where such data can be obtained.

If the data are coded in some way, the rules used to code the data should be supplied. If judgment on the part of the coders is required, procedures for ensuring accuracy should be discussed.

The audience will be judging the adequacy of a measure. The section on measurement should include any evidence the researcher has that the measures are reliable and valid. If the measures have been used in other studies, the other studies should be cited. If we have different measures of the property, we can show that all tend to classify the units in the same way. This is evidence of the validity of the measures. If a compound measure is used, it may be appropriate to evaluate the homogeneity of the items used in the measure. Information on such evaluations should be included in this section of the research report.

Collect Data

In the research design, the section on gathering the data deals primarily with the method of sampling used. As with measures, the procedures by which the sample is chosen must be communicated so that another researcher could replicate the method exactly. It is not enough to say that a random sample of students will be picked. The exact way in which the random students are selected should be specified. The researcher should discuss the adequacy, and perhaps the liabilities, of the sample. This can be expanded in the final research report to include information on problems encountered in observation of units and on possibly unrepresentative aspects of the sample.

The consideration of the method used to collect the data may overlap with some of the discussion of the measures. General data-collection procedures applying to several of the properties might be discussed here. Methods of interviewing, and how interviewers were trained, should be discussed if a survey is used.

Analyze the Data

The analysis section should do four things. First, it generally should present a description of the properties. Though a description of the properties is not always necessary in the testing of hypotheses, providing frequency distributions and indicators of central tendency and dispersion may often be useful. Second, the relationships specified in all the hypotheses should be reported. These may take the form of percentage comparisons or comparisons of central tendencies. Usually, appropriate measures of association are reported even when the tables are presented. Sometimes only the measures of association are presented. When they are presented, they must be appropriate both for the level of measurement and for testing the hypotheses. Third, alternative explanations need to be considered. Other properties should be used as controls, and chance should be evaluated as a factor through application of tests of significance. The tests of significance should also be appropriate for the level of measurement and the hypotheses being tested. Finally, the hypotheses should be evaluated as to whether the data support them or not. If the data do not support the hypotheses, other explanations should be suggested.

Difference Between Research Design and Research Report

In the research design, the entire analysis should be laid out in as much detail as possible without the data present. From the hypotheses, we know the variables that will be observed and the relationships that are expected. From these it is possible to prepare blank tables that will be filled in after the data are collected. It is even possible to specify what the data will look like if the hypotheses are supported. The design should also specify the tests of statistical significance to be used and the level of significance to be accepted. The design should indicate which measure of association are going to be used. If alternative statistics are available, the design should discuss why the ones selected are being used rather than the others.

The final research report is a simple extension of what has been prepared in the research design. The figures from the actual data are placed in the appropriate tables. The tests of significance are inserted, as are any other statistics that have been computed.

The conclusions drawn from the data analysis are made through consideration of whether the hypotheses are supported. If all of the expectations are supported, the researcher can conclude the report easily. However, one or more of the hypotheses may not be supported. Then the researcher must reevaluate his or her explanation in light of the new evidence. Sometimes the analysis will lend itself to new explanations.

Remember that new explanations that seem to fit the data do not have the same authority as explanations offered in advance and then verified. As you may recall, we argued that such post hoc explanations are more likely to be artifacts of the particular set of data than are explanations offered in advance. The revised explanations should be viewed as suggested hypotheses from exploratory research; additional verification is necessary.

Summary of a Research Report

The outline below summarizes what is expected in a research report.

    I. Develop explanatory statements
       A. Search for explanation.
          1. professional literature
          2. nonprofessional commentary
          3. exploratory research
       B. Specify hypotheses.
          1. units of analysis and theoretical population
          2. two properties precisely related
       C. Note interrelationships among hypotheses.
       D. Specify properties as alternative explanations.
       E. Specify properties having conditioning effects.
   II. Develop measures.
       A. Define properties.
       B. Specify procedures for measures.
 III. Collect data.
       A. Specify procedures for selecting sample.
       B. Specify procedures for carrying out primary data collection or secondary data retrieval.
  IV. Analyze data.
       A. Present description of properties.
       B. Report relationships between properties.
       C. Consider alternative explanations.
          1. other causal properties
          2. chance
       D. Consider conditioning effects.
       E. Conclude whether hypotheses are supported.
   V. Reevaluate explanations.

For stylistic reasons, different topics in the outline may be discussed in an order different from the one presented here. Also, in some research reports some of the sections may not be relevant and may be omitted. The outline is intended as a checklist of steps to remember when you are deciding what to write.

You will seldom see a published research report as detailed as the checklist. Space limitations usually force authors to omit some of the discussion. Since a researcher is writing for a professional audience, some steps can be assumed.

For example, it may be reported that a cluster sample of the national electorate was used. We may have enough confidence in the researcher to assume it was adequate, even if the details of the procedures are not given. Often, however, critical pieces of information are omitted, and this makes replication of the research difficult. A researcher must be prepared to supply the omitted information even if it cannot be published. As students, you will generally be required to be more explicit. When you are in a position to evaluate research, either in academic circles or in business or government, insist that the information missing from a presentation be made available if there is any question as to the way the research was done, or if it must be replicated.

SUMMARY

Though we have covered much information in this book, and hope you have learned a great deal, we also have not mentioned many things. Enough has been presented to enable you to perform acceptable research, but problems will frequently arise in research that require the application of techniques we have not been able to present in a general introduction. This book has laid the foundation for additional learning; it has not provided all the necessary information.

Though you may learn more by taking additional courses in statistics, design, and so on, the real way to develop an understanding and appreciation for empirical-research methods is to do some empirical research. The way to learn and appreciate empirical research lies not in the context of learning methods but in answering a question of substantial interest to you. You will appreciate and understand the methods you must use to answer interesting questions far more than you would when taught in a classroom. As a student, you should now feel confident of your ability to do a small empirical research project when given the choice in a course of doing traditional "library" research or empirical research. Use these opportunities. It is by doing research that you will complete your education in social science methods. We wish you well.

LABORATORY EXERCISES

The purpose of this laboratory is to give you an opportunity to draw together everything you have learned and apply it in evaluating and constructing research projects.

Task 1. Below is a fictitious research report. Read and evaluate the report, using the following outline. In your evaluation be sure to give specific reasons for any objections you raise. Assign a grade to each section, basing it on the quality of the work and on the total points possible for that section.

OUTLINE FOR EVALUATING RESEARCH

Indicate the number of points assigned to each section in the grade blank. Write NA if the section is not applicable to the article. Give reasons for the evaluation in each section.

I. Explanatory statements
   A. Search for explanation (5 points)
      Are there convincing reasons for advancing the hypotheses? Does other empirical research support the hypotheses? Do the hypotheses follow from the professional literature, informed commentary, or exploratory research?
   B. Specification of hypotheses (10 points)
      Are there hypotheses? Do they all relate two distinct properties? Is it clear how the properties are related? Is the theoretical population clear and as extensive as is reasonable? Are value statements involved in the hypotheses?
   C. Relations among hypotheses (10 points)
      When more than one hypothesis is presented, is the interrelationship among the hypotheses clear and reasonable? Are alternative explanations offered and appropriate controls suggested? Are variables considered that would be expected to have conditioning effects on the hypothesized relationships?
II. Measures
   A. Definition of properties (5 points)
      Are properties defined appropriately?
   B. Measurement procedures (15 points)
      Are the measures likely to be valid? Are they likely to be reliable?
III. Collection of the data
   A. The sample (10 points)
      Is the sampling procedure well specified? Is the procedure free from bias? Is it likely to produce a sample representative of the theoretical population? Is it of sufficient size to be useful?
   B. The data sources (5 points)
      If primary sources were readily available, did the researcher use them? If he or she relied on secondary sources, were they the sources most likely to yield reliable and valid data?
IV. Analysis of data
   A. Presentation of relationships (10 points)
      Are the independent and dependent variables correctly distinguished?
      Are the statistics used appropriate for the level of measurement of the variables? Are the tables correctly set up and labeled?
   B. Alternative relationships, conditioning effects, and chance (10 points)
      Are controls correctly applied so that the researcher can evaluate conditioning effects and other possible causal variables? Are tests of significance applied and are the ones used appropriate?

C. Conclusions about hypotheses (20 points)
Are the conclusions of the analysis correct? Check the relationships, effect of controls, and the determination as to whether the results are significant.

Overall Evaluation

Add the points assigned for each section. Subtract the points in sections not applicable from 100. Divide the total number of points assigned by the total number possible in the applicable sections. Reject the article if the resulting figure is below 70%. Reject the article if any applicable section is assigned 50% or fewer of the points available in the section.

FICTITIOUS REPORT: THIRD-PARTY VOTERS

With the emergence of a strong third party in the United Kingdom and recent attempts at creating third parties here, many researchers have attempted to determine what causes people to vote for third-party candidates. Cyrus Key has hypothesized that people who see little difference between the major-party candidates are more likely to vote for third-party candidates than are those who see an important difference between the major-party candidates.[1] Ralph Black has argued for a different hypothesis: Strong ideologues (i.e., extreme liberals and extreme conservatives) are more likely to vote for a third-party candidate than are those who are not strong ideologues.[2]

Both of their explanations cannot be correct. This research is designed to determine which of the two hypotheses is better supported by the data.

The analysis will be based on data from the 1976 American National Election Study done by the Center for Political Studies at the University of Michigan. The center surveyed 2248 individuals throughout the United States. Complete details regarding the sampling technique can be found in the codebook for the 1976 election distributed by the center.

The dependent property, vote for third-party candidate, is measured by responses to the question "Who did you vote for in the election for president (in 1976)?" Anyone who voted for a candidate other than Ford or Carter is classified as voting for a third-party candidate. Ford supporters are coded 1; Carter supporters, 2; third-party supporters, 3.

The first independent property, whether or not respondent sees a difference between the major-party candidates, is measured by responses to the question "Do you think there are any important differences in what the Republicans and Democrats stand for?" Those responding yes are coded 1; no, 5; all others are deleted.

The second independent property, whether respondent is an ideologue, is measured by responses to the question "Where would you place yourself on this scale (a seven-point scale arranged from extremely liberal to extremely conservative)?" Responses are recoded so that liberal and extremely liberal are 1; conservative and extremely conservative are 6; and slightly liberal, slightly conservative, and moderate are 3.

There is no support for the hypothesis that ideologues are more likely to vote for third-party candidates than are those who are not ideologues. The bivariate table, shown below, has a del_l of $-.20$.

		Liberal	Neither	Conservative
	Ford	16%	50%	78%
Vote	Carter	82%	48%	19%
	Third Party	2%	2%	2%
	(N)	(62)	(419)	(134)

Controlling for whether respondents see a difference between candidates has little effect: The del_l is $-.26$ for those who see an important difference, and $-.10$ for those who do not. Clearly there is no support for Black's hypothesis.

In contrast, there is support for Key's hypothesis among both liberals and conservatives. The bivariate table shows a positive del_k:

		See a Difference?		
		Yes	No	
	Ford	46%	53%	$del_k = .01$
Vote	Carter	53%	45%	$\chi^2 = .054$
	Third Party	1%	2%	
	(N)	(411)	(338)	

The control tables show a del_k of .11 ($\chi^2 = .214$) for liberals and .07 ($\chi^2 = .445$) for conservatives.

In summary, it is those who see little difference between the major-party candidates, and not those who are ideologues, who are most likely to vote for third-party candidates.

Notes

[1]Cyrus Key, *The Rise of the Third Party* (New York: Random House, 1979).
[2]Ralph Black, "Ideologues," *Journal of Politics,* 56 (March 1981), 42–50.

Task 2. Use the outline in the chapter to prepare a brief research design, as assigned by your instructor. Look at the example of a student's research paper reproduced in Appendix I. Nonapplicable sections of the outline may be omitted, and its order modified. Be careful, however, to include all of the relevant discussion.

APPENDIX I

The following paper is a slightly edited version of a research paper submitted by Jerry Mitchell, a student in our introductory methodology course. It is an example of the kind of research that a good student with no prior training can do during a one-semester methodology course. We think it is a good model for you to follow when you do your own research.

SUPPORT FOR OSHA BUDGET CUTS

Explanation

Hypothesis 1. Republican congressmen are more likely to vote for spending cuts in the Occupational, Safety, and Health Administration (OSHA) than are Democratic congressmen.

The news media, general public, and a number of political scientists cite party affiliation as a primary determinant of congressmen's votes. Conventional wisdom holds that Republicans represent support for less government and consequently, for reduced appropriations for regulatory agencies.

No research could be found that specifically examined the relationship between party identification and congressional votes on regulatory-agency appropriations. However, research has been done on the relationship between congressional party affiliation and votes on other issues. For example, William Shaffer (1980) found distinct differences in congressional votes on appropriations bills based on party identification. He found that Republicans were more likely than Democrats to cut funds in social programs and social regulations. (p. 27)

Hypothesis 2. Congressmen with low seniority are more likely to vote for spending cuts in OSHA than are congressmen with high seniority.

Senior congressmen are more likely to view the appropriation process as incremental than are junior congressmen. Thus, senior congressmen tend to maintain the status quo and rarely favor budget cuts. Junior congressmen are more likely to view the appropriations process as a new problem in resource allocation, one that may require budget cuts.

No empirical research could be found specifically linking seniority to support for regulatory-agency funding. But there is research that shows how seniority generally affects policy decisions in the budget process. Aaron Wildavsky (1979) notes that congressmen tend to develop mutually beneficial relationships with certain agencies. Those "cozy relationships" build up over time and cause the budget process to become incremental. (p. 130)

Hypothesis 3. Conservative congressmen are more likely to vote for spending cuts in OSHA than are liberal congressmen.

In the past two decades conservative philosophy has had a basic tenet that "less government is the best government." That belief should result in votes to reduce government spending by conservative congressmen.

There is ample research indicating the importance of ideology in determining voting decisions, although none of it specifically deals with votes on funding regulatory agencies. Shaffer (1980) concluded that congressional votes on appropriations bills reflected ideological differences. Conservatives have consistently voted for reduced appropriations for social regulations over the past decade. (p. 48)

Hypothesis 4. Congressmen who are not lawyers are more likely to vote for spending cuts in OSHA than are congressmen who are laywers.

Lawyers are more likely than others to believe that rational expertise can solve most problems. They are more likely than nonlawyers to believe that agencies should be given a freer rein because those agencies have expertise in their areas. Thus, lawyers are less likely than nonlawyers to cut agency budgets.

John Plumlee (1981) studied the influence of legal training on civil servants and congressmen and found that legal training influences congressmen more than it does other public servants. He found that lawyers are more likely than nonlawyers to support the status quo. (p. 327)

Research Justification

Little research has been done on congressional support for regulatory agencies. This study can help determine if properties that have been found to affect other congressional behavior will also affect support for those agencies. The research specifically focuses on the OSHA vote because it was close, recent, and not packaged with other amendments.

Sample

The sample consists of all those members of the House of Representatives who voted on the 1980 amendment that proposed to cut OSHA appropriations by $10 million.

Measures

The source for all data is the *Almanac of American Politics,* 1982.

1. Support for OSHA Budget Cut: Each member's vote on the 1980 amendment to cut OSHA funding.
   Coded: 1 = favored cut; 2 = against cut.
2. Party Affiliation: Representatives are classified as Republicans or Democrats.
   Coded: 1 = Republican; 2 = Democrat.
3. Seniority: Representatives are classified according to the number of years they have served in the House. The categories are those used by John Kingdon (1981).
   Coded: 1 = junior (1–6 years); 2 = senior (> 6 years).
4. Ideology: Representatives are classified as conservative or liberal based on their ratings by the Americans for Democratic Action (ADA). The categories are those used by Kingdon. Coded: 1 = conservative (ADA = 0–60); 2 = liberal (ADA > 60)
5. Legal Background: Classification is based on whether or not the representative has a law degree.
   Coded: 1 = nonlawyer; 2 = lawyer.

Design of Analysis

Each hypothesis is tested in order. For each, a bivariate table is constructed, followed by tables controlling for each one of the other independent variables. A del_k correlation is computed for each table as a measure of the association between the independent and dependent variables. The χ^2 value for the del_k is computed for each table to determine the statistical significance of the correlation coefficient.

Findings

Hypothesis 1. Republican congressmen are more likely to vote for spending cuts in OSHA than are Democratic congressmen.

		Party Affiliation		
		Republican	*Democratic*	
Budget Cut	Favors	77%	26%	del_k = .49
	Opposes	23%	74%	χ^2 = 78.6
(*N*)		(132)	(215)	

Controlling for seniority:

		JUNIOR		SENIOR	
		Party		Party	
		Rep.	*Dem.*	*Rep.*	*Dem.*
Budget Cut	Favors	85%	29%	70%	24%
	Opposes	15%	71%	30%	76%
(*N*)		(53)	(79)	(77)	(136)
		Del$_k$ = .47	χ^2 = 38.2	Del$_k$ = .54	χ^2 = 39.9

Controlling for ideology:

		CONSERVATIVE		LIBERAL	
		Party		Party	
		Rep.	*Dem.*	*Rep.*	*Dem.*
Budget Cut	Favors	84%	53%	19%	5%
	Opposes	16%	47%	81%	95%
(*N*)		(116)	(94)	(16)	(121)
		Del$_k$ = .32	χ^2 = 20.2	Del$_k$ = .17	χ^2 = 0.8

Controlling for legal background:

		NONLAWYER		LAWYER	
		Party		Party	
		Rep.	*Dem.*	*Rep.*	*Dem.*
Budget Cut	Favors	80%	31%	72%	22%
	Opposes	20%	69%	28%	78%
(*N*)		(75)	(104)	(57)	(111)
		Del$_k$ = .55	χ^2 = 41.1	Del$_k$ = .49	χ^2 = 34.3

Some support for the hypothesis is shown in all tables. However, the χ^2 value for the liberals indicates that we cannot be confident that the support shown in the sample is representative of the behavior of liberal congressmen in general. Among conservatives, Republicans are more likely to vote for spending cuts in OSHA than are Democrats.

Hypothesis 2. Congressmen with low seniority are more likely to vote for spending cuts in OSHA than are congressmen with high seniority.

		Seniority	
		Junior	*Senior*
Budget Cut	Favors	52%	41%
	Opposes	48%	59%
(*N*)		(134)	(213)
Del$_k$ = .11	χ^2 = 4.05		

Controlling for party affiliation:

		REPUBLICAN		**DEMOCRATIC**	
		Seniority		Seniority	
		Junior	*Senior*	*Junior*	*Senior*
Budget Cut	Favors	85%	70%	29%	24%
	Opposes	15%	30%	71%	76%
(*N*)		(55)	(77)	(79)	(136)
		Del$_k$ = .02	χ^2 = .03	Del$_k$ = .05	χ^2 = .44

Controlling for ideology:

		CONSERVATIVE		**LIBERAL**	
		Seniority		Seniority	
		Junior	*Senior*	*Junior*	*Senior*
Budget Cut	Favors	77%	66%	10%	3%
	Opposes	23%	34%	90%	97%
(*N*)		(84)	(126)	(50)	(87)
		Del$_k$ = .02	χ^2 = .03	Del$_k$ = .09	χ^2 = .55

Controlling for legal background:

		NONLAWYER		**LAWYER**	
		Seniority		Seniority	
		Junior	*Senior*	*Junior*	*Senior*
Budget Cut	Favors	57%	48%	47%	35%
	Opposes	43%	52%	53%	65%
(*N*)		(76)	(103)	(58)	(110)
		Del$_k$ = .09	χ^2 = 1.39	Del$_k$ = .12	χ^2 = 1.99

The support shown for this hypothesis could have occurred by chance. Based on this research, we cannot conclude that congressmen with low seniority are more likely to vote for spending cuts in OSHA than are congressmen with high seniority.

Hypothesis 3. Conservative congressmen are more likely to vote for spending cuts in OSHA than are liberal congressmen.

		Ideology	
		Conservative	Liberal
Budget Cut	Favors	70%	6%
	Opposes	30%	94%
(N)		(210)	(137)
$\text{Del}_k = .60$	$\chi^2 = 129.5$		

Controlling for party affiliation:

		REPUBLICAN		DEMOCRATIC	
		Ideology		Ideology	
		Cons.	Lib.	Cons.	Lib.
Budget Cut	Favors	84%	19%	53%	5%
	Opposes	16%	81%	47%	95%
(N)		(116)	(16)	(94)	(121)
		$\text{Del}_k = .47$	$\chi^2 = 12.3$	$\text{Del}_k = .51$	$\chi^2 = 48.6$

Controlling for seniority:

		JUNIOR		SENIOR	
		Ideology		Ideology	
		Cons.	Lib.	Cons.	Lib.
Budget Cut	Favors	77%	10%	66%	5%
	Opposes	23%	90%	34%	95%
(N)		(84)	(50)	(126)	(87)
		$\text{Del}_k = .64$	$\chi^2 = 53.3$	$\text{Del}_k = .57$	$\chi^2 = 74.8$

Controlling for legal background:

		NONLAWYER		LAWYER	
		Ideology		Ideology	
		Cons.	Lib.	Cons.	Lib.
Budget Cut	Favors	74%	10%	67%	4%
	Opposes	26%	90%	33%	96%
(N)		(117)	(62)	(93)	(75)
		$\text{Del}_k = .58$	$\chi^2 = 59.8$	$\text{Del}_k = .61$	$\chi^2 = 64.5$

This hypothesis is supported in all of the control tables. The associations are very strong. It is clear that conservative congressmen are more likely to vote for spending cuts in OSHA than are liberal congressmen.

Hypothesis 4. Congressmen who are not lawyers are more likely to vote for spending cuts in OSHA than are congressmen who are lawyers.

		Legal Background	
		Nonlawyer	*Lawyer*
Budget Cut	Favors	77%	26%
	Opposes	23%	74%
(N)		(179)	(168)
$Del_k = .51$ $\chi^2 = 5.59$			

Controlling for party affiliation:

		REPUBLICAN		**DEMOCRATIC**	
		Legal Background		**Legal Background**	
		Nonlaw	*Law*	*Nonlaw*	*Law*
Budget Cut	Favors	80%	72%	31%	22%
	Opposes	20%	28%	69%	78%
(N)		(75)	(57)	(104)	(111)
		$Del_k = .09$	$\chi^2 = .83$	$Del_k = .09$	$\chi^2 = 1.80$

Controlling for seniority:

		JUNIOR		**SENIOR**	
		Legal Background		**Legal Background**	
		Nonlaw	*Law*	*Nonlaw*	*Law*
Budget Cut	Favors	57%	47%	48%	35%
	Opposes	43%	53%	52%	65%
(N)		$Del_k = .10$	$\chi^2 = 1.30$	$Del_k = .13$	$\chi^2 = 3.61$

Controlling for ideology:

		CONSERVATIVE		**LIBERAL**	
		Legal Background		**Legal Background**	
		Nonlaw	*Law*	*Nonlaw*	*Law*
Budget Cut	Favors	58%	56%	45%	36%
	Opposes	42%	44%	55%	64%
(N)		(84)	(18)	(95)	(149)
		$Del_k = .02$	$\chi^2 = .03$	$Del_k = .09$	$\chi^2 = 1.8$

This hypothesis is not supported when controlling for party or ideology. The associations are so weak they could easily have occurred by chance. We cannot be confident that nonlawyers are more likely to vote for spending cuts in OSHA than are lawyers.

Conclusion

Of the properties investigated, ideology has the most independent influence on congressional voting on OSHA. Conservative congressmen are more likely to vote for spending cuts in OSHA than are liberal congressmen.

Among the conservative congressmen, party affiliation has an independent influence on voting. Among conservatives, Republicans are more likely to vote for spending cuts than are Democrats.

References

BARONE, MICHAEL and GRANT UJIFUSA, eds. (1982) *The Almanac of American Politics.* Washington: Barone & Co.

KINGDON, JOHN (1981) *Congressmen's Voting Decisions.* New York: Harper & Row.

PLUMLEE, JOHN (1981) "Lawyers as Bureaucrats." *Public Administration Review* 41 (March/April):220–28.

SHAFFER, WILLIAM (1980) *Party and Ideology in the United States Congress.* Lanban, Md.: University Press of America.

WILDAVSKY, AARON (1979) *The Politics of the Budgetary Process.* Boston: Little, Brown.

APPENDIX II

A. LEVELS OF SIGNIFICANCE FOR χ^2

Degree of Freedom	Probability			
	.1	*.05*	*.01*	*.005*
1	1.64	2.71	5.41	6.63
2	3.22	4.60	7.82	9.21
3	4.64	6.25	9.84	11.34
4	5.99	7.78	11.67	13.28
5	7.29	9.24	13.39	15.09
6	8.56	10.64	15.03	16.81
7	9.80	12.02	16.62	18.47
8	11.03	13.36	18.17	20.09
9	12.24	14.68	19.68	21.67
10	13.44	15.99	21.16	23.21
11	14.63	17.27	22.62	24.72
12	15.81	18.55	24.05	26.22
13	16.98	19.81	25.47	27.69
14	18.15	21.06	26.87	29.14
15	19.31	22.31	28.26	30.58
20	25.04	28.41	35.02	37.57
25	30.67	34.38	41.57	44.31
30	36.25	40.26	47.96	50.89

Source: Sampling distribution of chi-sqaure values *for those tables supporting the hypothesis.* Abridged from R. A. Fisher, *Statistical Methods for Research Workers,* 14th ed. (New York: Hafner Press, copyright © 1970, University of Adelaide). Reprinted by permission of Macmillan Company.

B. 100 RANDOM DIGITS

5	4	7	9	3	3	0	6	4	1	9	9	4	3	9	6	9	5	3	4
0	1	4	9	3	5	2	0	2	7	9	2	6	3	2	0	6	7	0	2
2	3	9	3	1	7	5	2	5	7	7	6	8	5	1	0	9	0	4	4
6	0	5	7	9	0	9	4	6	7	0	4	5	0	9	2	2	1	8	9
3	1	3	2	2	0	1	7	6	6	4	4	1	5	1	7	5	4	5	7
8	8	4	1	9	4	5	0	2	4	1	3	1	8	7	2	8	9	7	9
5	9	2	0	7	8	6	1	3	8	3	6	6	5	8	4	1	4	0	4
8	0	5	8	4	6	5	5	0	8	8	6	3	8	3	3	1	7	5	6
7	9	0	5	8	0	5	8	1	9	8	9	6	7	8	2	5	6	5	1
0	3	7	3	0	7	1	5	4	3	1	2	5	0	3	5	1	3	2	0
0	1	7	4	4	8	5	4	1	5	2	1	2	1	2	2	9	1	4	5
9	2	5	3	3	8	0	1	1	4	8	5	0	7	5	6	4	1	5	5
1	6	7	0	8	3	3	9	9	2	2	6	5	3	3	7	1	2	1	9
9	2	3	7	7	9	6	0	0	6	7	3	7	2	2	5	7	8	9	8
0	7	1	8	6	3	8	1	8	0	7	7	8	7	3	3	2	3	2	3
3	9	4	7	6	3	8	2	4	4	4	6	2	8	8	5	1	1	4	2
6	8	4	6	4	4	5	7	6	6	5	5	6	7	9	6	7	3	3	4
2	2	0	5	0	6	5	4	3	5	3	0	8	3	6	4	4	1	9	7
3	4	0	7	0	7	1	3	5	1	9	8	2	2	5	4	2	0	3	7
2	8	9	5	9	8	0	2	2	5	9	4	4	9	4	6	7	6	3	3
2	4	7	1	6	3	6	9	8	4	2	7	9	9	8	2	7	9	5	5
4	5	8	7	1	3	4	3	6	9	0	4	9	1	9	6	5	4	2	3
4	9	8	0	8	6	3	3	8	4	0	6	1	0	7	7	5	1	1	7
2	3	5	7	3	8	7	8	4	9	8	4	5	9	3	6	1	8	0	9
9	5	2	0	7	6	2	5	2	3	3	2	9	7	7	4	3	3	6	7
7	3	8	2	8	9	3	8	0	5	3	0	9	4	2	5	9	5	4	2
9	5	0	5	6	5	2	7	8	6	0	0	7	9	8	4	8	4	8	1
6	5	6	2	4	1	2	1	3	6	0	3	6	4	5	5	7	9	5	5
7	8	7	1	4	3	1	7	2	7	6	9	5	7	2	5	9	7	3	5
8	0	8	2	0	3	3	9	6	7	4	1	1	2	6	1	3	9	9	8
2	9	4	0	7	7	9	3	2	5	7	2	6	7	7	5	5	1	0	5
9	4	9	2	4	1	6	7	4	5	5	0	0	1	1	6	8	0	3	5
0	3	1	4	4	8	0	1	8	9	6	8	9	4	9	4	1	4	3	2
3	9	8	3	6	9	8	0	7	6	4	8	9	3	2	2	9	4	0	0
5	4	1	0	3	2	4	5	8	0	4	7	4	3	3	9	4	3	3	5
4	4	5	8	4	2	9	9	4	6	9	7	8	6	4	4	3	0	2	4
5	3	3	5	5	5	2	4	7	3	7	2	4	0	7	5	4	2	0	3
1	4	7	8	1	7	3	9	0	7	1	7	0	4	8	5	2	5	8	2
9	5	6	7	2	6	6	9	4	5	7	8	0	1	5	6	1	8	8	9
8	5	6	1	5	5	3	6	9	1	1	0	0	2	8	4	9	1	4	1
7	1	4	6	1	4	0	5	4	2	1	6	8	2	2	1	9	2	1	6
9	8	5	9	3	4	1	1	2	3	1	1	5	8	6	6	3	8	9	8
5	2	7	6	0	3	3	0	6	1	2	5	9	5	5	5	5	2	0	6
8	8	9	0	5	7	0	1	8	8	8	6	4	5	4	5	6	6	3	5
8	3	0	3	5	1	1	2	6	9	5	3	3	3	2	6	6	6	6	3
8	7	3	1	6	8	3	9	0	6	4	6	7	7	1	8	3	9	5	6
8	2	3	9	2	4	7	5	6	4	2	1	7	5	6	9	9	7	4	1
5	1	7	8	6	0	4	6	5	3	0	5	9	5	4	2	1	8	8	3
1	4	3	0	9	0	8	0	4	7	2	4	1	1	3	2	3	6	4	3
6	1	5	0	7	0	8	5	1	0	6	4	4	1	0	3	7	0	4	8

C. LEVELS OF SIGNIFICANCE FOR *t*

df	.05	.01
1	6.314	31.821
2	2.920	6.965
3	2.353	4.541
4	2.132	3.747
5	2.015	3.365
6	1.943	3.143
7	1.895	2.998
8	1.860	2.896
9	1.833	2.821
10	1.812	2.764
11	1.796	2.718
12	1.782	2.681
13	1.771	2.650
14	1.761	2.624
15	1.753	2.602
16	1.746	2.583
17	1.740	2.567
18	1.734	2.552
19	1.729	2.539
20	1.725	2.528
21	1.721	2.518
22	1.717	2.508
23	1.714	2.500
24	1.711	2.492
25	1.708	2.485
26	1.706	2.479
27	1.703	2.473
28	1.701	2.467
29	1.699	2.462
30	1.697	2.457
∞	1.644	2.326

Source: *Assumes the direction of the relationship has been hypothesized in advance of the test.* Abridged from D. B. Owen, *Handbook of Statistical Tables* (Reading, Mass.: Addison-Wesley, copyright © 1962). Reprinted by courtesy of the U.S. Department of Energy and with permission of the author and publisher.

D. ESTIMATED LEVELS OF Δ_I REQUIRED FOR STATISTICAL SIGNIFICANCE

Assumes the direction of the relationship was hypothesized in advance. Estimated through the use of 2400 randomly produced tables for each sample size drawn from uniformly distributed populations. These tables had the same number of categories for each variable; the del needed for significance will be slightly different from that shown above if there are significantly more categories for one variable than for the other.

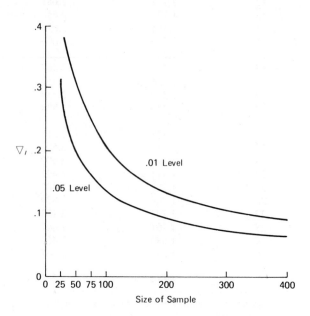

E. F DISTRIBUTION

.05 Level

df for denominator (N − C)	df for numerator (C − 1) 1	2	3	4	5	6	8	12	24	∞
1	39.86	49.50	53.59	55.83	57.24	58.20	59.44	60.70	62.00	63.33
2	8.53	9.00	9.16	9.24	9.29	9.33	9.37	9.41	9.45	9.49
3	5.54	5.46	5.39	5.34	5.31	5.28	5.25	5.22	5.18	5.13
4	4.54	4.32	4.19	4.11	4.05	4.01	3.95	3.90	3.83	3.76
5	4.06	3.78	3.62	3.52	3.45	3.40	3.34	3.27	3.19	3.10
10	3.28	2.92	2.73	2.61	2.52	2.46	2.38	2.28	2.18	2.06
20	2.97	2.59	2.38	2.25	2.16	2.09	2.00	1.89	1.77	1.61
30	2.88	2.49	2.28	2.14	2.05	1.98	1.88	1.77	1.64	1.46
40	2.84	2.44	2.23	2.09	2.00	1.93	1.83	1.71	1.57	1.38
60	2.79	2.39	2.18	2.04	1.95	1.87	1.77	1.66	1.51	1.29
120	2.75	2.35	2.13	1.99	1.90	1.82	1.72	1.60	1.45	1.19
∞	2.71	2.30	2.08	1.94	1.85	1.77	1.67	1.55	1.38	1.00

.025 Level

df for denominator (N − C)	df for numerator (C − 1) 1	2	3	4	5	6	8	12	24	∞
1	161.4	199.5	215.7	224.6	230.2	234.0	238.9	243.9	249.0	254.3
2	18.51	19.00	19.16	19.25	19.30	19.33	19.37	19.41	19.45	19.50
3	10.13	9.55	9.28	9.12	9.01	8.94	8.84	8.74	8.64	8.53
4	7.71	6.94	6.59	6.39	6.26	6.16	6.04	5.91	5.77	5.63
5	6.61	5.79	5.41	5.19	5.05	4.95	4.82	4.68	4.53	4.36
10	4.96	4.10	3.71	3.48	3.33	3.22	3.07	2.91	2.74	2.54
20	4.35	3.49	3.10	2.87	2.71	2.60	2.45	2.28	2.08	1.84
30	4.17	3.32	2.92	2.69	2.53	2.42	2.27	2.09	1.89	1.62
40	4.08	3.23	2.84	2.61	2.45	2.34	2.18	2.00	1.79	1.51
60	4.00	3.15	2.76	2.52	2.37	2.25	2.10	1.92	1.70	1.39
120	3.92	3.07	2.68	2.45	2.29	2.17	2.02	1.83	1.61	1.25
∞	3.84	2.99	2.60	2.37	2.21	2.10	1.94	1.75	1.52	1.00

Source: *Assumes direction of relationship was hypothesized in advance.* This table is taken from Table 5 of Fisher and Yates, *Statistical Tables for Biological, Agricultural, and Medical Research,* published by Longman Group Ltd., London, previously published by Oliver and Boyd, Edinburgh. Reprinted by permission of the authors and publishers.

F. LEVELS OF PEARSON'S r REQUIRED FOR STATISTICAL SIGNIFICANCE

df*	Level of Significance	
	.05	.01
5	.67	.83
10	.50	.66
15	.41	.55
20	.36	.49
25	.32	.44
30	.30	.41
35	.27	.38
40	.26	.35
45	.24	.34
50	.23	.32
60	.21	.29
70	.20	.27
80	.18	.26
90	.17	.24
100	.17	.23
500	.07	.10

*df $= N - 2$.

Source: *Assumes direction of relationship hypothesized in advance of test.* Computed using

$$r = \frac{t}{\sqrt{N - 2 + t^2}}$$

G. ESTIMATED LEVELS OF Δ_n REQUIRED FOR STATISTICAL SIGNIFICANCE

df*	Level of Significance	
	.05	.01
5	.73	.89
10	.52	.72
15	.43	.58
20	.38	.51
25	.34	.46
30	.30	.41
35	.28	.38
40	.27	.38
45	.25	.35
50	.23	.33
60	.22	.30
70	.20	.28

*df $= N - 2$.

Source: Above df $= 70$, use significance level for Pearson's *r. Assumes direction of relationship hypothesized in advance of test.* Estimated by drawing 1000 random samples at each df from a normally distributed population of 100,000 and computing Δ_n on each.

GLOSSARY

Appropriateness: degree to which the definition given for a property is consistent with the way the word is generally used by those viewing the research.

Association: when variation in one property generally coincides in a consistent way with variation in a second property.

Bar Graph: a figure using different size bars to represent the number of units in each category of a measure.

Batch Processing: a mode of data processing in which all instructions are submitted to the machine at one time; the machine processes them all and returns the output.

Bell-Shaped Distribution: a distribution of a measure that resembles a bell in that most of the units are found near the midpoint with symmetrical distributions to either side.

Bimodal Distribution: a distribution where two nonadjacent categories or two groups of nonadjacent categories have approximately equal numbers of units and have more units in them than there are in the other categories.

Categorization: separating units according to the level or amount of the property present.

Causal Association: when the variation in one property independent of variation in other properties, causes (leads to, results in, influences, affects, etc.) variation in the second property.

Central Tendency, Indicators of: indicate the middle or center position of a distribution of a measure. Indicators of central tendency include mode, median, and mean.

Chi-Square (χ^2): a statistic with known sampling distributions used for determining the statistical significance of bivariate tables.

Cluster Sample: a sample in which identifiable groups of units (clusters) are first randomly chosen from among all groups; then units are randomly chosen from within the clusters.

Coding: assigning numbers to represent categories of a property.

Compound Hypothesis: a statement that relates three or more properties.

Compound Measures: measures of a single property that are combinations of several variables.

Compound Question: a question which asks two or more questions at the same time.

Computer: any automated device that does calculations.

Conditional Support: when the hypothesis is supported for only some categories of the control variable.

Confounding Effects: when the control variable indicates that the apparent bivariate relationship is misleading, and controlling for it indicates a consistent effect on the relationship in all categories of the control variable.

Content Analysis: research using measures based on written or verbal communication.

Controlling: holding the effects of other variables constant while observing a relationship between two variables.

Control Variable: a variable the effects of which are held constant while testing the relationship between the independent and dependent variables.

Conversational Interaction: interactive computing in which the machine prompts the user in ordinary language and the responses are also in ordinary language.

Correlation Coefficient: a single number which indicates the extent to which the variables are related.

Coverage (of measure):   the extent to which all aspects of a property are reflected in the measure.

Crossproduct: the value of a unit on one variable multiplied by the corresponding value on another variable.

Del_k: a correlation coefficient used to measure association between qualitative variables.

Del_j: a correlation coefficient used to measure association between relative variables.

Dependent variable: the variable, variation in which is said to be caused by variation in another variable (the independent variable).

Directions of Association: a measure of which Y values tend to be paired with which X values, usually indicated by the sign of the correlation coefficient.

Discrimination (of measures):   the degree to which a measure distinguishes units as belonging to different categories.

Dispersion, Indicators of: indicate the extent to which units of analysis are distributed across categories, or how far apart the units are. Indicators include range, interquartile range, variance, and standard deviation.

Elite Survey: a survey of people defined by their position as being central or important in some way.

Eta: a correlation coefficient used to measure association between an interval variable and a categorical variable.

Exploratory Research: empirical research that proceeds without hypotheses and/or involves looking at a smaller amount or different kind of data than would be appropriate for testing hypotheses.

Factor Analysis: a family of techniques used to determine the weighting of items for a compound measure by a mathematical procedure for evaluating the interrelatedness of the items.

Fixed Format: where the data for the same variable is recorded in the same place on the line or card for each unit of analysis.

Free Format: where data is entered with individual numbers separated by blanks or commas and without having to be placed in specific locations on the line.

Frequency Distribution: a table showing the number of units falling in each category of a measure.

Gamma: a correlation coefficient used to measure association between relative variables.

Generality of a Hypothesis: the size of the theoretical population for a hypothesis.

Guttman Scaling: a procedure for creating compound measures when the response to the items to be combined conform to a specified pattern. A Guttman scale communicates more information than other scales and provides a procedure for determining correct scores for cases with missing or erroneous data.

Hardware: all machines used in automated data processing.

Homogeneity (of measures): degree to which several different measures of the same property tend to classify the units in the same way.

Hypothesis: an assertion of a causal association between two properties.

Independence (of measures): the extent to which the classification of a unit on one measure does not determine its position on others.

Independent Property or Variable: the property or variable, variation in which is said to cause variation in another variable (the dependent variable).

Indirect Measure: when a property is measured by observing some other property that is assumed to be related to it.

Interaction: when the control variable has a conditioning effect on the relationship between independent and dependent variables. The relationship between the independent and dependent variables is different for different categories of the control variable.

Interactive Processing: a mode of computer processing where the commands are entered into the machine one at a time producing the response to each command immediately.

Intercept: the estimated value of Y when the X variables are zero.

Interquartile Range: a measure of dispersion usable with ordinal and interval level measures that indicates the high and low categories of the middle 50% of the units.

Interval Level Measures: measures in which the numbers distinguish units into categories that can be ordered and also indicate how far apart the categories are.

Level of Measurement: indicates the amount of information communicated by knowing in which category an object is. We distinguish nominal, ordinal, and interval levels.

Level of Statistical Significance: the likelihood that a relationship could have occurred by chance which a researcher is willing to accept and still have confidence in the relationship. It is also used to refer to the actual likelihood that a relationship could have occurred by chance.

Likert Scaling: a technique for combining ordinal indicators to form a compound measure. Respondents indicate how strongly they agree or disagree with a series of statements. The agreement categories are given values that are then averaged over all of the items used in the compound measure.

Linear Function: one variable is a linear function of another when the values of one variable can be predicted from those of the other using the equation for a straight line, $Y = a + bX$.

Linear Relationship: a relationship between two variables that can be described by the equation for a straight line, $Y = a + bX$. It occurs where a unit increase on the independent variable produces a constant increase on the dependent variable.

Line Graph: a figure using the height of a line to indicate the frequencies of units at different values of an interval level measure.

Loading Questions: wording questions so as to encourage a particular response.

Marginals: the numbers at the bottom of the columns or on the right of the rows of a percentage crosstable that indicate the total number in each column or row.

Mass Survey: a large survey dealing with a wide variety of respondents.

Mean: a measure of central tendency for interval level measures, computed by adding the scores on a measure and dividing by the number of units.

Mean Deviation: a measure of dispersion for interval measures computed by averaging the distances between the mean and each of the values (ignoring the signs).

Median: a measure of central tendency usable for ordinal and interval level measures indicating the middle category of the distribution.

Mode: a measure of central tendency usable for all levels of measurement indicating the category with the most units in it.

Negative Relationship: a relationship where as the value of one variable increases, the value of the other tends to decrease.

Nominal Level Measures: measures that do nothing more than separate the units into different categories of the property.

Observation (as a method of measurement):   consists of the researcher watching units and categorizing and coding their properties.

Ordinal Level Measures: measures that separate the units into categories and order the categories according to the amount of the property that is present.

Partial: a correlation coefficient measuring the extent of association between two interval variables while controlling for the effects of other interval variables.

Participant Observation: observation occurring while the researcher is a participant in the group he is observing.

Pearson's r: a correlation coefficient used to measure association between interval-level variables.

Percentage Crosstable: a table comparing the percentage distributions among categories of an independent variable.

Percentage Distribution: a table showing the percentage of units falling into each category of a measure.

Perfect Association: the relationship which exists when the X and Y variables are paired in such a way that the absolute or relative value of Y for each unit can be predicted perfectly by knowing either the absolute or relative value of X.

Positive Relationship: a relationship where as the value of one variable increases, the value of the other also tends to increase.

Primary Data: data collected by the researcher for his own study.

Probability Sample: a sample in which each unit of the theoretical population has a known probability of being selected for the sample.

Program: a set of instructions to do a particular task on a computer.

Program Packages: groups of programs designed to do a large variety of interrelated tasks.

Property: any observable (directly or indirectly) characteristic, attribute, or behavior of a unit.

Qualitative Properties or Variables: properties or variables that can classify units by type, but not amount.

Quota Sample: a sample in which units are selected in such a way that the distribution of an important property or properties is set by the researcher.

Random Digit Dialing: a method of sampling using random numbers to determine which phones will be called for a telephone survey.

Random Sample: a sample in which each unit or combination of units of the theoretical population has an equal probability of being selected for the sample.

Range: a measure of dispersion usable for ordinal and interval levels of measurement indicating the highest and lowest value of a measure.

Regression Coefficient: the slope of an X variable in a multiple regression equation, it shows how much Y is estimated to increase for every increase of one in the value of the X variable.

Regression Equation: an equation for estimating interval Y values from the values of one or more interval X variables.

Regression Line: a line visually representing the regression equation.

Relative Properties or Variables: properties or variables that can classify units by degree or amount.

Reliability: degree to which measures would yield the same results when applied by different researchers to the same units under the same circumstances.

Replication: retesting of a previously tested hypothesis.

Representative Sample: a miniature of the theoretical population with respect to the properties and relationships being measured.

Residual: the difference between the estimated and the observed Y value of a unit.

Response Rate: percentage of the people contacted who answer the questions.

Response Set: the tendency of a person to respond to a set of questions in a patterned way that has little to do with the substance of the questions.

Reversal: when upon controlling for the effects of one or more variables a relationship between two variables is shown to be the opposite of that observed without the controls.

Sample: any subset of the theoretical population.

Sample of Convenience: a sample in which the units have been chosen only because they happen to be available.

Sampling Distribution: a distribution of the probabilities of a descriptive statistic that occur in all unique samples of a specific size from a specific population.

Scatterplot: a graphic representation of a relationship between two interval variables.

Secondary Data: data originally collected by a researcher other than the one reporting it.

Simulation: when units of analysis different than those hypothesized about are substituted for the appropriate ones because they are believed to behave in similar ways.

Skewed Distribution: a distribution that is not symmetrical around a midpoint. The skew is right or positive when the outlying cases have high values; it is left or negative when those cases have low values.

Slope: the amount that Y is estimated to increase for every increase of one in X.

Software: the instructions, programs, and so on that control the machines in automated data processing.

Spurious Association: when two properties are associated because variation in a third property causes consistent, coincident variation in each of the first two properties.

Standard Deviation: a measure of dispersion for interval level measures computed by taking the square root of the average squared distances between the mean and each of the values. It is the square root of the variance.

Statistical Independence: the relationship which exists when each Y value is equally likely to be paired with each X value.

Stratified Random Sample: sample in which independent random samples are drawn from different groups (or strata) that make up the population.

Strength of Association: a measure of how closely the observed relationship matches perfect association, usually indicated by the magnitude of the correlation coefficient.

Sum of Squares: the sum of the squared differences from the mean.

Survey: any data collected by asking individuals to respond to questions.

Symmetrical Distribution: a distribution in which roughly the same number of cases are above and below the mean.

Systematic Sample: a sample in which every nth object is selected from a list after determining a random starting point.

Table of Random Digits: a list of digits constructed by selecting digits one at a time so that each digit has an equal chance of occurring.

Terminals: devices that allow the user to communicate directly with the computer; usually similar to a typewriter.

Tests of Statistical Significance: statistical operations that allow us to estimate what the probability is that the association found between variables was found by chance.

Theoretical Population: all of the units of analysis to which an explanation is meant to apply.

Theory: A general explanation that is constructed from a series at interrelated hypotheses.

Thurstone Scaling: a technique for forming compound measures in which judges decide the weight to be given to each variable.

Uniform Distribution: the shape of a distribution in which roughly the same number of units are included in each category of a variable.

Unit of Analysis: the kind of object being observed in empirical research.

Unit Record Devices: machines which do operations on computer cards; included are keypunches, verifiers, reproducers, interpreters, and countersorters.

Validity: degree to which a measure measures the property as defined.

Value Statement: a statement indicating or implying how units *should* behave rather than how they do behave.

Variance: a measure of dispersion for interval measures computed by averaging the squared distances between each value and the mean of the values.

Variation (in a property): the differences observed among the units of analysis with respect to the level or amount of the property exhibited.

Washout: when an apparent relationship between two variables disappears when the effects of one or more other variables are controlled.

Zero Association: the relationship which exists when the X and Y variables are paired in such a way that knowing the X value of a unit is of no help in predicting its Y value.

Z-score: the amount by which the unit's value is above or below the mean value for that variable divided by the standard deviation of the variable.

INDEX

A

Accuracy, 36–37
Almanac of American Politics, 79
American Statistics Index, 80
America Votes, 81
Analysis
  content, 74–75, 274
  data, 116–22, 253, 254
  factor, 86–87, 275
  units of. *See* Units of analysis
Appropriateness, 55–56, 273
Archival data, 75–81
  reliability of, 76–77
  sources of, 78–81
  validity of, 77–78
Assertions, 8
Association, 13–14
  causal, 14, 273
  directions of, 199–200, 227, 274
  extent of, 198–200
  indirect, 167–68
  perfect, 198–99, 227
  spurious, 167, 168, 279
  strength of, 199, 227, 279
  zero, 198–99, 224, 225, 280
Automated data processing, 111–23
  data analysis and, 116–22
  facilities for, 112–16
  positive and negative aspects of,
    111–12
Averaging responses, 100–102

B

Bar graph, 127, 273
Batch processing, 113–14, 273
Bell-shaped distribution, 136, 273
Bernstein, R.A., 171
Bimodal distribution, 135, 273
*Biographical Dictionary of the Federal
    Judiciary,* 79
Bivariate table, 162, 166–67
Black, G., 206
BMD package, 115
Bollen, K., 64
Bond, J.R., 15
Branching questions, 98

C

Card interpreters, 113
Card reproducers, 113
Catalog of U.S. Census Publications, 80
Casual observation, 25–26
Categorization, 57–58, 273
Causal association, 14, 273
Causation, multiple, 14–15
Census, United States Bureau of the, 76
Census of Agriculture, 80
Census of Government, 80
Census of Housing, 80
Census of Population, 80
Center for Political Studies, 75